Swiss America
Rich Cromwell - Phil Gordon
John Marshall - Tom Stornelli
1-800-289-2646

# The Inflation Deception

Also by
## Craig R. Smith

*Rediscovering Gold in the 21st Century:*
*The Complete Guide to the Next Gold Rush*

*Black Gold Stranglehold: The Myth*
*of Scarcity and the Politics of Oil*
(co-authored with Jerome R. Corsi)

*The Uses of Inflation:*
*Monetary Policy and Governance in the 21st Century*

*Crashing the Dollar:*
*How to Survive a Global Currency Collapse*
(co-authored with Lowell Ponte)


Also by
## Lowell Ponte

*The Cooling*

*Crashing the Dollar:*
*How to Survive a Global Currency Collapse*
(co-authored with Craig R. Smith)

# The Inflation Deception

Six Ways Government Tricks Us...
and Seven Ways to Stop It!

## Craig R. Smith

Swiss America

and Lowell Ponte

Foreword by Pat Boone

Idea Factory Press
Phoenix, Arizona

# The Inflation Deception:
## Six Ways Government Tricks Us...
## and Seven Ways to Stop It!

Copyright © 2011 by Idea Factory Press
All Rights Reserved, including the right to reproduce this book,
or parts thereof, in any form except for the inclusion of brief quotations
in a review. Printed in the United States of America.
For more information contact publisher.

Cover art by Linda Daly, Dalybread.com
Based on a design concept by Lowell Ponte
Copy editing by Ellen Ponte

Portions of this book originally appeared in
*Crashing the Dollar: How to Survive a Global Currency Collapse*
by Craig R. Smith and Lowell Ponte
Copyright © 2010 by Idea Factory Press.
All Rights Reserved.

Portions of this book originally appeared in
*The Uses of Inflation: Monetary Policy
and Governance in the 21st Century* by Craig R. Smith
Copyright © 2011 by Swiss America Trading Corporation
All Rights Reserved.

Library of Congress Data
ISBN Number 978-0-9711482-2-2
First Edition. June 2011

Idea Factory Press
President, David M. Bradshaw
*13232 North 1st Avenue, Phoenix, AZ 85029
Tel. (602) 918-3296 * Ideaman@myideafactory.net*

*Updates, reviews and more posted at*
http://www.inflationdeception.com

# Table of Contents

Foreword: Pat Boone.........................................................................vii

Introduction: Craig R. Smith..............................................................1

**Part One: Grand Theft Dollar**

Chapter One: "Inflation Is Theft" ........................................7

Chapter Two: CSI – Crime Scene: Inflation .......................................21

Chapter Three: Ways Inflation Deceives.............................................47

**Part Two: Inflation's Method of Operation**

Chapter Four: A Compressed History of Inflation...........................75

Chapter Five: Inflation in America .............................................91

Chapter Six: The Money Illusion .................................................111

Chapter Seven: Under Inflation's Spell ...........................................137

**Part Three: The Uses of Inflation**

Chapter Eight: Inflation as Taxation .............................................153

Chapter Nine: Inflatocracy – Inflation as Ideology and Power......169

**Part Four: Arresting Inflation**

Chapter Ten: Three Political Ways to Rein in Inflation .................193

Chapter Eleven: Three Ways Alternative Money
Can Handcuff Inflation .................................................................215

Chapter Twelve: How to Escape from the Inflatocracy ..................233

**Sources** ...................................................................................243

**Additional Background Sources** ...............................................255

## Dedication

To my wonderful wife and best friend
Melissa Smith, who makes me better
each day and raised our daughters
Holly and Katie to love the Lord
with all their hearts.
Also to my Pastor Tommy Barnett,
who taught me that doing the right thing
is always the right thing to do,
and to always hold onto the vision.

# Foreword
## by Pat Boone

*"The wicked man earns deceptive wages,*
*but he who sows righteousness reaps a sure reward."*
– Proverbs 11:18

The Framers of America's Constitution followed the Biblical standard for money, specifying that it be an honest measure of silver or gold.

So long as America kept faith with this standard, between the 1820s and the creation of the Federal Reserve Board in 1913, the purchasing power of the U.S. Dollar over that time gradually increased in value. American prosperity grew in part from keeping our money a medium of exchange and a store of intrinsic value trusted around the world. You could actually redeem this paper for a fixed amount of gold or silver.

In 1913 we began the turn from gold to today's Federal Reserve Notes, paper money based only on politician promises. In less than a century the buying power of our paper dollar has plunged to only two cents of its 1913 value.

In this book my long-trusted friend and advisor Craig Smith and former *Reader's Digest* Roving Editor Lowell Ponte explain how this happened, why we feel like the man the Prophet Haggai described as earning wages but seeing his money vanish as if put "in a purse with holes in it," and how our government now deliberately creates inflation as a deceptive way to tax and control us.

During the same era that politicians adopted un-Biblical fiat money, they in 1957 added the words "In God We Trust" to U.S. paper currency. Craig and Lowell show how to free our nation, and protect our families, from already-skyrocketing prices and declining values created by our ruling Inflatocracy – government of, by and for inflation. In this excellent book, you'll discover why today's paper money should say: "In God We Trust, Not in This Paper."

*Pat*

*"Believe me that the whole system of credit and finance
which is carried on here at Rome in the Forum,
is inextricably bound up with
revenues of the Asiatic province.*

*If those revenues are destroyed,
our whole system of credit
will come down with a crash."*

– Cicero
Roman Republic statesman
66 B.C.

# Introduction
## by Craig R. Smith

*"History is largely a history of inflation,*
*usually inflations engineered by governments*
*for the gain of governments."*

– Friedrich A. Hayek
*Nobel Laureate Economist*

High, or even hyper, inflation is rapidly approaching.

After 30 years of helping people hedge against financial risk, I can feel
the tremors of this oncoming economic tidal wave rumbling beneath
my feet. It is far bigger than I have ever felt.

The coming devastation will put America's economy underwater and
destroy the U.S. Dollar as we have known it, as the world's Reserve
Currency.

For those who have not prepared, the economic devastation about to
arrive will bring hardships that make the Great Depression look like
a summer picnic.

Most of us have been deceived into thinking that high inflation is the
inadvertent by-product of misguided or unlucky government policies.

As this book will show you, inflation *is* the government policy.

The approaching tidal wave has been deliberately set in motion. This
investigation will show you how and why.

Our aim is to show you why inflation is much more than higher prices,
and what steps you and your family can take to survive, thrive and
even prosper during the hard economic times in America's immediate
future.

In this book you will also learn how you have been systematically deceived about what inflation really is, how much it has taken from you, and how many ways our politicians and central bankers use it.

Inflation, we will show you, is quietly being used as a tool, an ideology, and a form of taxation that secretly extracts the earnings not only of Americans but also of unsuspecting people in other countries. It has also become a means of wealth redistribution, a mode of social engineering, a device to weaken some and strengthen others both within our nation and in the global community of nations, and a way to seize and exercise power.

Inflation and its monetary impact can, as recent scientific brain scans suggest, literally affect our perceptions, judgment and decision-making ability like a mind-altering drug....just one of the ways inflation can be used to manipulate us through what economists and scientists call "Money Illusion."

Inflation is being deliberately created and used to trick us out of:

1. Our earnings, savings, investments and property
2. Our opportunities to pursue happiness
3. Our independence and self-reliance
4. Our security and peace of mind
5. Our freedom and our rights, and
6. Our children's and grandchildren's future in what used to be a much freer America.

The welfare state depends on inflation to fund its unlimited craving for expansion. If we can curtail inflation, this would be a huge step towards halting and reversing the ballooning growth of Big Government.

This book offers seven ways we can rein in inflation and government – including a path that, come what may, can protect you and your family from inflation and even hyperinflation.

Fasten your seatbelt, dear reader. You are about to take an amazing journey through empowering information and horizon-expanding ideas. After reading this, you will never again see inflation or money the way you do now.

Craig R. Smith

# Part One
# Grand Theft Dollar

# Chapter One
# "Inflation is Theft"

*"Inflation is as violent as a mugger,*
*as frightening as an armed robber*
*and as deadly as a hit man."*

– Ronald Reagan

Ryan and Peggy Jones have been robbed, but they are confused about how this crime happened.

They awoke one day to find that their home had been turned upside down. Despite all the effort and savings they have sacrificed to keep their home, like more than 11 million American families they now owe more on their mortgage than the market value of their house.

Most of the purchasing power of their life savings is gone – gone with the wind and storms that have swept through the U.S. economy in recent years.

The average American family's income has fallen by more than 18 percent – almost one-fifth – since 2007. [1]

Family average net worth has declined by about $100,000 since

2008, with more being lost every day in home values that continue to sink and savings value that continues to evaporate. [2]

Total household net worth in America is $12 Trillion less today than it was in 2008, with most of this loss in the homes that for millions were their largest repository of family investment and savings.

Gone, too, is Ryan's and Peggy's American Dream of owning their home free and clear, and of a secure retirement with leisure time, of a little travel in their twilight years, and most of all of spending their last days with one another instead of being forced to continue working until they drop dead in harness.

## Debt from the Start

This mysterious robbery troubles Peggy and Ryan, too, because they had hoped to help their two children go to college and to begin their lives a few steps ahead through a gift of a little money or perhaps even an inexpensive small starter home for each of them.

Their children instead had to take out student loans. Ryan and Peggy earned too little to afford the schooling, but too much for their children to qualify for scholarships.

Their kids began adult life hobbled by several tens of thousands of dollars in debt. It is hard to see how they, like every previous American generation, will do better than their parents.

Like Ryan and Peggy, their kids are troubled by how President Barack Obama expropriated the nation's private bank student loan programs.

In 2010 student loan debt for the first time topped credit card debt. In 2011 college debt is projected to exceed one trillion dollars as the cost of college is now growing faster than health care costs. [3] The average student college loan exceeds $23,186, and total student loan debt in the U.S. is increasing by $2,853.88 per second. [4]

One reason for this is a tightening of credit restrictions, limits and issuance on credit cards and other lines of credit. Another reason may be more ominous.

Mr. Obama has announced that his aim is to forgive the student loan debts of those who go to work for government or for "non-profit" political activist organizations – but not the student loan debts of those who choose instead to work in the free marketplace, even though they on average will earn only half as much in wages and benefits as Federal Government employees.

We used to call this ruling class "public servants." Thomas Jefferson said that he regarded his stepping down after two terms as President as a "promotion," because it meant he would again be one of the People, the true rulers of our democratic republic, and no longer just a servant of the People.

Jefferson's sincere words today taste bitter on our tongues. Today's ruling class of bureaucrats and regulators (but thankfully not yet the brave soldiers, police and firefighters who protect us) has acquired a status superior to most other Americans – in income, pensions, job security, privileges and capricious power.

## To Catch a Thief

Who stole the Jones family's life savings, dreams and their and their children's future?

The chief suspect is inflation, a thief whose fingerprints can be seen everywhere by those who know the secrets of how to recognize them.

Inflation itself, however, is a master of disguise and deception. Who or what is it? Most people have been tricked into mistaking its true identity.

Who does inflation serve? As you are about to discover, inflation has friends and allies in high places and low who enrich and empower themselves from what inflation steals from you.

Like most Americans victimized by inflation, Ryan and Peggy sense that it is something more mysterious and disturbing than just another way to say "higher prices."

Their intuitive fear of inflation is justified. It comes from our survival instinct.

You might feel the same fear, and with good reason. You probably see Ryan or Peggy each morning in your bathroom mirror.

## The Carter Nightmare

To Ryan and Peggy, inflation is the name of a monster they have dreaded since the year they wed, 1980.

In that year President Jimmy Carter presided over a rate of inflation that soared above 18 percent and a prime interest rate that topped 21 percent.

Millions of homeowners, desperate to sell, saw the value of their biggest lifetime investment plummet, and the cost of everything else they needed, from food to gasoline, soar.

Millions more, like the Jones family (not their real name) were eager to buy their first home but – with interest rates at their highest level in American history – were unable to qualify for a mortgage.

Mr. Carter won office in 1976 by citing what he called his opponent's "Misery Index," the combined rates of inflation and unemployment.

By 1980 Carter had blamed the American people for his economic shortcomings in his so-called "Malaise" speech – while his own "Misery Index" of unemployment and inflation climbed to 21.98 percent.

President Carter's four years in the Oval Office produced one of the greatest acts of theft in history. His nightmare inflation stole half the purchasing power from the life savings of every American.

Carter lost in 1980 to Republican Ronald Reagan, who with great discipline and political courage forced the inflation genie back into its sinister magic lamp and thereby laid the foundation for many years of prosperity.

However, the Carter legacy has returned, crippling the economic futures and dreams of millions of struggling homeowners, would-be home buyers, businesses and workers. Mr. Carter's housing policies – forcing banks to give billions of dollars in mortgages to high-risk borrowers – sowed the seeds of today's global economic problems and America's current financial crisis.

President Bill Clinton doubled down on Mr. Carter's redistributionist housing policies, arm-twisting banks into funding more than a trillion dollars of loans and mortgages to people unworthy of credit.

Our 2010 book *Crashing the Dollar: How to Survive a Global Currency Collapse* lays out the details of how this happened, and how it triggered the Great Recession. [5]

## The Squeeze

Ryan and Peggy have worked hard for more than 30 years and now, like many typical American families, from two jobs they earn $1,150 a week. The Federal, state and local governments snatch a third of this in direct and hidden taxes, leaving them about $770 per week on which to live.

Each week, groceries cost $100 and gasoline now another $120 for their two commuting cars, so they have only around $550 left to pay the utilities and mortgage.

Squeezed dry, they have almost nothing left to save or invest for retirement or to spend for their children or grandchildren. They are not alone. According to the Employee Benefit Research Institute's (EBRI) latest survey, nearly 30 percent of workers have less than $1,000 saved for retirement, and 56 percent – more than half – have saved less than $25,000.

This is why economist Hans F. Sennholz minced no words in describing it: "Inflation is Theft." [6]

President Barack Obama's Administration tells them not to worry about inflation, which it officially declares to be close to zero.

In 2010, 2011 and 2012 the Obama Administration denied or thwarted Cost-of-Living Adjustments (COLAs) to those who depend on Social Security, claiming that there is no increase in the cost of living. The government's official "core inflation" index (which conveniently ignores food, gasoline and energy costs) shows inflation nearly dormant at around 1.1 percent per year.

Ryan's and Peggy's elderly parents are among the millions Mr. Obama has denied any Social Security increase, but every week prices threaten to go higher at the gas pump and the supermarket.

Nowadays Ryan and Peggy have only $35 left at the end of each week while, like a floodtide, prices around them keep rising. What will they do if an emergency hits, with their savings drained and the limits on their remaining credit cards already maxed out?

## The America We Lost

Ryan and Peggy used to feel more optimistic. After all, they were earning a lot more dollars than their "Leave It To Beaver" fathers did while Mom stayed home with the kids.

Today they see growing evidence that Jimmy Carter's inflation monster is stealthily returning, and that it is again devouring their income, hopes and dreams. It also could soon devour the U.S. Dollar and America's economy.

What cost only $1 in 1971 now costs on average more than $5.65, but how many of us have seen our incomes increase during the past four decades by 565 percent?

Ryan remembers 1973, just before the first Oil Embargo, when gasoline cost 27 cents a gallon and service station attendants were eager to wash your windshields, check your engine fluids and tire pressure, and give you a free set of elegant drinking glasses or other inducements to attract your business as a customer.

American cars were roomy and powerful back then, virtual ships of the land, and gasoline was so cheap that the Sunday drive and long-haul driving vacations were enjoyed by millions of us.

Ryan remembers childhood summer vacations. His father would proudly drive to fishing lakes and streams hundreds of miles from home, pitch tents, and prepare amazing meals over campground woodstoves.

The towering pines, woodsmoke and sizzling trout or salmon, Ryan remembers, smelled like freedom in a vast, open America.

## "Your Land Is My Land"

Ryan once tried to take his children to a national park. The Rangers who had been so friendly decades earlier now demanded a steep admission price and pre-booked campsite reservation. When did Yosemite turn into Disneyworld?

Didn't the old left-liberal folk song say "This land is your land?" Why is government demanding that the people pay to visit our own public land, supposedly set aside from development for the free use of the People?

And who, Ryan finds himself wondering, are these environmental regulators and taxers who have re-written the song to mean "Your land is my land" and behave as if all private property and earnings in America have already been expropriated and collectivized? And what does President Obama mean by "tax expenditures," as if letting taxpayers keep a few more dollars of their own money was an expense to, and an unjustified gift to us from, the government?

Ryan remembers during such long vacation drives what happened every time they went through some tiny town or village.

"How do you suppose people make a living there?" his father always asked.

"They take in each other's laundry," his mother always replied, followed by his parents laughing.

Nowadays Ryan finds himself looking at America and asking the same question. How do Americans make a living? Increasingly the answer is "They get a government check."

Ryan once saw a quote by the 19th Century French lawmaker-philosopher Frederic Bastiat: "Government is the great fiction by which everyone tries to live at the expense of everyone else."

"Everyone wants to live at the expense of the state," added Bastiat. "They forget that the state wants to live at the expense of everyone."

If more and more people keep getting government checks, wonders Ryan, then where is government getting the money to pay all those checks?"

## BoomerWorld

Ryan and Peggy have probably never understood that they grew up in a kind of Eden or utopia, a rare golden moment in a place we might call BoomerWorld.

After World War II the United States was the only major industrial nation whose cities and factories were untouched by the horrors of enemy attack.

Pearl Harbor and the Aleutian Islands were then in American territories, but not yet in states inside our mother country. More than 416,000 Americans died fighting Germany and Japan, and government spending by 1945-46 reached 122 percent of our Gross Domestic Product – a pinnacle of indebtedness never again approached in America's entire history until today's stratospheric-spending by President Barack Obama.

World War II had done what President Franklin Delano Roosevelt's other government programs failed to accomplish. It ended the Great Depression that their parents knew.

American soldiers, sailors and fliers returned home to prosperity, the G.I. Bill, and new suburban tract homes that cost $6,990, and that could be bought for $100 down and a five percent 30-year fixed mortgage in Levittown, New York. [7]

Europe, the United Kingdom, Japan and China had experienced war on their soil, high casualties both civilian and military, and economic devastation from the horrifying conflict.

## The Last Land Standing

The U.S. was the sole colossus still standing at the end of World War II. Our dollar had become the standard of global currency. Our movies, cars and Coca-Cola were the measure of success and style worldwide.

To Americans with American dollars, the whole world was for sale at bargain basement prices. Saudi Arabian light sweet crude back then cost $1 per barrel or less, not the more than $100 per barrel it hit in spring 2011. Our huge, muscular automobiles cruised the landscape, pulled by hundreds of horsepower.

In 1952 the average American working family paid less than three percent of its income in income taxes.

We were safe, free, powerful and by world standards wealthy. We grew up in a sheltered bubble of history, a bubble that developed cracks and in the 21st Century burst. Many of us remain Baby Boomers, but BoomerWorld – the America of our childhood and adolescence – is rapidly fading into history.

We grew up with no thought that such a wonderful world might end. Our success, we assumed, came from American Exceptionalism and our faith that we are a nation under divine blessing – not just from being lucky.

Boomers never paused to ask what would happen when those other nations that had been knocked down by World War II got back up on their feet and began to compete with us.

We never considered the possibility that our wealth and power had limits, that we could not fight and spend everywhere without our life blood and treasury eventually being depleted.

We never asked what would happen if America stopped praying on its knees as our pioneer ancestors had done – and turned instead to profligacy and pleasure-seeking, abandoning the heritage and values of our Founders.

## Resourceful

Since the 1960s leftists have prated endlessly about how unjust it is that Americans, now only four percent of Earth's population, have controlled 25 percent of the world's resources and ought to give them away to others.

This leftist statement is inaccurate in any event, yet for sake of argument let's say it is quasi-correct. At our peak we never controlled 25 percent of the world's resources – but we were invested in nearly 25 percent of the world's *developed* resources.

Why? Because *we* were the people who *developed* them. We made unused natural resources available, then watched dictators in nations such as Mexico expropriate our achievements to enrich themselves.

Because we had little ambition to build an empire, we usually let such thieves rob us.

Other nations in the past sought colonies because they needed resources beyond their own shores. The United States has from its birth been blessed with abundant resources of its own, one key to our spirit of independence.

## The Six

The United Nations has 192 member states. Of these, only six major nations could, if they wished, be entirely and reliably self-sufficient in both food and fuel for decades and centuries to come.

We are the richest of those six nations, able to produce at least four times more food than we consume and to power our engines and industry entirely from resources within our own borders.

If needed, America has a thousand-year supply of coal that could be converted into automotive and truck fuel. We have ample uranium. We could by some accounts be "the Saudi Arabia of natural gas." And as to food, we remain a breadbasket to the world, even with up to 40 percent of our corn crop diverted to make alcohol fuel.

(How odd that the same legal system that prohibits driving under the influence of alcohol now requires the cars we drive to guzzle alcohol.)

Created by worldwide immigration and ideals, we prefer to trade with the world. We are, after all, an experiment, a remarkably successful tryout for what a future united states of the world could be like. For the most part, people from every nation, religion and clime live here together in harmony.

We were then, and remain, one of the few countries that, if we wished, could simply build a giant wall on our borders and be completely self-sufficient without trade. Nor need we fear foreign invasion – except by foreign missiles or nuke-toting terrorists – because we are a natural castle with 3,000-mile-wide ocean moats protecting our East and West Coasts.

No nation in history has been in such an advantageous position as that of Ryan's and Peggy's childhood America.

## Looking for Clues

Ryan drove around America in spring 1973 in a 5-speed Toyota Corolla, wheeling from Southern California to Boston, Boston to Miami, and Miami to Southern California with lots of sightseeing along the way. The total cost of his new Toyota: $1,500. The cost of all the gas he burned on this trip while putting 10,000 miles on his Odometer: $140.

Today the cost of gasoline in several states has passed $4. As of May 2011 on one Hawaiian island gas hit $6 per gallon. A mideast crisis could send gas prices into the stratosphere and cause shortages.

Ryan and Peggy shudder to think what will happen to the price of keeping their jobs, and of everything they buy that shipped by truck, if gasoline and diesel fuel jump to $6 or more per gallon.

In inflation-adjusted dollars, Ryan and Peggy are earning almost exactly the same income they did more than 30 years ago on their wedding day – despite both of them running hard in a succession of uncertain and stressful jobs just to stay in the same financial place.

What will happen if and when Peggy and Ryan retire and no longer receive meaningful raises to their Social Security? What happens when their fixed income cannot offset the dollar's shrinking purchasing power? How long will it be before the marauding inflation monster devours them – and us?

Like most typical Americans, Ryan and Peggy feel but do not fully understand why they seem to be in a financial trap. They have been misled by the Inflation Deception, and, like you, their first step to escape from this trap is to read this book.

## Obamalaise: Obama's "Misery Index"

If we combine the U.S. Bureau of Labor Statistics (BLS) December 2010 U6 measurement (roughly the way unemployment was measured during the Great Depression) of unemployed, underemployed and discouraged workers – 16.7 percent – with the estimate of real (not "official") inflation by highly-regarded *Shadowstats.com* economist John Williams – today at 8.5 percent annually – President Barack Obama's own current "Misery Index" is 25.2 percent.

If we use the more reliable Gallup Poll's January 2011 data equivalent of U6, combining part-time and unemployed workers – which was 18.9 percent – and combine this with John Williams' estimate of real annual inflation of 8.5 percent, Mr. Obama's "Misery Index" jumps to 27.4 percent. [8]

The President's "Obamalaise," as *Investor's Business Daily* calls it, is 3.22 to 5.42 percentage points *higher* than what prompted American voters overwhelmingly to reject President Jimmy Carter for re-election in 1980.

# Chapter Two
# CSI – Crime Scene: Inflation

*"Inflation is not an act of God...*
*not a catastrophe of the elements*
*or a disease that comes like the plague.*
*Inflation is a policy."*

– Ludwig von Mises
*Economic Policy*

To hunt down the inflation monster, we must track its cloven hoof prints and recognize its claw marks on our ravaged economy and body politic. Only then will we see the path down which those who have spawned inflation are taking us, and what their hidden motives, deceptive tactics and real destination are.

*( WARNING: If you are easily frightened by reality or prone to nightmares, stop reading now. If the information below enters your head, you will never again see the world as you now do. )*

The United States is already effectively bankrupt, as the International Monetary Fund reported in Summer 2010.

Our national debt as of April 2011 is $14.3 Trillion, approximately $128,666 for each American taxpayer. [9]

America's entire Gross Domestic Product (GDP), the sum of all our productivity combined according to government statistics, is $14.67 Trillion. America's debt, therefore, is nearly 97.5 percent of its annual income.

However, as we shall discover many times in this book, the government's politicized, cooked and gimmicked statistics are a major part of the Inflation Deception.

## Gross Domestic Politics

As much as 40 percent of America's claimed Gross Domestic Product comes not from genuine productivity, but from spending by Federal, state and local governments. [10]

Because governments produce almost nothing except bureaucratic paperwork, and must tax or borrow from others the money they spend, we can reasonably infer that almost all state and local spending was counted once in the GDP when taxpayers earned it – and a second time when government snatched and spent it.

In real terms, in other words, up to 40 percent of America's entire Gross Domestic Product is a kind of fiction. It is a double-counting shell game, a hollow illusion that we are richer than in fact we are.

Our economic condition may be deceptive in other ways as well, as *Washington Post* reporter Steven Pearlstein explores in his February 1, 2011, article "Much of Nation's Recent Growth May Have Been a Mirage." [11]

Moreover, state and local governments reportedly face a shortfall of at least $2.5 Trillion in having money enough to pay the retirement benefits promised to their public employees, along with another trillion dollars to pay current benefits such as healthcare.

By 2011 some states and cities have begun to make up this shortfall by imposing crushing new tax burdens on citizens, businesses, and even nonprofit entities. By one estimate, 2006 American home prices have fallen on average by 18 percent per year, but state and local property taxes during these years have risen by an average of 7 percent per year.

The Federal Government distinguishes between discretionary spending (which, oddly, includes national defense) and mandatory spending for things such as entitlement programs.

In 2011 mandatory spending alone will be approximately 101 percent of total federal receipts. Even for government's mandatory spending, Uncle Sam is now living beyond his income and will have to borrow yet more money.

This shortfall had been predicted by economic planners. What is shocking is that it has arrived in 2011, 50 years ahead of schedule.

Mandatory spending, according to White House numbers, reportedly devoured only 47 percent of government revenues in 2000, 61 percent in 2005, and 90 percent in 2010.

This took the Obama Administration by surprise, suggested Jeffrey Anderson in *The Weekly Standard*, because it wildly overestimated how much revenue the government would reap American taxpayers for during the current economic downturn. [12]

## $58,000 A Second

At the Federal level, since 2007 when Democrats took over control of Congress, approximately 42 cents of every dollar the U.S. Congress has spent is borrowed money that must be repaid with interest.

More than 40 percent of this debt is relatively short-term and must be paid off or refinanced within the next three years.

How fast is the Federal Government borrowing to fill the gap between its revenues and the amount it is spending? By the higher end of expert estimates, here are a few chilling numbers:

The Federal Government is currently borrowing roughly $58,000 every second, 24 hours a day, seven days each week. [13]

This increases our national debt by roughly $3.5 Million per minute, and $210 Million every hour.

The Federal Government, according to Jill Schlesinger of *CBS MoneyWatch*, by November 2010 was routinely borrowing money at a rate of approximately $5 Billion every day. [14]

This is roughly $150 Billion per month, equivalent to $1.8 Trillion per year.

What does this mean in historical perspective?

According to Reuters investigative reporter Emily Stephenson, it means that every hour the U.S. Government is borrowing more, in inflation-adjusted dollars, than our nation paid Russia to buy all of Alaska in 1867. [15]

It means that every two hours we borrow more than what the U.S. in 1803 paid France to buy the entire Louisiana Purchase.

The Louisiana Purchase bought the U.S. land that today includes the states of Louisiana, Arkansas, Missouri, Iowa, Oklahoma, Kansas, Nebraska, and South Dakota, as well as sizable portions of what today are Texas, New Mexico, Colorado, Wyoming, Montana, North Dakota and Minnesota.

Every two hours we borrow nearly double the $15 Million ($219 Million in 2010 dollars) Thomas Jefferson authorized to buy 828,800 square miles from needy Napoleonic France.

The dollar back then really *did* have more purchasing power than it does today. What happened that has cost our dollar its once-great buying power?

## Much Obliged

Who has been buying spendthrift America's current debt?

Japan, recently devastated by natural and subsequent other disasters that will require at least $300 Billion in reconstruction, has been the second biggest foreign buyer of U.S. debt, holding nearly $900 Billion in Treasury paper.

The first, the People's Republic of China, now facing inflation and other economic problems of its own as well as doubts about whether the U.S. intends to repay its obligations with devalued dollars, has begun selling off its more than one trillion dollars of United States obligations at a pace calculated to avoid destroying their value.

In early 2011 Bill Gross, the head of PIMCO, announced that this largest independent private purchaser of U.S. debt paper would buy no more.

Gross has said he expects that the U.S. Dollar could lose 20 percent of its purchasing power in the immediate future, and that he fears that the U.S. might outright default on its debts.

Gross is not just selling off PIMCO's U.S. Treasury bills; he reportedly is selling them off short.

So who is left to buy America's debt paper, especially after July 1, 2011, when the Federal Reserve ceases buying under its stimulus program Quantitative Easing Two (QE2)? With few other likely customers eager to buy shaky U.S. debt, the Fed will be forced to continue buying under some new name, guise, or secret intermediaries.

"Knowledgeable people in finance are quite aware that the Federal Reserve has been buying roughly 70 percent of all new Treasury paper, making the government by far the largest client for its own debt," wrote billionaire investor Mortimer B. Zuckerman in late April 2011.

"This is only possible by increasing the money supply and the balance sheet of the Federal Reserve," wrote Zuckerman, "and is, in essence, a national Ponzi scheme that sooner or later will blow up." [16]

America's debt load does not end – indeed, it scarcely begins – here.

President Barack Obama's proposed budget path would add at least another trillion to trillion-and-a-half dollars of debt each year until at least 2021.

If the cost of borrowing money remains unchanged, by that year the *interest* alone on money borrowed to pay Federal debts will be nearly a trillion dollars each year, much of it leaving the country in payments to foreign nations such as the People's Republic of China, Japan and the United Kingdom.

## Loan Sharking

The likelihood, however, is that today's interest rates will rise dramatically in the immediate future. In April 2011 one of America's two largest credit agencies, Standard & Poor's, warned that the U.S. is at risk of losing its AAA credit rating. If that happens, America might find its credit cut off – or, at best, its cost of borrowing money going up sharply.

How sharply? Greece, whose debt-to-GDP ratio is only slightly higher than that of the U.S., in 2011 refinanced much of its international debt at a loan shark effective annual interest rate in excess of 21 percent.

International money analysts have given two to one odds that Greece will find this interest burden unsustainable.

Much of Greece's debt is owed to German banks, and in 2010 two German lawmakers called on Greece to give several of its sunny islands to Germany to repay what it has borrowed.

In recent years the Federal Reserve has held bank interest rates close to zero and now purchases 70 percent or more of U.S. Government debts. This has unleashed our politicians as well as key international speculators to continue spending wildly in the name of stimulating the economy while paying rock-bottom interest rates for their profligacy.

These artificially-low Fed-induced interest rates, of course, have deterred banks from lending to businesses, thereby taking risks for almost zero profit. (They have also driven ordinary people to put their money at risk in investments instead of near-zero-interest bank accounts, thereby benefitting the stock market.)

At least the government can be relied upon to pay, so the government has crowded out most other potential borrowers and left America's productive private small business sector gasping for investment and hiring capital.

Could the United States afford to pay the equivalent of 21 percent annual interest on more than $20 Trillion in debt - piling up $4.1 Trillion in interest every year - which could be the next stop on America's economic road to ruin?

Even without an interest rate increase, if President Obama's current budgetary spending trends continue, the Federal debt will by year 2037 be eight times larger than America's entire GDP. Our whole economy will be swallowed up by financial quicksand, leaving America as a disempowered nation.

Governments never declare bankruptcy, however, so long as they have taxpayers who can be squeezed to pay the debts run up by politicians. Our country's obligation becomes our obligation.

# One Nation, Under Debt

Historians will note that by year 2011 less than 53 percent of working Americans paid Federal income tax. The other 47 percent paid hidden taxes, passed on as higher prices, but they were propagandized to vent their envy and dissatisfaction at "the rich" and the "greedy corporations" whose products they bought.

This privileged 47 percent was encouraged to think of the government as a big goody-dispensing machine that gave them stuff for free.

As Kenneth Minogue of the Fabian socialist-founded London School of Economics has warned, today's "social democratic" welfare state depends on a dwindling minority of economic generators, but once 51 percent of the people in such a society become "public clientage," i.e., welfare recipients, decline of the society inevitably sets in. [17]

America, as *Wall Street Journal* economics writer Stephen Moore observed, has become "a nation of takers, not makers." [18]

By 2011 more than twice as many people (22.5 million) worked for local, state or Federal government than in all of manufacturing.

Many obtained government jobs during President Bill Clinton's 1990s welfare "reform," which in many cases got people "off the welfare rolls" by giving them the same or bigger government check for make-work, paper-shuffling jobs in Federal, state or local bureaucracies.

# A Financial Pearl Harbor

According to Defense Department consultant Kevin D. Freeman, America in September 2008 suffered a financial "Pearl Harbor," an internationally-launched coordinated computerized attack designed to drain overnight trillions of dollars from our most important financial institutions. The resulting panic gulled Federal lawmakers into approving vast emergency bailout funds for banks, brokers and key corporations.

This remarkably-timed attack and resulting economic confusion persuaded voters to renew the liberal Democratic control of Congress and to elect a fresh, unknown, untested anti-capitalist radical community organizer as president.

According to Freeman, this attack was the culmination of three co-ordinated assaults that began in 2007 with "a speculative run-up in oil prices that generated as much as $2 Trillion of excess wealth for oil-producing nations, filling the coffers of Sovereign Wealth Funds, especially those that follow Shariah Compliant Finance."

Oil prices soaring to $147 per barrel devastated the American economy, already vulnerable from the housing boom hitting a ceiling and the negative economic influence of a new and imperious Democratic Congress.

"The rapid run-up in oil prices," wrote Freeman in his 2009 analytic study *Economic Warfare: Risks and Responses: Analysis of Twenty-First Century Risks in Light of the Recent Market Collapse*, "made the value of OPEC oil in the ground roughly $137 Trillion (based on $125/barrel oil) virtually equal to the value of all other world financial assets, including every share of stock, every bond, every private company, all government and corporate debt, and the entire world's bank deposits." [19]

## Economic Terrorism?

"This means that the proven OPEC reserves," wrote Freeman, "were valued at almost three times the total market capitalization of every company on the planet traded in all 27 global stock markets."

The second phase of this assault on U.S. financial entities began in 2008 with a series of "bear raids" against companies such as Bear

Stearns and Lehman Brothers and seemed clearly coordinated to collapse the companies.

"The bear raids were perpetrated by naked short selling and manipulation of credit default swaps, both of which were virtually unregulated," wrote Freeman. "The short selling was actually enhanced by recent regulatory changes...."

"The source of the bear raids has not been traceable to date due to serious transparency gaps for hedge funds, trading pools, sponsored access, and sovereign wealth funds," wrote Freeman.

"What can be demonstrated, however, is that two relatively small broker dealers emerged virtually overnight," he wrote, "to trade 'trillions of dollars worth of U.S. blue chip companies. They are the number one traders in all financial companies that collapsed or are now financially supported by the U.S. Government. Trading by the firms has grown exponentially while the markets have lost trillions of dollars in value.'"

## "Financial Jihad"

The risk of phase three of this attack could involve "a potential direct economic attack on the U.S. Treasury and U.S. Dollar....," wrote Freeman.

"A focused effort to collapse the dollar by dumping Treasury bonds has grave implications including the possibility of a downgrading of U.S. debt forcing rapidly rising interest rates and a collapse of the American economy," Freeman wrote. He also noted that authorities had recently seized counterfeit U.S bonds with "a face value of $134 billion."

A year before Freeman's study, the American Center for Democracy published a detailed analysis, "The Fifth Generation Warfare," of what its analysts Dr. Rachel Ehrenfeld and Alyssa A. Lappen identified as the risk, tactics, strengths and weaknesses of what they called

"Financial Jihad." [20]

As evidenced by Freeman's study for the Department of Defense, the Pentagon is acutely concerned about the prospects for economic warfare against the United States. [21]

The Pentagon has also been "war gaming" possible scenarios of social breakdown caused by an economic collapse, with one of the most recent of these war games called "Unified Quest 2011." [22]

The world's two billion Internet users already suffer $1 Trillion annual losses to cyber crime. [23]

"Just as our reliance on critical infrastructure has grown, so have the threats," said Deputy Assistant Secretary of Defense for Cyber Policy Robert J. Butler in testimony before the Senate Committee on Homeland Security and Governmental Affairs in May 2011. [24]

America's staggering debt remains the "single biggest threat to our national security," warned Admiral Mike Mullen, chairman of the Joint Chiefs of Staff in April 2011. It weakens our capabilities, makes us more fragile and vulnerable, and makes others in the world perceive us as a world power in decline. [25]

## Our "Flash Crash" Future

On May 6, 2010, the New York Stock Exchange suffered what came to be called "the Flash Crash," when the Dow Jones Industrial Average plummeted unexpectedly by nearly 1,000 points in only minutes, reportedly from a human entering a computerized market order with a few too many zeroes. [26]

This order purportedly set off a cascade of computerized buy-and-sell programs around the world that are designed to respond instantly, and without consulting human beings, to sudden large changes in a stock's price. As each major trading computer reacted, it could have triggered programmed reactions in similar computers.

These automated computer programs, some pundits suspect, have put the modern computer-driven global stock markets on a hair trigger, not unlike nuclear missiles of the early 1960s that were to be launched at the first sign of preemptive enemy missile attack because military planners believed they had to "use it or lose it." Only with the development of solid fuel rockets and invulnerable hardened missile silos did this hair trigger policy change.

Our weakening economy and the U.S. Dollar are becoming more vulnerable because, as Mr. Butler warned, we rely on ever-more-centralized systems.

Decentralizing our technologies would make America much less vulnerable to high-tech terrorism and breakdowns. What left-liberals condemn as "urban sprawl" would make us much harder for terrorists to attack and shut down. [27]

America's ruling Democratic Party, however, is ideologically committed to forcing more and more centralized control onto every aspect of life in the United States. Decentralization and self-reliance would make Americans too independent, too free, and socialists want to replace individual liberty with collectivist control.

These centralized systems of control make our economy and society vastly more vulnerable to many kinds of "flash crashes," inadvertent or deliberate, in the technological systems on which we depend.

The risk that a "flash crash" could cascade into a massive crash of the dollar and economy therefore grows bigger every day.

If the weakening U.S. Dollar and our financial institutions have been targeted for disruption and destruction by global power brokers and terrorists, then it would be prudent to move a portion of our personal investments and life savings out of their bull's-eye. This saving remnant should be converted into something with value that will survive – and even grow in the wake of – an economic collapse.

An easy and secure way to do this is by converting a portion of our paper dollars into a universal investment medium such as gold coins that America's enemies will not, and cannot successfully, attack....and inflation cannot devalue.

## Anti-Capitalists Seize Control

When Democrats took over Congress in January 2007, unemployment stood at 4.6 percent. It thereafter quickly worsened.

In January 2009, when Democrats tightened their congressional control and President Obama took office, on Inauguration Day the nationwide average price per gallon for regular unleaded gasoline was $1.79, and unemployment stood at about 6.7 percent.

Since Mr. Obama took office, the national debt has grown by more than $5 Trillion and has reached its highest debt-to-GDP ratio since World War II. The national deficit tripled, sinking to nearly Minus $1.5 Trillion.

Gasoline prices have more than doubled since Mr. Obama's inauguration, and in some states have pushed beyond $5 per gallon towards $6. The ripple effects of such a jump in fuel prices increase the cost of everything that must be transported, including food and other goods at local stores and markets.

In April 2011, strategist Richard Hastings at Global Hunter Securities in Charlotte, North Carolina, warned that the weakening dollar makes gasoline prices so vulnerable that hurricane disruptions of output at even a few refineries during the 2011 season could easily send summer gas prices to $6.50 a gallon. At this price, the cost of filling a family car's 18-gallon gas tank would be $117.00. [28]

Financial analyst J. Kevin Meaders of Magellan Planning Group and ING Financial Partners in April 2011 predicted that inflationary forces evident in government data charts point to gasoline soon reaching $7 per gallon. At that price, a single 18-gallon fill-up would cost $126. [29]

Unemployment under President Obama quickly surged to double digits, despite what appeared to be gimmicking to make the numbers look better by the Administration-controlled Bureau of Labor Statistics. The non-politicized unemployment tracking done by the Gallup polling organization has relentlessly shown numbers higher than the Obama Administration's.

If we measure unemployment using the same methodology as during the Great Depression, under President Obama we find depression levels of underemployed, discouraged and unemployed workers.

## The Obama "Anti-stimulus"

President Obama has been active in pursuing his vision of job growth. He spent the first two years of his presidency preserving existing government jobs while hiring approximately 10,000 new Federal Government employees per month.

Such Federal civil servants in 2009 earned on average $123,049 per year in wages and benefits, more than double the $61,051 average annual wages plus benefits of private sector employees. [30]

Had Mr. Obama chosen instead to provide comparable tax incentives for private employment, he could have helped twice as many people find jobs.

These new government workers, of course, will be paid with money taxed away from private workers and companies. Obamacare all by itself directs the eventual hiring of an additional 16,000 Internal Revenue Service agents to enforce this one law. Of these new IRS agents, 81 reportedly will work only to enforce Obamacare's 10% tax on tanning salons. Many of these new IRS agents will doubtless increase the government's rate of auditing businesses to collect the ever-greater taxes a growing government requires.

Obamacare and the president's other policies will greatly increase the private sector's cost of complying with government taxes and regulation, a compliance cost that already exceeds $1.1 Trillion each year.

Incidentally, 16,000 is roughly the number of people in an ancient Roman Legion, a military force used to subdue and collect taxes in conquered provinces of the Roman Empire.

## Welfare Stated

Instead of creating jobs, President Obama and congressional Democrats created 99 weeks – nearly two years – of unemployment benefits. In effect, he put the unemployed on welfare and gave them an incentive to turn the social safety net into a hammock until their job skills and work habits dissipated from disuse, and their willpower turned to won't-power.

The European social welfare state Denmark used to offer its unemployed citizens benefits that lasted for five years. What it discovered was that when such benefits were cut to four years, people miraculously found work as soon as their government benefits ran out. The same thing usually happened when benefits were cut to three years, then to two years. [31]

Many employers have spoken to reporters about people applying for jobs who refuse to take a job unless paid under the table so that their unemployment and welfare checks can continue.

One might say that Mr. Obama, a veteran of Chicago politics, has tried to turn America into a giant version of the Windy City's ward heeler politics, where votes are bought with government money, and even the graveyards vote Democratic.

In 2010 in Obamerica, reported Fox Business Channel's Elizabeth MacDonald, households received $2.3 Trillion in one or another kind of government support – in extended unemployment benefits, Social Security, Medicare, Medicaid, stimulus spending programs and more.

What makes this striking, MacDonald notes, is that Americans in 2010 paid only $2.2 Trillion in taxes, a full $100 Billion fewer dollars than the government "redistributed" in checks to them.

These "government cash handouts," she writes, "account for a whopping 79% of household growth since 2007, even as household tax payments – for things like the income and payroll tax, among other taxes – have fallen by $312 Billion."

## Changing America's DNA

"Somehow the DNA of our country is changing," writes MacDonald. "Wealth creation is coming from D.C., not from America's entrepreneurs." [32]

This prompted Fox's Director of Business News, Ray Hennessey, to raise some tough questions in MacDonald's report:

If more households have the government to thank for their wealth, does that mean those households are more inclined to re-elect politicians who are pushing for more government handouts?

(For the answer, look in this month's issue of the scientific journal of the obvious, *DUH!*)

Does America's workforce erode because it is easier to collect a check than answer to an alarm clock each morning?

Is our competitiveness as a nation hurt because profit is generated not by American capitalism but by European-style socialism?

Can we, as taxpayers, afford to carry the burden of government-sponsored wealth creation?

## Welfare State Wages

More than one-third – 35 percent – of what we now call American "wages" and "salaries" now come from government entitlement programs, according to a March 2011 analysis by Madeline Schnapp, the Director of Macroeconomic Research at the investment research company TrimTabs. [33]

Such entitlement spending comprised only about nine percent of American wages and salaries in 1960, rose to 20 percent in 1975, reached 25 percent by 1993, and began a skyrocket ride soaring to today's 35 percent when President Obama was elected.

This rise in social welfare benefits has occasionally leveled off or even declined slightly, as it did during the last five years of Ronald Reagan's presidency.

For most of the last half-century, however, such social benefits have relentlessly ratcheted upward, going up during economic downturns but not retreating when good economic times return.

This enormous increase in transfer payments has come at the expense of private sector workers and companies which create the productivity on which government feeds.

This immense expansion of the welfare state has taken more than wealth from working Americans. It has also robbed them and their children of the resources that could have provided them a longer, happier and more pleasant life. It has robbed our most productive people of the ability to fulfill their own personal American dreams, their own individual pursuit of happiness.

Schnapp expects social welfare payments to remain at 35 percent or higher even after the economy improves. One reason for this, she writes, is that "the oldest of the 78 million Baby Boomers turn 65 this year and are eligible for Medicare."

# Pig in the Python

The Baby Boom has long been called America's demographic "pig in the python," a post-World War II reassertion of life and love that crowded maternity wards, then public schools and universities, then the job and housing markets, and soon retirement homes and then graveyards.

For the next several decades, however, retiring Baby Boomers shift from being taxpayers to tax takers and become a huge additional strain on a fragile economy. Younger Americans must wonder if geezer Boomers will become bigger pigs than ever before at the government trough.

One of the worst effects of the Baby Boom is already arriving, warned the National Inflation Association (NIA) in March 2011. The President of NIA is investment advisor Gerard Adams. [34]

"The fact is, the last baby-boomer turned 46 years old in 2010," NIA wrote, "and 46 is the age in which the average American reaches peak consumer spending."

"Therefore, even though most baby-boomers might not be retired, baby-boomer spending is now in free-fall while baby-boomers are simultaneously signing up for entitlement programs at record pace."

"This," wrote NIA, "will begin to affect our economy today, not 15 years from now." [35]

In recent years, consumption has accounted for 70 percent of America's Gross Domestic Product, and therefore a decline in Boomer spending will almost certainly cause a drop in GDP.

Baby-boomers may be America's Greatest Generation when it comes to self-indulgence. Many of its members will doubtless continue to spend on themselves and to buy "new and improved" – this generation's guiding motto – gadgets till their dying breath.

Many boomers will keep working to the end, as well, thereby block-ing the promotion ladder for many younger people and denying them what would have been a larger piece of the earnings pie when they turn age 46.

## On Uncle Sam's "Payroll"

Daniel Indiviglio, Associate Editor for the Atlantic Business Chan-nel, has drawn a striking conclusion from Schnapp's analysis of data from the Bureau of Economic Analysis.

With government social benefits and entitlements now 35 percent of American wages and salaries, he writes, "the U.S. government's transfer payment burden will, indeed, begin to resemble that of a European welfare state." [36]

In 1960 more than half of every tax dollar was spent for national de-fense. Today more than half of every tax dollar goes for "transfer payments," the fruits of your labor taken from your pocket so they can be put into the pocket of someone the politicians deem more de-serving of your money than you are.

Politicians such as President Obama have followed a transparent po-litical strategy in the tradition of left-liberal President Franklin D. Roosevelt's motto: "Tax and tax, spend and spend, elect and elect."

The key to this "progressive" politics is to buy the winning votes of a majority by massively, and selectively, tax-targeting minorities who do not vote for candidates of the Democratic Party.

In May 2011 the news broke that the Obama Administration plans to require all applicants for every kind of government contract work to provide details of all candidates, political parties and independent political expenditure organizations to which they have ever given contributions.

Skeptics wonder if this is being done to make politics cleaner, or as a way to threaten to deny contracts to those who support Republicans and conservatives, thereby drying up corporate contributions to Mr. Obama's opponents. [37]

After Mr. Obama expropriated General Motors and Chrysler, many long-established car dealerships were terminated. Critics noted that these terminations seemed not to correlate with a poor sales record, but with which dealership owners had been campaign contributors to the Republican Party.

This is state-capitalism-with-a-partisan-vengeance when we see that the Obama Administration has apparently likewise injected politics into government decisions about banks and investment houses, thereby threatening to cut off credit, the lifeblood of business, from other businesses targeted for political reasons. Meanwhile, 1,400 Obamacare waivers went mostly to Obama allies.

## Targeting the "Rich"

Chief among left-liberal targets are the so-called "rich," a tiny minority now burdened – in violation of both the U.S. Constitution's equal protection clause and liberal ideals of equal treatment before the law – with paying a huge share of the nation's taxes far beyond their share of income or wealth.

The top one percent of America's income earners now pays 34 percent of all Federal income taxes, a proportion far larger than their share of income.

American companies in our purportedly free market United States now pay the highest business tax rates in the world. Many businesses have responded by relocating to more tax-friendly countries such as Switzerland.

By one estimate, several trillion dollars on the books of such companies are not being transferred to the United States to create jobs and prosperity because, if they were, they would be taxed at a confiscatory 35 percent rate.

President Obama insists that only military spending, not entitlement spending, must be cut, and that the rich must bear the brunt of the massive tax increases he wants in order to sustain the 25 percent increase he in only two years has made to the size of our Federal Government's share of GDP.

Mr. Obama briefly proposed a Federal spending "freeze" after Republicans won control of the House of Representatives in November 2010. His apparent reason was not to limit government spending, but to lock in place the huge increases that he and the voter-rejected Democratic House of Representatives had made in social spending.

The dogma of the Big Government party is that – like the mysterious "arrow of time" that flies only into the future, never into the past – spending that increases dependency on government must go in only one direction: up, up, up.

Hennessey's question deserves an answer: Can we, as taxpayers, afford to carry the burden of government-sponsored wealth creation?

The Great Recession that began in 2008 may already have cost the United States 26 percent of its Gross Domestic Product.

"The impact of the next crisis will be greater," as MIT Sloan School of Management Professor Andrew Lo told *The Huffington Post* in 2011, "because the economy is in a much more fragile state...."

"Next time around, if we see another systemic shock, it will be very difficult for us to depend on our foreign trading partners to cushion that kind of blow," says Professor Lo. "The world economy is not as resiliant as it was just a few years ago." [38]

## Conjuring Cash

Pushed to the brink, America's leaders will have three choices to stave off insolvency, according to the International Monetary Fund:

– They can double all Federal taxes.

– They can cut all Federal Government spending by half.

– Or they can "monetize the debt," turn on the printing press and simply create however much money is needed to "pay" the politicians' obligations.

This money will have no real value, of course. And doing this will ruin our credit for generations to come, wreck our economy and crash the U.S. Dollar.

"Government," wrote Austrian economist Ludwig von Mises, "is the only institution that can take a valuable commodity like paper, and make it worthless by applying ink."

One key to unlocking The Inflation Deception is that America's Federal Reserve Board and Federal Government are monetizing our nation's debts right now.

Their aim is to accomplish this while using disinformation and distraction to prevent foreign bankers from panicking and American voters from seeing trillions of dollars being conjured from thin air by our money magicians.

Such sleight of hand by the Fed and Obama Administration would be tricky during good economic times. With the economy fragile and people frightened, this legerdemain is being played out in a dangerous environment with America's Rube Goldberg debt and America's borrowing on a short leash.

"About 40 percent of our federal debt is scheduled to mature by midyear 2011," write financial advisor Peter J. Tanous and CNBC's Jeff Cox in their 2011 book *Debt, Deficits and the Demise of the American Economy.* "Seventy percent of the debt will mature within five years."

"If investors smell even a whiff of inflation," write Tanous and Cox, "they will demand higher interest rates when the government attempts to roll over (reissue) the debt as it matures."

"For a strategy of 'inflating our way out of debt' to work," Tanous and Cox write, "we would need to have a much higher proportion of long-term debt to short-term debt. Indeed, we can't inflate our way home if inflation causes us to roll over existing debt at much higher interest rates." [39]

## Long Bondage

Is this why Treasury Secretary Timothy Geithner has been considering the issuance of new U.S. debt paper with 40, 50 and 100 year terms, or tied to GDP – to give Washington's politicians a longer leash on financial life and more running room to keep spending? [40]

In May 2010, write Tanous and Cox, the major credit rating agency Moody's "estimated that the cost of servicing the U.S. national debt could rise to as much as 23 percent of federal revenues by 2013...."

If this happens, the annual cost of interest alone on the national debt could exceed $4 Trillion!

This is roughly equivalent to more than $53,000 for every American family of four, just in annual interest on the national debt alone. Median U.S. household income in 2009 was $49,777.

"When the debt servicing costs for a nation reach 18 percent or more," write Tanous and Cox, "that country is on the equivalent of a 'credit watch' by the rating agencies."

"Indeed, none of the major credit agencies wants to see sovereign debt service in excess of 20 percent," they write. "If that happens, the credit agencies will downgrade that country's debt," as Standard & Poors warned in early 2011 could soon happen with the United States.

# Concealing Inflation

For a policy of deliberate inflation to work with optimal success, its victims must not fully understand what is happening. If they did, everyone would instantly try to adjust their prices and wages to off-set it – and the game could be over, or at least must be modified to keep average working Americans at a disadvantage.

"When people begin anticipating inflation, it doesn't do you any good anymore," said former Chair of the Federal Reserve Board Paul A. Volcker, "because any benefit of inflation comes from the fact that you do better than you thought you were going to do."

A key consideration was not whether the Fed "flooded liquidity in the marketplace," said Franklin Delano Raines – a Democratic oper-ative and Clinton Administration insider, who was made Chief Exec-utive Officer of the government-backed mortgage lender Fannie Mae – because "the mortgage rate is based much more on expectations of inflation. So if the average investor believes that there is inflation coming, they'll move that rate up."

Raines pocketed $90 Million for his role in Fannie Mae's notorious enabling of the mortgage mess that triggered our current economic problems. In the controversy that followed, Raines reportedly gave back approximately $7.1 Million of this.

Fannie Mae and Freddie Mac – which continue to siphon billions in taxpayer dollars for toxic mortgages they absorbed – became vehi-cles for funneling vast amounts of money into the pockets of Demo-cratic apparatchiks, from Jamie Gorelick to Rahm Emmanuel, as we explored in our previous book *Crashing the Dollar*.

"You could not buy a house in those days [of soaring home prices prior to 2007] without just assuming that the house was not only a place to live, but it was a good investment," said Volcker, "because it was going to keep up with inflation or get ahead of inflation, and it was just – that was America."

# The Invisible Depression

America today is very different. With 44.5 million on Food Stamps – up by nearly 40 percent since President Obama took office – and combined unemployment and underemployment stuck at 1930s levels, we are already living in an Invisible Depression.

We might not see people's belongings heaped in their front yards for non-payment of rent or mortgages, as was common during the 1930s, because banks now do slow-motion foreclosures. We see job-seekers only when they swarm places that publicize job openings, not standing outside factory gates every day to show their allegiance to the old work ethic, because millions now receive 99 weeks – nearly two years – of unemployment checks.

Today's bread lines and soup lines are likewise invisible, but nonetheless real. As famed Chief Economist for Gluskin Sheff, David Rosenberg, put it: "The modern day soup line is a check in the mail."

These government checks are directly or indirectly drawn against Federally borrowed and printed-from-thin-air paper fiat money. This feeds the inflation that has caused our problems, regressively taxing all of us via inflation to feed people harmed by government's inflationary policies. Thus the spiral feeds on itself as it drags us downward to a poorer, less free future of Big Government dependency.

Later in this book you will discover how the founder of the Soviet Union Vladimir Lenin, influential economist John Maynard Keynes and others understood many of the secret and subversive uses of deliberate inflation. To succeed, a policy of inflation requires gullible patsies it can deceive and rob.

This book was written to immunize you and to help you protect yourself and your loved ones against being taken in by the Inflation Deception.

# Chapter Three
# Ways Inflation Deceives

*"All the perplexities, confusion and distresses in America*
*arise not from defects in the Constitution*
*or confederation, nor from want of honor or virtue,*
*as much as from downright ignorance*
*of the nature of coin, credit and circulation."*

– John Adams
in a letter to Thomas Jefferson

Most of today's dictionaries, and even some economics textbooks, define inflation as a rise in the general level of prices of goods and services over a period of time.

This was not inflation's original meaning and is not its proper definition today.

"For many years, the word inflation was not a statement about prices but a condition of paper money – a specific description of a monetary policy," writes Michael F. Bryan, Vice President and economist at the Federal Reserve Bank of Cleveland. [41]

"What was once a word that described a monetary cause now describes a price outcome," writes Bryan, and this confuses people as to cause and effect and to inflation's cause and origin.

A six-year-old Federal Reserve Board was not confused in 1919 when its *Bulletin* said: "Inflation is the process of making addition to currencies not based on a commensurate increase in the production of goods."

"Substantial inflation is always and everywhere a monetary phenomenon," famously said Nobel-laureate economist Milton Friedman, meaning that inflation is an undue increase in the supply of money, just as the classic definition of inflation says. The rise in prices that can result from this is an effect of inflation, not inflation itself.

"As a condition of the money stock," writes Bryan, "an inflating currency has but one origin – the central bank – and one solution – a less expansive money growth rate."

Inflation occurs, in other words, when a government or its central bank – in America's case, the nominally private bank cartel called the Federal Reserve – authorizes the printing of more paper money than the value of newly-produced goods and services.

## "Magic" Money

Like the fabled genie, the Fed can create paper money by fiat, an order, out of thin air. Conjuring and spending this "magic" money is what early economists meant by inflation, and it has serious consequences.

Paper money is, in one sense, just another commodity subject to a law that can no more be repealed than the Law of Gravity – the economic Law of Supply and Demand. If consumers are willing and able to pay two dollars for the same number of potatoes that a day earlier cost one dollar, then the price of potatoes will soon dramatically increase.

Since 2008 the U.S. Government and Federal Reserve Board have pumped more than four trillion new dollars into the economy.

This was purportedly done to prevent key companies and banks from collapsing or going bankrupt, and to fill the nearly-bottomless hole in consumer demand caused by plummeting home values, soaring unemployment, and economic and government policy uncertainties that made people too afraid to spend as they previously had done.

Fed Chair Ben Bernanke recently implemented a policy of flooding an additional $600 Billion, conjured out of thin air, into the economy by July 2011 in a policy he calls Quantitative Easing 2 (QE2).

Will this increase consumer prices? $600 Billion is more than double the entire quantity of actual physical paper dollars in all American wallets, piggy banks, mattresses and home safes in the United States.

This is only a fraction of the electronic money in our economy that records in transactions (and your bank account) as computer blips, but QE2 is adding a huge amount of money that will dilute the purchasing power of every other dollar in circulation.

QE2 will compound the huge dormant inflation caused by QE1, both with its tidal wave of money and via speculation done to hedge the market, as happens with commodity futures trading.

Mr. Bernanke says that one of his aims is to stimulate the economy by deliberately generating roughly two percent inflation.

The Fed Chairman has, of course, already succeeded. Real inflation, as we mentioned earlier, according to *ShadowStats* is running at least 8.5 percent.

And in the pipeline headed to consumers' wallets, the Producer Price Index in April 2011 showed finished goods prices up 6.8 percent. The Bureau of Labor Statistics reported April 2011 intermediate goods prices rising at an annual rate of 9.4 percent.

Combine these rising prices with unemployment stuck at around 9 percent, observed Stanford University economist Ronald McKinnon in May 2011, and we are experiencing the return of the Jimmy Carter malaise of the 1970s. Stagnation and inflation are now again producing Stagflation. [42]

## Inflation Intoxication

Among the first effects and symptoms of inflation is an illusion of prosperity, abundance and well-being that tricks most of the people sometimes and some people all of the time.

This effect of inflation is addictive and requires ever-increasing doses of stimulus money, soon thereafter followed by a crash when people lose faith in their paper money and then a hangover that can last for years, even decades. [43]

This Inflation Deception happened in Germany's Weimar Republic after World War I, where vast quantities of paper money run off the printing presses first intoxicated, then addicted, and in its hyperinflationary crash devastated the society as people needed wheelbarrows full of money to buy a single loaf of bread.

Social values were destroyed in the upside-down Weimar world where hard work and thrift led to poverty, while irresponsible borrowing made wastrels wealthy as they paid off debts with devalued worthless currency. Weimar's hyperinflation and moral breakdown thus paved the path to the depravity of Adolf Hitler.

In a healthy, productive society, each working person, on average, produces at least as much as he or she consumes. The money a person earns for productive work is an honest claim on goods and services in the marketplace.

One of the fundamental problems with inflation is that politicians concoct vast quantities of paper money in excess of what people are actually producing.

This concocted cash is created so that the politicians can give them-selves and other unproductive people a dishonest claim on available goods and services that others worked to produce.

This effectively transfers much of the earnings of productive people into the pockets of the unproductive, while bidding up the price of everything for consumers.

Those who get the biggest gain from such newly-made fiat money are the ones who receive it first. They can buy at the lower old prices, before the marketplace adjusts by the irrevocable Law of Supply and Demand to the larger supply of paper dollars available to buy things.

As these new dollars go from hand to hand, they lose value because sellers recognize this growing supply of dollars as a sign that the value of dollars is in decline.

## Stopping the Heartbeat

British economist John Maynard Keynes studied how various nations fared after World War I. He developed the idea that governments could prevent the up and down, boom and bust economic roller coaster ride of the business cycle if governments and/or their central banks borrowed to inject economic stimulus into their economies at the low point in such cycles.

Such borrowing could be repaid by increasing taxation or interest rates at the prosperous high points of such cycles, he wrote, thereby reducing what one Fed chairman later called investor "irrational ex-huberance" and investment bubbles.

The first problem with Lord Keynes' theory is that in our age of paper fiat money, the business cycle has become the heartbeat of the economy. This cycle weeds out weak companies and entrepreneurs while making strong ones stronger.

The business cycle is a way of recycling workers and investment money to newer and better purposes. It has become part of the dynamism that churns up and thereby helps renew the modern economy.

## Unnatural Cycles

According to pure free market economists such as Murray N. Rothbard, the market's boom-bust cycle "began in the 18th Century with the beginnings of central banking, and has spread and intensified ever since, as central banking spread and took control of the economic systems of the Western world."

"Only the abolition of the Federal Reserve System and a return to the gold standard can put an end to cyclical booms and busts," according to Rothbard, "and finally eliminate chronic and accelerating inflation."

"Inflation, credit expansion, business cycles, heavy government debt, and high taxes," wrote Rothbard, "are not, as Establishment historians claim, inevitable attributes of capitalism or of 'modernization.'"

"On the contrary," Rothbard wrote, "these are profoundly anticapitalist and parasitic excrescences grafted onto the system by the interventionist State, which rewards its banker and insider clients with hidden special privileges at the expense of everyone else." [44]

## "Socialism Through the Back Door"

By choking off the business cycle through political monetary redistribution, Keynesian policies disrupt our paper economy's process of economic recycling and renewal.

This government interference in the economy then further degenerates as politicians redirect stimulus money, tax breaks, government contracts and other benefits to individuals, industries and specific companies they favor, often for arbitrary, ideological or corrupt self-serving reasons.

Such stimulus can become a permanent and regular feature of government policy and swiftly become "socialism through the back door" as marketplace winners and losers are picked not by consumers and investors but by politicians.

Government intervention also creates malinvestment by companies and individuals whose decisions are based upon government policy, not what makes economic sense. How many self-employed people used to purchase computers they did not need simply because this could be deducted from their income taxes?

And government has learned to use aptly-named "Pigovian" taxes and inflation not only to raise revenue but also to impel taxpayers to do things the government wishes.

"We don't have a market economy now," says Thomas Hoenig, retiring President of the Federal Reserve Bank of Kansas City, Missouri. "I hate to use this term, but it's almost crony capitalism – who you know, how big your political donation is." [45]

When the business cycle heartbeat of the economy is thus manipulated and suppressed, free market capitalism dies and is replaced by crony capitalism. Giant companies such as General Electric become so close to politicians and the government that they have effectively merged with and become extensions of government.

The stimulus policies of recent years merged with TARP, the spending of nearly a trillion dollars to bail out companies the government deemed "too big to fail."

## Unnatural Markets

One of the ugliest, but least noticed, aspects of today's crony capitalism is that it encourages reckless high-risk investing by companies that know they will be rescued when their economic bets go bad.

Some liberals have rightly described this as high-stakes gambling in a rigged capitalist casino. When a risky investment wins, those marketplace winnings are pocketed by private companies and individuals. When such gamblers lose, however, they receive socialist-like government repayment for their losses using taxpayer money bailouts and other policies.

Sound investing is based on a balance of risk, reward and prudence. In recent years government bailouts and risk-spreading devices such as derivatives have largely erased risk. This turned Wall Street capitalism into a reckless high-stakes game where the unspoken motto was: heads I win, tails the taxpayers lose.

"By manipulating the supply of money and setting interest rates, the Fed has practiced backdoor economic planning," writes Rep. Ron Paul (R.-Texas) in his 2009 book *End the Fed*. [46]

"The Fed essentially keeps interest rates lower than they otherwise would be," Rep. Paul continued. "In a free market, low rates would indicate adequate savings and signal the businessperson that it's an opportune time to invest in capital projects."

"But the system the Fed operates discourages savings, and the credit created out of thin air serves as the signal for investors to spend, invest, and borrow excessively, compared to a system where interest rates are set by the market."

The Fed and government thus create malinvestment in the economy and produce economic distortions that cripple the free market's ability to invest rationally based on consumer wants and needs.

This, at best, creates a phony prosperity prone to speculation, bubbles, and a destructive misallocation of resources based not on genuine consumer wants and needs but on political considerations and caprice. Businesses and individuals invest, for example, based on what can be written off for taxes – even when such investment makes little or no economic sense.

A few years ago, for example, politicians created a short-term tax policy that allowed businesses to write off in one year the cost of a new SUV. Many small companies rushed to buy SUVs, and both they and the nation now bear the cost of more dependence on oil imports for these poor-gas-mileage vehicles.

Such political manipulation of the market, ironically, produces many of the same problems as socialist centralized planning because, as Rep. Paul wrote, it is "backdoor economic planning" by government-empowered bureaucrats and Federal Reserve commissars.

## The Speed of Unsound Money

Keynes taught that stimulus would work because money in an economy has at least two attributes – quantity and velocity, the speed at which it passes from hand to hand in transactions.

A wise government, neo-Keynesian theory still teaches, will provide money to the poor who, because they must spend it immediately to buy food and other necessities, will increase its velocity. This speed, Keynes believed, creates a "multiplier effect" in stimulating a slow economy. It also revives people's optimistic "animal spirits" essential to feeling the confidence to invest and spend. [47]

The economists in the Obama Administration are devout Keynesians who calculated that their stimulus spending would have a "multiplier effect" of 1.5 to 1.6 and produce rapid economic growth.

They were wrong. Massive government spending produced little growth and few jobs, not the millions of jobs they expected. We got a multiplier of less than 1.0 as recipients used government money to pay down existing debt, and governments used it to "save" jobs and pensions of public employees – using money taxed and inflated away from $60,000-per-year average private sector workers to safe-

guard government workers, many of whose pay-plus-benefits average $123,000 per year.

President Obama signed into law an $862 Billion stimulus package
that he said would fix America's deteriorating infrastructure and provide "shovel-ready jobs." The money was spent, but only $4 Billion
of the $862 Billion – less than one-half of one percent – was spent on
infrastructure.

Senator Tom Coburn (R.-Oklahoma) has documented some of the
wasteful projects funded by tax dollars. Such wild spending ranges
from $41,000-apiece woodland potties in outback Alaska to video
games, to museums for parachutes, neon signs and other oddities,
and to paying prisoners $112 Million in bogus tax refunds. To see
his 2010 Wastebook findings with 100 outrageous examples of
where the taxes taken from you and your family at gunpoint are
being spent, download his booklet. [48]

The Obama Administration sent $173 Billion to state and local gov-
ernments, where most was squandered. *Investor's Business Daily* concluded that all this spending produced few jobs and generated little
economic stimulus, calling it "a huge repudiation of the ideas behind
Keynesianism." [49]

The lion's share of this stimulus money went to "transfer payments,"
taking the dollars you earned and saved from your pocket so they
could go into the pockets of people more likely to vote for President
Barack Obama and others in his Big Government political party.

In some ways Mr. Obama's stimulus produced negative growth, because government, by hook or by crook, must take money in taxes,
available loans or monetary value away from other potential investors,
who then will be unable to spend it. [50] Government stimulus thus
can, and often does, produce less economic stimulus, not more. And
whatever stimulus it does create is chosen by partisan politicians and
their cronies, not by you who earned the money.

## Keynesian True Believers

Keynes apparently was somewhat mistaken about stimulus and its multiplier effect, according to new research by economists Ethan Ilzetzki of the London School of Economics and Enrique G. Mendoza and Carlos A. Vegh of the University of Maryland. They studied how it worked in 44 different countries and found that the Keynesian fiscal multiplier can be effective in emerging countries with low debts, fixed exchange rates and closed economies. [51]

In advanced nations like the United States with high debt, floating exchange rates and open economies, however, Keynesian measures are often much less effective.

Lord Keynes came from an earlier era in which people were productive and saved – a time long before middle-class people lived on credit cards instead of earnings, and long before 70 percent of America's Gross Domestic Product (GDP) was created, as it is today, by consumer and government spending.

This new analysis of today's spendthrift era of living on credit makes it clear that Mr. Obama's stimulus policies have wasted trillions of dollars on a wrong-headed left-liberal Keynesian dogma. Obama and Fed Chair Bernanke via QE2 created a process that wasted another $600 Billion in another failed attempt to stimulate the U.S. economy.

Let's be clear. Today's Neo-Keynesians will never be persuaded by the evidence that they are wrong. For them Keynesianism is a religion that promises them the keys to a heavenly utopia in which government, run by a chosen elite of superior people like themselves, will control all aspects of human society, including the economy.

As True Believer religious zealots possessed by their own bestial "animal spirits," the Keynesians' response to all contrary evidence is that "we didn't spend enough on stimulus."

If only government would tax away everything from the rich and spend another $100 Trillion on stimulus to redistribute that wealth, they say, a glorious new age will dawn.

## Atlas Is Shrugging

Even if Keynes' theory were correct, such stimulus is both immoral for robbing those who earn society's wealth and the wrong medicine for what currently ails the American economy. His stimulus is supposed to create liquidity to lubricate a dry economy, but today's economy is not dry – it is frozen.

Corporations and banks reportedly have been holding back at least $3 Trillion on their books, reluctant to hire or invest because of uncertainties about how President Obama's unspecified tax, regulatory and other policies will affect their future costs of doing business.

In addition to such uncertainty, some corporate leaders may unconsciously be living out the fantasy set forth by philosopher Ayn Rand in her novel *Atlas Shrugged* – a strike by society's "productive" people, a work stoppage to protest ever-higher taxes and oppressive mandates that force them to pull the wagon millions of others feel entitled to ride in for free.

We may be seeing Atlas shrugging right now in the ongoing slowdown by investors and employers against an Obama Administration that is openly hostile towards business and capitalism.

When this $3 Trillion regains velocity in the economy, and when hundreds of billions of stimulus money now hoarded by recipient entities is again being spent, the economy will be awash in money and a dangerous excess of liquidity.

Explosive inflation will likely then send prices soaring, perhaps leading to Weimar-like hyperinflation in which prices double every month, thereby turning the United States into Weimerica.

By following a QE2 policy deliberately intended to ignite inflation, Mr. Bernanke and the Federal Reserve are literally playing with fire in a room full of frozen gasoline.

## Housing's Potemkin Village

QE2 may have caused the stock market to inflate its values, perhaps by using Fed money secretly channeled through its 18 insider lending institutions. [52]

Housing – which has been the biggest form of savings by middle-class Americans and the biggest source of their spending of borrowed money prior to the Great Recession that began in 2008 – continues to lose value and drag down the economy. Improvements in the housing market, which affects roughly one-third of American jobs, have usually led the way out of past recessions.

Fully 28 percent of borrowers as of April 2011 were "underwater" on their mortgages, according to the home pricing service Zillow.com, with people owing more than the market and appraisal value of their homes. In the Fourth Quarter of 2010 average home prices plunged another 5.9 percent [46] and have continued to fall. [53]

Housing by May 2011 was suffering a worse decline than it did during the Great Depression of the 1930s.

This should concern even non-homeowners, because America has never in its history recovered from a recession or depression until the housing market recovered.

The continuing fall of home prices may have a silver lining for young people who used to think they could never afford a home, but for those with life savings tied up in an upside-down home this is a prolonged nightmare.

America is rapidly turning from a nation of homeowners into a nation of renters. This, too, is troubling when we recognize that it means more shallowly rooted and transient communities of people who have less sense of permanence and investment in the place where they live.

Meanwhile, at least 11 percent of the nation's homes – and 20 percent of Florida homes – stand empty. The "shadow inventory" of unsold homes may be as high as 6 to 7 million, many of which have yet to be put on the market lest oversupply drag prices down even further and faster. Even if the rest of the economy recovered this afternoon, it will take at least two years to clear this glut of houses to be sold.

The fact that the housing market continues to lose value suggests that today's "recovery" is either anemic or part of a Potemkin Village, a fake structure of the kind originally built to fool Russian Czarina Catherine the Great.

Today's Potemkin Village masquerades as a solid economic recovery, fabricated through media reports and low-volume stock exchange activity as an illusion to fool consumers into spending again.

## The Unemployment Deception

Unemployment remains stuck at or near double-digit levels. In early February, 2011, Mr. Obama's Executive Branch reported January growth of only 36,000 jobs, but declared at the same time that unemployment had dropped from 9.6 to 9.0 percent of the workforce. It based this seeming contradiction on evidence that nearly two million people in January gave up, ceased looking for jobs, and thereby were no longer counted as unemployed.

By this reasoning, wrote financial columnist John Crudele of the *New York Post*, "the jobless rate will end up zero when everybody who is unemployed throws in the towel and simply stops sending out resumes or looking in the help-wanted ads." [54-57]

Like many other government economic numbers, the Bureau of Labor Statistics (BLS) employment information is a mix of hard data and out-of-thin-air guesses and assumptions that is not necessarily reliable.

The yardsticks chosen to measure unemployment sometimes change in ways that appear political.

In January's report, for example, if BLS had used the same assumption about job losses that it used a year earlier, writes Crudele, its "headline number could have been negative instead of showing the paltry 36,000 job growth." [54]

The U.S. Commerce Department reported that sales were up in December 2010, data that many in the media reported as evidence that consumer activity was increasing and the economy was growing.

But a deeper look, writes Crudele, reveals that this rise came not from happy consumers "but instead from rising prices on things like energy. That isn't growth; it is inflation. And inflation is bad." [55]

Crudele's wise words apply to nearly the entire economy, throughout which Mr. Obama's media allies and operatives are busy selling the symptoms of inflation as if rising costs were signs of emerging prosperity. People are being deceived, like a pilot lost in fog who believes he is flying higher when in fact he is plummeting downward towards a crash.

"Despite all the inflation that you and I see in the real world," writes Crudele, "the Commerce Dept. barely noticed that prices were rising in its GDP (Gross Domestic Product) calculations.... The December estimates put into the GDP are about as solid as a Jello mold." [56]

This lack of growth begets a lack of jobs. Today our economy has at least 7.2 million fewer jobs than before the Great Recession. Many of these jobs are never coming back. They have moved overseas, vanished in the disappearance of unsuccessful businesses, or been eliminated by companies that learned how to produce more with fewer workers.

# Governmental Cannibalism

Unemployment, the decline in housing, and slow economic activity have combined to reduce the tax revenues of states, counties and cities – which, unlike the Federal Government, cannot simply print whatever amount of money they desire.

In recent years states such as California have engaged in governmental cannibalism as counties have seized city property tax revenues, and the state government has seized county revenues. California, whose legislature has been run by liberal redistribute-the-wealth Democrats for many decades, is now at least $25 Billion in debt, despite its use of every bookkeeping trick in the books to remain solvent.

Nationwide, the fat paychecks and pensions politicians promised to government employees and their unions during more prosperous times have left state, county and city governments a bitter legacy of at least $3.5 Trillion in underfunded promises. Federal bailouts in 2009 and 2010 largely went to keep these government retainers from losing pay and benefits, or from being fired like their lower-paid private sector counterparts in downsizing and failing companies.

In 2011, with the dawn of a Republican-majority House of Representatives, the likelihood that such Federal bailouts will continue should have largely vanished.

This should be likely for at least three reasons. Republicans generally find it distasteful to make one person or state pay for the irresponsibility of another person or state. States that have been profligate – and especially those run into the ground by liberal Democrats elected with union help – should bear the price of their vote-buying, spendthrift behavior.

Republicans also say they believe in states' rights, local sovereignty and the Constitution's separation of powers. These would be lost if states and localities became mere dependencies, bowing and scraping for the money to survive from the Federal Government in Washington, D.C. It would turn individual states and localities into welfare recipient governments, or into beneficiaries of partisan or ideological preference in a new national scheme of wealth redistribution.

And many elected Republican lawmakers now depend on the Tea Party Movement to secure their current House majority and have a chance of winning back the U.S. Senate and White House.

Although Republican lawmakers in the past have supported their own versions of Big Government and stratospheric spending, they logically should vote for government reductions that Tea Party members seek.

Republicans took conservatives for granted in the late 1990s, forgetting that disgusted voters might vote with their feet by not showing up at the polls to cast ballots. Have these politicians learned their lesson? We can only hope that, as the old political saying goes, "When they feel the heat, they see the light."

## Breaking Point

The other elephant in the room today that few are willing to face is whether economic collapse in America will begin at the top with the Federal Government monetizing its debt, thereby sending prices into the stratosphere and the U.S. Dollar into history's garbage can – or at the bottom with a spate of city, county and state bankruptcies as local and state officials attempt to re-write public employee union contracts to slow what nationwide has become a public employee union gravy train.

In 2010 in Greece, where government has run up debts equivalent to $250,000 per Greek taxpayer, this latter scenario led to public strikes, lethal violence, and a breakdown of social and civil order that further damaged the climate for investment. The resulting uncertainty made bonds and loans more expensive, pushed up the cost of living, and depressed the prospects for future economic growth. These tectonic forces may yet collapse the fledgling currency of the

European community, the Euro, and start economies falling like dominoes from Dublin to Palermo.

In 2011 in Madison, Wisconsin, the nation witnessed a nationally-organized union attack, complete with death threats and other intimidation, against state officials who dared to impose even tiny limits on lavish public employee benefits.

The union concern is politically understandable. Union membership in the private sector over the past 60 years has shrunk from more than 30 percent to less than seven percent of workers. Organized labor has become so desperate that it now has the politicians dependent on its huge campaign contributions trying to enact "card check," which would deny company workers a secret ballot election to decide if they wish to become unionized.

Under "card check," union goons carrying baseball bats could surround individual employees after work and demand that they sign a card in support of unionization. When a bare majority of such employees has been intimidated into signing, unionization of their company and imposition on all employees of union dues – a fat chunk of which gets kicked back to liberal politicians – becomes automatic.

Roughly one third of government workers, by contrast, are unionized – not via secret ballot nor even "card check," but merely by the fiat of politicians who pocket fat union campaign contributions. Public employees are the fastest – indeed, almost the only – growing segment of the labor movement.

## Government Gimmickry

Government's gimmickry with data and statistics suggests that no piece of good economic news from the government can be trusted. All such data now appears to be massaged, manipulated and tailored to serve President Obama's 2012 re-election campaign already underway.

By contrast with Obama Administration numbers, the Gallup polling organization does its own tracking of unemployment and in early February reported that unemployment had increased to 9.8 percent. [58]

The cost and uncertainty caused by Obama Administration policies and its open hostility to capitalism and business have produced poor results.

By adding more than $4 Trillion to our nation's debts and deficit – the largest infusion of stimulus money in human history – Obama boasts that he has driven economic growth to somewhere between one and three percent.

At best, the anemic 1.8 percent "growth" reported in May 2011 following this huge stimulus is being devoured by concealed inflation running at perhaps 8.5 percent, more than four times our economic rate of growth.

Factor in today's real inflation and the U.S. is now suffering negative growth, an unreported economic contraction of at least 6.7 percent.

As noted earlier, Mr. Obama's government-expanding expenditures and legislative agenda therefore could be called an "anti-stimulus" because they frightened businesspeople away from investing and hiring.

The housing, employment, economic growth and inflation data coming from the Obama Administration may or may not be politicized. It is certainly unreliable. Genuine data might show what an astonishing failure the current Administration is.

"The Bureau of Labor Statistics is lying...[and Fed Chairman] Mr. Bernanke is a liar," famed investment analyst Marc Faber told cnbc.com in February 2011. "Inflation is much higher than what they publish." [59]

Because of this failure, we could be on the verge of inflation or hyperinflation that will bring hardships and horrors even worse than the nightmare of the Jimmy Carter years.

## "It's the Economy, Stupid!"

The winning slogan of Democratic candidate Bill Clinton's 1992 presidential campaign was "It's the economy, Stupid!"

Throughout American history, incumbent presidents have usually won re-election when the economy is good and voters feel prosperous and optimistic.

Challenger Clinton and his media allies defeated incumbent President George H.W. Bush by deceiving the public into believing that the 1992 economy – which we now know was well into full recovery – was "the worst economy in 50 years."

That same left-liberal mainstream media will do all in its power to create the illusion of economic recovery in 2011 and 2012 to help re-elect President Barack Obama.

The Federal Reserve, the government bureaucracy, and of course the Democratic Party and its apparatchiks have the means and motive to rig statistics and generate short-term improvements in parts of the economy to bolster this illusion.

This illusion will be carefully orchestrated to reach its crescendo in the months just prior to the election. It will, in fact, appear in the media as a powerful surge of economic improvement.

This will be exactly the reverse of the precisely-coordinated attack on America's banks and other financial institutions that caused the economy to plunge in September 2008, stampeding frightened Americans into voting for hope and change by electing an unproven Senator Barack Obama as our new Chief Executive and Commander-in-Chief.

This attempt to herd Americans a second time will be full of tricks, but it will also be tricky to carry off successfully.

The hurdles President Obama and his allies must clear to win the 2012 presidential run are high, hard and numerous – in part because of how the Fed, inflation and related historic and financial changes have reshaped the playing field of our politics.

## Dilemmas of Our Politicized Economy

"The perfection of interest-group politics," writes Federal Circuit Court Judge Richard Posner in his 2010 book *The Crisis of Capitalist Democracy*, "seems to have brought about a situation in which…taxes can't be increased, spending programs can't be cut, and new spending is irresistible." [60]

President Obama and Federal Reserve Chairman Ben Bernanke, true to the dogma of neo-Keynesian economics, believed that injecting more than $4 Trillion dollars into the economy would produce explosive growth and prosperity.

This largest Keynesian stimulus in history failed for a host of reasons we explore here and in our previous book *Crashing the Dollar: How to Survive a Global Currency Collapse*.

What remains is the cost of this vast expenditure, a crushing addition to the national debt – and the coming very high inflation this flood of money already has begun to unleash.

Here are a few of the dilemmas Mr. Obama and his comrades now face.

The Fed has held interest rates close to zero to encourage borrowing, spending and growth.

Certain giant banks and other financial institutions have been delighted to borrow vast sums at essentially no cost – but rather than take the risk of lending it to homeowners and businesses, most have simply bought government paper that pays a few percent interest with 100 percent safety.

Rather than go out into the free marketplace, many hundreds of billions of dollars simply made a U-turn back to the government, which used this turnaround cash to stay solvent and expand government payrolls.

## "Crowded Out"

This, along with Federal Government borrowing from other nations, has largely "crowded out" of the lending market those capitalists seeking loans to sustain or enlarge their own enterprises.

By pressuring banks to tighten their lending standards for private borrowers in the wake of the 2008 mortgage paper nightmare, the government gave banks and others a double incentive to lend mostly to the one borrower who could always make good on its loans – because it has the legal power to print money: the Federal Government.

Government, however, produces nothing of real value. Whatever the government has, it has gotten by taxation, confiscation, conquest or fiat.

Tax-paying private companies and people do make things and are the source of whatever genuine wealth the government spends or redistributes.

Growth in the private sector is, therefore, what government must depend on for the means to pay its debts. This is where President Obama must look for the green shoots of economic growth that could persuade voters to re-elect him.

Trouble is, the Obama Administration's anti-business policies have choked off the credit businesspeople need to recover, grow and hire.

The Obama Administration arbitrarily seized control of many banks, expropriated two of America's biggest motor vehicle companies, capriciously shut down oil drilling in much of the country, and now says it intends to increase taxes on businesses – when America already has the highest business taxes in the world.

This has created uncertainty and fear among potential investors and companies in the private sector and, even using the government's optimistic rigged numbers, has reduced the growth of the U.S. economy to 1.8 percent....an anemic rate at which economic recovery could take decades, if it survives at all. Unless current profligate government spending changes, our economy will self-destruct at the latest by 2037 – but probably much, much sooner, whenever others decide to stop lending the freespending United States money.

Even House Democratic minority whip Rep. Steny Hoyer (D.-Maryland) in March 2011 acknowledged that the Federal budget may not be balanced for 20 years, and even then only if economic growth turns robust. "We've dug such a deep hole," says Hoyer. [61]

In Spring 2011, real estate specialists pronounced that home prices – already down on average by at least 30 percent from their 2006 prerecession peak – have at least 5 percent to 20 percent farther to fall.

## America Underwater

As we noted earlier, the Seattle-based home-value-tracking service *Zillow.com* in May 2011 reported that more than 28 percent of mortgage holders are now "underwater," owing more on their mortgages than their homes – for most families their most valuable asset – are worth.

Analysts now predict that home values may not recover for at least 10 years.

No past recession or depression in American history has ended until home prices recovered.

Non-partisan economic analysts in Spring 2011 were describing

America's housing market as entering the second dip of a double-dip recession.

Official government unemployment statistics, meanwhile, dipped to 8.8 percent in March 2011 – thanks to some bookkeeping sleight of hand that conjured more than 100,000 jobs out of thin air, the way the Fed creates money.

By June 2011, however, even official unemployment had risen again to 9.1 percent. The real number of unemployed-plus-underemployed is roughly double this, according to *ShadowStats* analysis.

## Obama-in-Wonderland

Our Obamanomics situation at this point takes a sharp turn to the left, and President Obama and Fed Chair Bernanke begin to look like Alice-in-Wonderland and the Mad Hatter.

High unemployment like that in the Eurosocialist welfare states is actually good, Mr. Bernanke assures us, because we cannot fall into runaway inflation with so many available workers keeping wages down.

Those of you who have not taken Alice's red pill will notice that this means the Obama Administration actually *wants* and *needs* high unemployment so that it can go on spending vast quantities of freshly-printed Federal Reserve Notes.

This means that the Obama Administration is deliberately crowding out private borrowers, not only to guarantee a huge supply of Federal cash but also to hold down the velocity of money so runaway inflation cannot ignite.

## The Obama Paradox

Paradoxically, this also means that Mr. Obama's re-election cannot afford any good news, such as his successful military strike that killed 9-11 terrorist mastermind Osama bin Laden.

The paradox is that good news will be perceived as favoring Mr. Obama's re-election.

The prospect of Mr. Obama winning re-election will further discourage private sector investors, most of whom regard four more years of the Obama presidency as the end of free market capitalism in America. Obama's re-election would also mean that a majority favored an anti-free enterprise government.

President Obama has already sworn that he will never again extend the tax cuts put in place by former President George W. Bush. If Mr. Obama wins reelection in 2012, this lame duck president will no longer be concerned about public opinion and will rule like an emperor, by executive orders and emergency decrees.

President Obama will veto any attempt to extend the Bush tax cuts. In January 2013 this will instantly add an additional, back-breaking $2 Trillion burden to American taxpayers and businesses on top of the nearly-fatal economic damage Mr. Obama has already done.

Any good news for President Obama's re-election would therefore become bad news by prompting businesses and investors to move their assets out of the United States, or at least to curtail investing and hiring.

He could win a second term as President of a country with lots of takers but few makers, with lots of welfare and entitlement recipients and other Big Government dependents but few taxpayers left to pull the wagon his voters expect to ride in for free.

If Mr. Obama and Fed Chair Bernanke raise interest rates from near-zero, they risk choking off the anemic economic recovery, the prospects for more private-sector jobs, and the already-drowning housing market. If Mr. Obama raises taxes, which in turn will be passed on as higher prices, the effect will be essentially the same.

Mr. Obama will have only one way left to govern, short of outright socialist dictatorship. Get ready for the printing presses to run night and day churning out debased dollars for an exploding population of government "employees" and dependents, as Alice moves us to the Twilight Zone.

There's the signpost up ahead that reads "Welcome to Weimerica." The hyperinflation of Weimar, Germany, will soon engulf America.

Looking at President Obama's and Fed Chair Ben Bernanke's free-spending policies, Credit Suisse UK economist Robert Barrie in April 2011 told his austerity-backing European clients: "The U.S. is on a different monetary planet from the rest of the world."

Can President Obama's media allies and other apparatchiks thread this needle of a good-news-is-bad-news political contest to win with the votes of the parasites, without scaring off the producers?

Democrats have worked similar political wonders – such as persuading African-Americans to vote for them, the party of the slave owners, the Ku Klux Klan, Jim Crow and Bull Connor, instead of for the Republican Party of the Great Emancipator. They have a knack for fooling some of the people all of the time.

Stay tuned.

# Part Two
# Inflation's Method Of Operation

# Chapter Four

# A Compressed History
# of Inflation

*"With the exception only of the period of the gold standard,
practically all governments of history have used
their exclusive power to issue money
to defraud and plunder the people."*

– Friedrich A. Hayek
Nobel Laureate Economist

Inflation is not new. The deliberate debasing of money by those who rule may be as old as money itself.

One of the earliest units of Biblical money – the Shekel, still used as the name of Israel's currency – began in Mesopotamia around 3,000 B.C. as both a unit of value and a measure of barley, which among Israelites became a measure of silver.

(Millennia later, the British Pound began as a piece of silver that literally weighed one pound.)

From the dawn of such proto-money, sharpers found ways to short-change those they traded with by using two sets of weights on scales. The Bible contains many passages against those who used dishonest weights and measures to inflate or deflate the true value of what was being traded.

The rulers of Middle Eastern kingdoms began making coins of gold or silver nearly 4,000 years ago, then quickly learned and employed the tricks of stealing back for themselves part of the value from their own coins.

A typical king would call in and melt down his nation's old coinage, dilute its precious metal with cheaper base metal, then issue new coins to honor himself or a local pagan deity.

Such kings reimbursed the old coins of their subjects with these new debased coins, as if the value of the two were the same. The kings then pocketed whatever diverted pure gold or silver, or however many additional coins containing precious metal, that such re-minting let them get away with, leaving their subjects to wonder where their king got all his new wealth.

Rulers, then as now, were eager to siphon off whatever of value that their people earned. These rulers, however, were furious and punished it as a crime when others clipped or filed off bits of precious metal from rough-edged royal coins or made their own counterfeits by melting, further diluting, and then recasting the king's coinage.

## Submerging the Crown

In the Third Century B.C. such anger flared in Heiro II, the king of Greek Syracuse on the now-Italian island of Sicily. The king had hired an artist to fashion a votive gold crown for a local temple and had provided a significant quantity of gold with which to make it.

This crown, according to the Roman architect Vitruvius, was beautifully made. King Heiro had been delighted with it, until he heard rumors that the artist had stolen part of his gold, disguising the theft by melting an equal weight of silver invisibly into the crown's gold. If these rumors were true, then the artist was a criminal and the crown was unfit for religious use.

The crown appeared to be solid gold, and its weight was identical to the gold the king provided. How could the truth be proven?

The king had a cousin named Archimedes, who at age 22 was already starting to be recognized in the Greek world as a great philosopher, scientist and mathematician. Was there a way, King Heiro asked him, to discern whether this crown was entirely gold without cutting, scraping on a touchstone such as slate, or otherwise damaging it?

Archimedes told the king he knew of no way to do this, yet he would ponder the question.

Days later Archimedes was at a local bath where, as he immersed himself in a full tub, he noticed that water ran over its edge and splashed onto the floor. A person of a different body density, with more fat or less, his scientific mind understood in a flash, would displace from the tub a different amount and weight of water.

## Debasement Detected

Archimedes jumped from the bathtub, the story goes, and ran stark naked through Syracuse streets to the king's palace shouting in Greek *Eureka! Eureka!*, "I have found it! I have found it!"

His naked shout has echoed in our civilization for more than 2,200 years. *Eureka* would become the official motto of the Golden State of California and the name of more than a dozen American towns and cities that either were or hoped to be the center of a gold or silver rush.

Scientists from Galileo's Renaissance era to our own time have questioned precisely how Archimedes used this insight.

Knowing that gold has far more density – more weight per volume – than silver and most other metals, Archimedes could have made two pieces of exactly the same weight as the crown, one piece gold and the other silver.

If the crown was pure gold, Archimedes surmised, it would displace exactly the same weight of water as the piece of gold. But if the crown was an alloy containing silver, it would have less density and more volume than gold, and would send more weight in water over the tub edge. In principle this would detect a silver alloy, but could the crude measurement tools of 265 B.C. have done this?

Galileo proposed that Archimedes could have balanced the crown and an equal weight of gold on a simple scale, then submerged the scales in water. If the crown contained silver, it would have more buoyancy and would rise while the gold sank. [62]

Archimedes, whose genius discerned some of the foundations of calculus nearly 2,000 years ahead of anyone else and who has a crater on the Moon named in his honor, wrote a treatise about buoyancy titled "On Floating Bodies."

Whichever method Archimedes used, his scientific evidence persuasively demonstrated that the crown was not pure gold, that the artist had diluted the crown's gold with silver – much as kings have done for centuries to debase their coinage.

## Worse than a Highwayman

Why does inflation happen? Human greed and deceit have always been with us. What we think of as inflation, however, almost always begins with government and the avarice of some ruler.

"Governments are inherently inflationary," wrote free market economist Murray Rothbard in his classic book *What Has Government Done to Our Money?* [63]

"Bankers know that history is inflationary," wrote Christian socialist historian Will Durant, "and that money is the last thing a wise man will hoard."

By "money" Durant apparently meant government fiat currency, which is indeed something wise people will distrust.

"Throughout history, governments have been chronically short of revenue," wrote Rothbard. "The reason should be clear: unlike you and me, governments do not produce useful goods and services that they can sell on the market; governments...live parasitically off the market and off society. Unlike every other person and institution in society, government obtains its revenue from coercion, from taxation." [64]

Taxation has limits, noted Rothbard, because beyond a certain level it prompts people to revolt against their rulers, as happened in colonial America. Oppressive taxation also gives people incentives to flee, or to hide what they have, or to become a lot less productive when the fruits of their labor are taxed away.

"If taxation is permanently short of the style of expenditure desired by the State," wrote Rothbard, "how can it make up the difference? By getting control of the money supply, or, to put it bluntly, by counterfeiting."

"On the market economy, we can only obtain good money by selling a good or service in exchange for gold, or by receiving a gift," wrote Rothbard. "The only other way to get money is to engage in the costly process of digging it out of the ground."

"The counterfeiter, on the other hand, is a thief who attempts to profit by forgery," Rothbard wrote; "e.g., by painting a piece of brass to look like a gold coin."

Such a government counterfeiter passing off money with no productivity behind it "is more sinister and more truly subversive than [a] highwayman" who cheats one victim, wrote Rothbard, "for he robs everyone in society, and the robbery is stealthy and hidden, so that the cause-and-effect relation is camouflaged."

## Forty Centuries of Inflation

Accompanying such government inflation is a repeating pattern of coercion, as Robert Schuettinger and Eamonn Butler lay out in their book *Forty Centuries of Wage and Price Controls: How NOT to Fight Inflation.* [65]

Over and over, for nearly four thousand years, rulers have debased their money. At first, their subjects accept this money and by doing so are robbed of a portion of what they sell to the ruler and his retainers.

The people then recognize, sometimes slowly and other times quickly, that the ruler's money has less value than it claims. Merchants begin to raise their prices denominated in the king's money. Workers demand more coins for a day's work.

The ruler then responds with laws requiring the populace to use only his money.

Such laws are usually accompanied by denunciations of businesspeople for raising their prices out of greed and making "windfall profits," of the worker for holding society for ransom by demanding higher wages, and of others for speculation or lack of patriotism when they resort to barter or other varieties of exchange.

The next traditional ruler response, ancient and modern, has been some variant of wage and price controls.

Ten pounds of turnips used to cost one coin. The king – who has debased and pocketed half the valuable metal these coins used to contain – now commands, through criminal penalties, that merchants continue to sell their turnips at the old price.

The merchants' response for forty centuries has been to offer smaller, cheaper turnips to retain their profit margin – or to stop selling turnips at all.

The king is always praised for his law in defense of the people, and for his crackdown on greedy, gouging businesspeople, until the people realize that turnip prices are controlled – but no turnips can actually be bought in the marketplace at any price.

"If you think health care is expensive now," wrote comedic journalist P.J. O'Rourke, "wait 'till you see what it costs when it's free."

## Roman Inflation

During the Roman Empire – a society chillingly similar to our own bureaucratic welfare state, as you might have inferred from the quote by Roman statesman Cicero opposite this book's Introduction – the debasement of government coinage began as early as the reign (54-68 A.D.) of the Emperor Nero.

By the Third Century A.D., wrote one historian, "as a result of mounting inflation, widespread hoarding of specie, and sharply reduced revenues, the emperors resorted to reckless adulteration of the imperial coinage to meet their military and administrative costs."

"As a result, distrust of new currency was widely manifested, by individuals as well as by banks. Ultimately the government refused to accept its own coinage for many taxes and insisted on payment in kind."

As one emperor overthrew another in an ongoing series of coups, "banks were understandably hesitant to accept the coinage issued by the usurpers."

Historians know this from a surviving official letter ordering banks to accept the coins of two such short-lived emperors, and from public emergency decrees setting forth the punishment for dealing in black market money. [66]

As the debased Roman Denarius coin disintegrated from inflation, and merchants and workers demanded many more of them in exchange for what they were selling, in 301 A.D. the Emperor Diocletian issued his famous Edict on Maximum Prices requiring citizens, on penalty of punishment or even death, to accept at face value Roman imperial currency. Penalties applied to those who bought as well as sold at a higher price than the Edict allowed.

Diocletian's Edict has survived. It laid out precise maximum prices that could be charged in denarii for various weights of grain and other foods, types of wine, lumber, wool and silk, job wages, shipping costs, as well as matters as small as how much a Notary could charge for putting his seal on a document (10 denarii) to what veterinarians could charge for trimming an animal's hooves (6 denarii).

These imperial price controls even specified the maximum a scribe could charge for 100 lines of "best writing" (25 denarii) and for 100 lines of "second-quality writing" (20 denarii). [67]

Even as Diocletian's fixed prices were being chiseled into stone for all to read, the denarius was losing value by the day.

One wonders if President Richard Nixon consulted Diocletian's Edict for the guidelines used in his own 1970s wage and price controls.

Succeeding Emperors of the Western Empire followed the socialist price-control path to its logical conclusion. Those who refused to grow food or perform other essential tasks for imperial wages were required to do such jobs for the empire.

The downward debasement slide of money became the first road to serfdom, not unlike the road we are travelling today to a new global feudal rule.

## Inflation's Golden Antidote

In 301 A.D., the Emperor Diocletian also issued very limited numbers of a new coin called the *solidus* (Latin for "solid") that later became Rome's golden antidote to inflation. Each new coin carried one-sixtieth of a Roman Pound of pure gold, about 5.5 grams, and had an initial value of approximately 1,000 denarii.

In 312 A.D. the Roman Emperor Constantine replaced Rome's earlier gold coin the Aureus with the solidus, which he redefined as 1 / $72^{nd}$ of a Roman pound in gold, around 4.5 grams of pure gold. It would become the most reliable coin in human history.

Most people recall learning that the Roman Empire fell around 476 A.D. This is only half true. Constantine, who gave Christianity the standing to become the imperial state religion, also split the Roman Empire into Western and Eastern halves. The Western half fell in 476 A.D.

The Eastern Half of the Roman Empire, with its capital Constantinople – now called Istanbul in Turkey – was renamed the Byzantine Empire and did not fall until 1453 A.D., less than 50 years before Columbus reached the New World.

Byzantium for many centuries avoided the dark and medieval feudal stagnation of the West. It was cosmopolitan, successful and rich. Only in its latter days of fighting Islam did its taxes become so high that a few in its empire welcomed Muslim armies as liberators.

## Coining Soldiers

The Eastern Empire's longevity came in part from its money. Constantine's solidus retained its weight and gold purity for six centuries, was then briefly debased, and then issued again in a purer form.

This reliable gold coin, which was the medium in which imperial taxes had to be paid, came to symbolize the wealth, power and stability of Byzantium throughout Europe, Asia and Africa.

Then as now, the integrity or debasement of a nation's money carries a powerful message about how honorable that nation and its government are.

Byzantium's government frequently reminted new solidi from old, not to debase or siphon off their gold content as most other governments had done for centuries, but to give the impression that fresh, new gold was always pouring in to enrich and empower the Byzantine Empire, a Christian empire blessed from Above.

The Islamic Caliphates, to demonstrate their own merit, minted gold coins that resembled Constantinople's. Both the Muslim coins and Byzantine solidi were widely used in international trade and nicknamed *Bezants*, a name that evoked Byzantium.

Our word "soldier" originally comes from Byzantium's gold solidus, a coin used during the late Western and long-enduring Eastern Empire to pay Roman Legionnaires. [68]

The word "soldier" thus originally implied that someone worthy of this title is as solid, valuable, reliable, strong and trustworthy as the Byzantine gold *solidus* coin that is its namesake.

Our word "salary" likewise comes from a Roman soldier's pay, from his regular ration of salt (*sal* in Latin).

## The Dawn of Paper Money

As it did in the West and Near East, money in the Far East transformed societies.

"Money is a spiritual thing," wrote Chinese scholar Lu Bao around 300 A.D. in his discourse *The Money God.*

"It has no rank yet is revered; it has no status yet is welcomed."

"Where there is money," he wrote, "danger will turn to peace and death will give life."

"Where money slips away, honour will turn to baseness and life will give death."

"They say 'Money holds power over the spirits,'" wrote Lu Bao. "If that is true, just think of its power over men!" [69]

Several peoples had previously used individual paper contracts signed from one person to another as a medium of exchange. Romans as early as a century before Jesus used written *praescriptiones* to transfer a promise of money or credit. Even earlier, India used paper bank notes called *adesha* to transfer money.

By the 3rd Century A.D., the Persian Sassanid Empire used letters of credit called *chak*, and six centuries after that the Muslim Abbasid Caliphate of Baghdad used similar paper money transfer documents called *sakk*. *Chak* and *Sakk* are probably the root name and idea behind your personal bank checks.

## Song Money

While much of Europe faced the Dark Ages, China's Song Dynasty invented paper and, by the 7th Century A.D., what we think of as paper money.

Using wood block printing, the Song at first produced what amounted to promissory notes that could be redeemed for metallic coins. When coin copper ran short, the government began issuing paper that simply took the place of hard money.

By 1175 A.D. China's government was operating at least four factories in different cities to churn out paper money. One of these factories, records show, employed 1,000 workers.

In some ways this paper currency was remarkably modern. By 1107 A.D., it was printed on a special paper with intricate designs and six different colors of ink to make counterfeiting difficult.

In other ways, the early Song notes seem odd to us today. Distinctly different paper notes were printed for use in specific regions of China. Each note carried a time limit of three years, which meant that they could not be saved, hoarded or hidden from the tax collector for a longer period than that while retaining their store of value.

Sometime around 1268 A.D. the Southern Song Dynasty began printing a single China-wide currency convertible to gold or silver, but their days were numbered.

## Khan Games

By 1279 the Song's last defenders were defeated by Mongol troops of the grandson of Genghis Khan, Kublai Khan, and his Yuan Dynasty. Kublai at first printed the restricted currency used by the Song, but the Yuan soon created a flood of currency unbacked by metal, but without time limits on when it could be spent.

The Mongol ruler required his subjects to accept his currency at face value.

"The Chinese government confiscated all gold and silver from private citizens and issued them paper money in its place," wrote anthropologist Jack Weatherford.

"Even merchants arriving from abroad had to surrender their gold, silver, gems, and pearls to the government at prices set by a council of merchant bureaucrats."

"The traders then received government-issued notes in exchange," wrote Weatherford.

# "Hell Money"

Marco Polo, a Venetian merchant who visited Mongol-ruled China, "saw clearly that this system of paper money could work only where a strong central government could enforce its will on everyone within its territory," wrote Weatherford. [70]

Inflation began rising as succeeding rulers enjoyed the royal prerogative of manufacturing money.

The Chinese took to calling paper money "wind money" because its value could blow away.

And to this day, many Chinese ritually burn a paper imitation currency called "Hell Money" as a way of sending spending cash to deceased loved ones in the afterlife, above or below.

By 1455 the Ming Dynasty, to stabilize its economy, banished paper money and curtailed most international trade.

The Dynasty also destroyed its large imperial Chinese fleet that decades before Columbus had traded Chinese goods as far away as the island of Madagascar in Africa. [70]

Former British Royal Navy submarine commander Gavin Menzies has laid out a speculative case that ships of this Chinese fleet might have reached Europe and influenced the Renaissance, and might have reached the New World more than 70 years before Columbus. [71]

Had the Ming Dynasty retained its large fleet and sailed to the New World more than three generations ahead of Columbus, this might have changed human history in many ways.

Had they continued, you might be reading this book – or more likely a very different book from a different culture and history – right now in Chinese.

The International Monetary Fund in April predicted that China's economy will surpass that of the United States by year 2016, and that the era of America's global supremacy is about to end.

China's treasure fleet has arrived to conquer the West more than 500 years late, but many now believe that a long-postponed age of Chinese world supremacy is about to begin.

If so, this could happen not because China is superior, but because Western civilization and its economies collapsed from within.

## Paper Hanging

Paper money was slow in coming to Western nations, but when it arrived it did so with a vengeance in the person of one of inflation's great heroes and history's great paper hangers, the Scotsman John Law.

One of the first major modern advocates of manipulable monopoly paper money as a medium of exchange, Law was born in 1671 into a family of Scottish bankers and metalworkers.

In 1705 Law published *Money and Trade Consider'd with a Proposal for Supplying the Nation with Money.*

The thrifty Scots rejected Law's plans for a national bank, but he persuaded King Louis XV to appoint him Controller General of Finances of France.

France was bankrupt from foreign wars and running out of gold and silver coin.

Law claimed that he could pay off the King's huge national debt with profits from a government-monopoly bank for national finance and a state company for commerce.

The King's council rejected this idea, but the eccentric Law found other ways to replace gold with paper credit.

Law converted much of France's national debt to paper shares of ventures such as "The Mississippi Bubble" investment scheme, created by consolidating French trading companies in and around Louisiana into a monopoly.

Speculation wildly inflated the values of these shares, followed by a crash in value that devastated aristocratic and middle-class investors and further damaged the French treasury.

Vilified in his own time, John Law is now widely seen by Keynesians as a pioneer who devised several key ideas of modern Big Government economics.
[73]

No wonder that free market economist Friedrich Hayek wrote: "Lord Keynes has always appeared to me a kind of new John Law." [74]

Were he alive today, Law would probably be invited to join President Obama's Council of Economic Advisers, or to chair the Federal Reserve Board to implement Mr. Obama's easy-money, bubble-creating inflationary policies.

The catastrophe of Law's governmental inflationary schemes of wealth created out of mere paper may be the reason his French contemporary Voltaire wrote: "Paper money eventually returns to its intrinsic value – Zero."

# Chapter Five
# Inflation in America

*"Instead of funding issues of paper*
*on the hypothecation of specific taxes...*
*we are trusting to tricks of jugglers on the*
*cards, to the illusions of banking schemes*
*for the resources of the war [of 1812],*
*and for the cure of colic to*
*inflations of more wind "*

– Thomas Jefferson
1814 letter to M. Correa de Serra

Native Americans already had various kinds of money made from shells and other aesthetic materials, called *wampum*, before the first Europeans arrived in the New World.

In England's North American colonies a mix of the gold and silver coins of various nations was used when available. Our dollar would later take its name from one of the most popular of these coins, the German gold Thaler.

In the colonies, more common mediums of exchange were maize and beaver pelts, dried codfish in New England, tobacco leaves in Virginia, rice in the Carolinas. Most were commodities that could be eaten, smoked or worn as well as traded. [75]

Paper money and the inflation it brings, however, would soon appear in America.

## "A Plentiful Currency"

Which of America's Founding Fathers would feel most at home in our 21st Century world? Many historians say it would be a freethinking scientist, Benjamin Franklin.

Ben Franklin could also be called the Founding Father of American inflation.

In April 1729, when Franklin was 23, he published *A Modest Enquiry into the Nature and Necessity of a Paper-Currency,* a broadside that advocated what he saw as the many benefits of Pennsylvania having "a plentiful currency." [76]

Abundant paper money, he argued in this pamphlet and before the colonial assembly, would make money cheap to borrow, stimulate employment and enterprise, and encourage local manufacture and thereby reduce dependence on costly imported goods.

Franklin's science was far sounder than his economics, but his public support for this inflationary policy produced the effect he apparently desired – a job printing large quantities of the Pennsylvania colony's paper fiat currency.

Franklin, a printer who in 1732 launched *Poor Richard's Almanac,* later wrote in his *Autobiography*:

"My friends [in the legislature], who consider I had been of some service, thought fit to reward me by employing me in printing the money; a very profitable job, and a great help to me." [77]

Ben Bernanke, meet your predecessor Ben Franklin.

## New World Disorder

Our Founders largely bankrolled the American Revolution with paper currency, printing so many Continental dollars that the fledgling nation's money was soon seen as "not worth a Continental."

Part of this inflation came from our own politicians' profligacy. Part came from the British, which as a tactic of war to weaken our revolution flooded the colonies and Europe with unbacked counterfeit copies of our bonds and paper fiat Continental currency.

"Paper money was in those times our universal currency," said Franklin. "It being the instrument with which we combated our enemies...[The British] resolved to deprive us of its use by depreciating it; and the most effectual means they could contrive was to counterfeit it." [78]

Under the highly-decentralized Articles of Confederation, our first form of government after winning our independence from the British Empire, the states continued to issue their own easily-cheapened currencies.

In that pre-computer era of slow communications, trade across state lines could be limited by uncertainty about how much paper money each state was printing – and hence how much, by the Law of Supply and Demand, each state's currency was really worth.

More reliable money was needed, according to many who favored a stronger central government. As Thomas Jefferson's protege, later to become America's fourth President, James Madison in #44 of *The Federalist Papers* began his 1788 defense of one part of the proposed new Constitution by quoting it:

*"No State shall....coin money; emit bills of credit; make any thing but gold and silver a legal tender in payment of debts...."*

"The right of coining money, which is here taken from the States," commented Madison, "was left in their hands by the Confederation, as a concurrent right with that of Congress, under an exception in favor of the exclusive right of Congress to regulate the alloy and value...."

"The extension of the prohibition to bills of credit must give pleasure to every citizen, in proportion to his love of justice and his knowledge of the true springs of public prosperity," he continued.

## Pestilent Paper Money

"The loss which America has sustained since the peace, from the pestilent effects of paper money on the necessary confidence between man and man, on the necessary confidence in the public councils, on the industry and morals of the people, and on the character of republican government, constitutes an enormous debt against the States chargeable with this unadvised measure, which must long remain unsatisfied; or rather an accumulation of guilt, which can be expiated no otherwise than by a voluntary sacrifice on the altar of justice, of the power which has been the instrument of it," wrote Madison of the debts and problems resulting from state currencies.

"In addition to these persuasive considerations, it may be observed, that the same reasons which show the necessity of denying to the States the power of regulating coin, prove with equal force that they ought not to be at liberty to substitute a paper medium in the place of coin," he wrote.

"Had every State a right to regulate the value of its coin," wrote Madison, "there might be as many different currencies as States, and thus the intercourse among them would be impeded; retrospective alterations in its value might be made, and thus the citizens of other

States be injured, and animosities be kindled among the States themselves."

Madison also wanted no foreign nation to blame the United States for debased paper money issued by a single state: "The subjects of foreign powers might suffer from the same cause, and hence the Union be discredited and embroiled by the indiscretion of a single member."

"No one of these mischiefs is less incident to a power in the States to emit paper money, than to coin gold or silver. The power to make any thing but gold and silver a tender in payment of debts, is withdrawn from the States, on the same principle with that of issuing a paper currency," wrote Madison. [79]

## Constitutional Coin

The new U.S. Constitution established what was supposed to be a reliable national currency. It gave to Congress the power "To coin Money, regulate the value thereof, and of foreign Coin....To provide for the Punishment of counterfeiting the Securities and current Coin of the United States..." and, alas, "To borrow Money on the credit of the United States" (Article I Section 8).

"I wish it were possible to obtain a single amendment to our Constitution. I would be willing to depend on that alone for the reduction of the administration of our government to the genuine principles of its Constitution," wrote Thomas Jefferson in 1789. "I mean an additional article, taking from the federal government the power of borrowing."

John Adams apparently agreed. "There are two ways to conquer and enslave a nation," he wrote. "One is by the sword, the other is by debt."

"The principle of spending money to be paid by posterity, under the name of funding, is but swindling futurity on a large scale," wrote Jefferson, whose opinion on this did not change over time.

"There does not exist an engine so corruptive of the government and so demoralizing of the nation as a public debt," wrote Jefferson in 1821. "It will bring on us more ruin at home than all the enemies from abroad...."

The Founders likewise generally felt revulsion at state paper money, which is why the new Constitution specified that money was to be coin and that the state standard of value had to be silver or gold coin, not paper currency.

"Paper money has had the effect in your state that it will ever have, to ruin commerce, oppress the honest, and open the door to every species of fraud and injustice," wrote George Washington in 1787 to a constituent in Rhode Island.

"Paper is poverty...," wrote Thomas Jefferson to a correspondent in 1788. "It is only the ghost of money, and not money itself."

## Dixie Dollars

Over the next half-century a political battle raged between Hamiltonian Big Government advocates who created in succession two central banks empowered to manipulate the country's money supply – and other leaders, including Jefferson and President Andrew Jackson, who favored decentralized power and who distrusted and brought down both national banks.

(In the end our current central bank the Federal Reserve and the government welfare state cynically took their revenge by putting paper-money-hating Andrew Jackson's face on the $20 bill and Jefferson's face on Food Stamps to lend their legitimacy to both pieces of fiat paper that Jefferson and Jackson would repudiate were they here today.)

When government currency was in short supply, people bought, sold and saved by using the paper notes issued by usually-small private banks.

This was risky for savers because government regulations typically confined such banks' lending to a single state or even town, meaning that these banks were usually too small to have large reserves and could quickly run out of money and collapse if customers panicked and started withdrawing their savings. Such bank runs were all too common in the young Republic.

A major cause of collapse for many such banks, however, was not customer demands for their money.

## Government-Caused Bank Failures

State governments "required banks to collateralize their notes by lodging specified assets (usually state government bonds) with state authorities," according to University of Georgia economist George Selgin and George Mason University economist Larry White.

"[C]lusters of 'free bank' failures were principally due to falling prices of the state bonds they held," write Selgin and White, "suggesting that the bond-collateral requirements caused bank portfolios to become overloaded with state bonds." [80]

Or as economist Robert P. Murphy explained in *The Politically Incorrect Guide to Capitalism*, "government regulation actually unbalanced the banking system." [81]

Government demands that banks buy large quantities of debased state bonds could push otherwise-solvent banks off a cliff, and as with today's Obama-Bernanke deliberate inflation, innocent savers paid the price for government's greed.

Despite this, some banks developed solid reputations for safety, and their private "currency" promissory bank notes, akin to today's private bank traveler's checks, were widely accepted beyond their states' boundaries.

In the years before the War Between the States, the $10 note issued by the Citizens' Bank and Trust Company of New Orleans, chartered in 1833, may have been the most popular and trusted paper currency in many Southern states. [82]

Because its customers included Louisiana Cajuns and many other French-speaking Americans up and down the Mississippi River, this bank note in one corner carried the large letters "DIX," French for ten.

These bank notes were quickly nicknamed Dixies, and the Southern states where they were in wide circulation came to be called "the land of Dixies," or Dixieland, or simply Dixie.

## Bankrolling a War

When war between the states came in 1861, both the Union and Confederacy lacked sufficient gold and silver to pay for it. Both began issuing huge amounts of unconvertible paper money.

The Union called its paper fiat money "Greenbacks," because of their color, the same color as most of our fiat paper money today.

Following the war, the victorious U.S. Government was willing to redeem these Greenbacks for a small amount of gold. Confederate money went the way of the paper money of America's first confederacy, the Continental.

Farmers and other creditors knew that Greenbacks kept being printed in huge quantities and therefore continued to lose value. This meant that Greenbacks were easy money. They could be borrowed and spent for a known purchasing value, then later repaid with cheaper inflated Greenbacks.

By the 1870s a new Greenback Party arose, largely in the West and upper Midwest, that urged government to print lots more of this cheap paper money that benefitted debtors and shortchanged creditors.

The Greenback Party soon made common cause with Western and

Midwestern populists known as "Silverites" such as William Jennings Bryan – a Democrat famed for his "cross of gold" speech – who wanted more abundant silver, "the poor man's gold," to be the Federal Government's main coinage.

The Federal Government turned to gold instead, ushering in an era of transformative prosperity for most Americans.

## "A Flood of Irredeemable Paper Currency"

In 1913, under Democratic President Woodrow Wilson, a new cartel of 12 private central banks called the Federal Reserve, would begin turning America's gold into paper – and soon use that paper fiat currency to reshape and rule the United States through chronic inflation.

The Fed was devised in secret, and secrecy has always been its preferred mode of operation.

A recent court order gave Americans a glimpse of why such secrecy is promoted by the Fed and President Obama. It turns out that many tens of billions of dollars in recent bailout money were channeled via insurance giant AIG not to Americans but to foreign banks in Europe, Asia and the Middle East, and the Fed funneled $5 Billion to a bank nearly 40 percent owned at the time by Libyan strongman Col. Muammar Gaddafi. [83]

The Fed has become the central bank not only of the United States but also, in some ways, of the world. This private banking cartel, therefore, does not always put America's national interests first.

The Fed's enabling legislation provided that American dollars, which until 1913 were supposedly 100 percent backed by the nation's gold reserves, under the Fed suddenly required only 40 percent gold backing.

Many Republicans in Congress were convinced that the Fed was designed to dethrone the gold standard and empower redistributionist progressives such as the Silverites who wanted easy money, cheap credit that could be repaid with devalued dollars, and government spending unchecked by gold.

One lawmaker who opposed the Fed's creation was conservative Republican and longtime Massachusetts Senator Henry Cabot Lodge – whose son also became a Senator and, in a losing 1960 race, Vice President Richard Nixon's vice-presidential running mate.

"The [Federal Reserve Act] as it stands seems to me to open the way to a vast inflation of the currency," Lodge prophetically warned in 1913.

"I do not like to think that any law can be passed," said Lodge, "that will make it possible to submerge the gold standard in a flood of irredeemable paper currency."

## "Inflation and Deflation Work Equally Well"

Another fierce opponent was Swedish-born Minnesota Republican Congressman Charles A. Lindbergh, father of the later-to-be-famous aviator.

"This [Federal Reserve] Act establishes the most gigantic trust on Earth," said Rep. Lindbergh.

"When the President signs this bill, the invisible government by the Monetary Power will be legalized," he said. "The people may not know it immediately but the day of reckoning is only a few years removed.... The worst legislative crime of the ages is perpetrated by this banking bill."

In 1913 Lindbergh authored *Banking and Currency and the Money Trust*. [84]

In 1917 he published *Why Is Your Country At War and What Happens to You After the War and Related Subjects,* in which he argued that international financial interests had dragged America into World War I for their own benefit. [85].

"The financial system....has been turned over to the Federal Reserve Board," wrote Lindbergh. "That board administers the finance system by authority of....a purely profiteering group. The system is private, conducted for the sole purpose of obtaining the greatest possible profits from the use of other people's money."

"To cause high prices, all the Federal Reserve Board will do will be to lower the rediscount rate..., producing an expansion of credit and a rising stock market," wrote Lindbergh. "Then when...business men are adjusted to these conditions, it can check...prosperity in mid career by arbitrarily raising the rate of interest."

The Federal Reserve, warned Rep. Lindbergh, "can cause the pendulum of a rising and falling market to swing gently back and forth by slight changes in the discount rate, or cause violent fluctuations by a greater rate variation and in either case it will possess inside information as to financial conditions and advance knowledge of the coming change, either up or down."

"This," he continued, "is the strangest, most dangerous advantage ever placed in the hands of a special privilege class by any Government that ever existed."

These self-serving private bankers care only about their profits, not the public, warned Lindbergh. "They know in advance when to create panics to their advantage," he wrote. "They also know when to stop panic."

"Inflation and deflation work equally well for them," Lindbergh warned, "when they control finance."

When he died in 1924, Lindbergh had left the Republican Party and joined the Minnesota Farmer-Labor Party to run for Governor as its standard-bearer.

# Politicizing Money

The rationalization for creating the Federal Reserve was that it would remove partisan and self-serving politics from policy decisions about America's money supply. Such decisions, America was told, would henceforth be made objectively by non-politicians uninvolved in the buying and selling of votes.

(As comic writer P.J. O'Rourke has observed, when government gets involved in buying and selling, the first things to be bought and sold will be politicians.)

The Fed's bankers, we were told, would be free to do what is best for the country, not the political party in power at the moment.

The Fed was supposed to give us separation of money and state because, despite its name, the Federal Reserve is scarcely more a part of the Federal Government than is the private shipping company Federal Express.

"The Federal Reserve Banks are not federal instrumentalities..." said the ruling in Lewis v. United States 9th Circuit Court in 1992.

The United States Budget in 1991 and 1992 affirmed in passing: "The Federal Reserve banks, while not part of the government...."

Trouble was, and is, that the Fed's seven-member Board of Governors is regarded as a Federal Government agency. Its members are appointed by the President of the United States and consented to by the U.S. Senate for staggered 14-year terms.

Out of these seven, the President appoints the Fed Chair, currently Ben Bernanke, and Vice Chair, currently Janet Yellen, and can reappoint them to a succession of four-year terms. Mr. Bernanke's current term as Chairman ends in January 2014 and as a member of the Board of Governors in January 2020.

## Caesar and Central Banks

"It is wholly impossible for a central bank subject to political control, or even exposed to serious political pressure, to regulate the quantity of money in a way conducive to a smoothly functioning market order," wrote economist Friedrich A. Hayek in his classic book *Denationalistion of Money*. [86]

"A good money, like good law, must operate without regard to the effect that decisions of the issuer will have on known groups or individuals," wrote Hayek.

"A benevolent dictator might conceivably disregard these effects," Hayek concluded. "No democratic government dependent on a number of special interests can possibly do so."

The Fed originally had one mandate – to protect the value and stability of the nation's money. In 1979 it was given a second mandate – to carry out monetary policy that produces full employment.

Some analysts now say the Fed has taken upon itself a third mandate – to boost, or in the words of one analyst, to "levitate" – market stock values.

A few commentators hint that Mr. Bernanke's Fed implicitly has a fourth mandate – to make the economy seem as good as possible in the months leading up to November 2012, thereby indirectly – and some suspect intentionally – helping re-elect President Barack Obama. [87]

(Mr. Obama, as we noted earlier, won the presidency during a perfectly-timed, mysteriously-induced economic crisis that undermined the Republican Party.)

# By Their Fruits

The Bible says to judge a tree by its fruits. What financial fruits has nearly 100 years of Fed meddling with America's money supply produced?

You can see where the Fed has taken us with a glance at the Federal Reserve Notes most people now call money. When the Fed began, a $50 gold certificate included the words "Will Pay to the Bearer on Demand $50," making it clear that this piece of paper was merely a promissory note held in lieu of real money, genuine money being a fixed and convertible quantity of gold.

Before the Fed became overseer of America's money, the economy rose and fell, with dollars slightly gaining or losing purchasing power. Overall the dollar grew in strength and value, so that what cost $100 in 1829 could be purchased for only about $64 in 1913.

The gold dollar was not only a reliable store of value, but also an excellent investment in an appreciating asset.

# Today's Two-Cent Dollar

After the Fed began to tighten its control over our money, the path of the dollar has been almost entirely downhill through inflation. Today's inflated dollar has the purchasing power of only two 1913 pennies, a scant 2 /100ths of the 1913 dollar.

During World War I President Woodrow Wilson effectively took the dollar off the gold standard by making it extremely difficult to convert dollars to gold.

After World War I the United States quietly transferred nearly $1 Billion in gold to Great Britain as a gesture of personal friendship between central bankers, a gesture American consumers paid for in lost dollar value, in inflation.

Conservative Republican Presidents Warren G. Harding and Calvin Coolidge brought America back quickly from a sudden sharp recession in 1920-21 by slashing government spending and the size of the Federal Government.

Under their successor, Progressive Republican Herbert Hoover, the Fed contracted the money supply when a fever of margin stock buying tanked the Stock Market in 1929.

The Fed's and Hoover's ill-advised attempts at economic engineering, as Milton Friedman later documented, turned what probably would have been just another short recession into a Great Depression that government interference in the economy made worse for more than a decade.

## FDR's Gold Grab

Among left-liberal President Franklin D. Roosevelt's first acts as President was to issue Executive Orders making it illegal for ordinary Americans to own gold bullion and confiscating people's ordinary gold coins (but not coin collectors' numismatic gold coins).

Ordinary gold coins were forcibly taken in exchange for Federal Reserve currency at just over $20 per Troy ounce of gold. Immediately after this expropriation, FDR raised the official exchange rate of gold to $32 per Troy ounce, with government immediately pocketing the value difference to fund his welfare state schemes.

While nations with freer economic systems rapidly recovered from this global economic downturn, the United States under Roosevelt's collectivist policies wallowed in high unemployment and a stagnant economy.

Pearl Harbor and World War II gave FDR the power to conscript unemployed men into the military. Approximately two out of every three American soldiers in this war were drafted, and more doubtless joined the Navy, Marines or Coast Guard to avoid conscription into the Army.

The wartime economy regimented us into a command economy, complete with rationing and austerity, on the homefront. Rosie the Riveter and many thousands of other women learned factory jobs.

By war's end America's ratio of debt to Gross Domestic Product was at least 122 percent, by some measures even deeper in debt than we are today at close to 100 percent.

## Sole Superpower

The United States, however, was still standing, with its factories and cities intact while the world's other once-powerful nations had been knocked to their knees and were severely damaged, weakened and impoverished.

The steps that President Harry Truman took at this history-turning moment continue to shape our world today.

A 1944 treaty called the Bretton Woods agreement provided that the United States Dollar would continue to be pegged at $35 per Troy ounce of gold, a convertibility redeemable only by mostly-European central banks. Other major nations in turn agreed to peg their currencies to the dollar, thereby creating what was supposed to be at least the faint shadow of the pre-World War I gold standard.

Out of Bretton Woods, too, came two enduring institutions: what today we call the World Bank, by custom run by an American, and the International Monetary Fund or IMF, supposedly the world's "lender of last resort," by custom run by a European.

The IMF gained widespread notoriety in May 2011 when its Managing Director Dominique Strauss-Kahn, the likely Socialist Party candidate for the presidency of France, was arrested in New York City for allegedly-felonious sexual behavior with a hotel maid.

# Europe Reborn – and Infantilized

In Europe Truman authorized the Marshall Plan, an outpouring of food, medicine and reconstruction aid worth in today's inflated currency perhaps a trillion dollars. Humane and well-intended, this aid for some beneficiaries became an addictive dose of government dependency.

During postwar reconstruction the United States established forward U.S. military bases in Western Europe and Japan, and pledged that our nuclear superpower arsenal would protect these nations from aggression by the Communist Soviet Union. This pledge that an attack on one was an attack on all was made explicit in the Atlantic Alliance and given a force structure in NATO, the North Atlantic Treaty Organization.

America's nuclear umbrella gave protection to a shattered Western Europe, but it also transformed politics there. Nations that previously had paid for their own defense now left this heavy responsibility mostly to the United States and the half-million troops or more that we left in Europe.

This Pax Americana gave Western Europe the longest period free from war that it had known since the Roman Emperor Augustus 20 centuries ago.

Money being fungible, what these nations saved on defense they mostly spent on creating socialist welfare states.

American left-liberals soon developed Euro-envy and an endlessly-repeated chant of "Why can't we have socialized medicine and welfare benefits like France or England?"

We could not, of course, because during the five decades of the Cold War against the Soviets, we chose to be the grown-ups who paid for Western Europe's and Japan's national security in a dangerous world.

Western Europeans enjoyed the luxury and ease of having American taxpayers pay for what otherwise would have been their biggest national expense.

## America the Enabler

By this act of generosity, however, we created a "pox Americana" in Western Europe: a huge constituency of government employees and welfare recipients dependent on government money.

The democratic votes of such Europeans empowered socialist Social Democratic, Labourite, Green and Communist political parties that were sometimes quick to bite the American hand that fed them.

In war-weary Western Europe, people living under our nuclear umbrella and the nearby Soviet Union's red shadow indulged themselves for decades as their culture and faith crumbled and their fertility rates declined to below-replenishment levels.

European Christian churches now stand nearly empty, while Muslims from what once were European colonies have become sizable and influential voting minorities in Germany, France, the Netherlands, Great Britain and several other European nations.

Europe has become a place, by American standards, of high taxes, soaring gasoline prices, chronic high unemployment, and a still-struggling attempt to create a united states of Europe and a rival to the U.S. Dollar's status as the world's reserve currency called the Euro.

It remains to be seen whether a European Union of profligate southern nations – the so-called "PIIGS": Portugal, Italy, Ireland, Greece and Spain – will remain yoked to fiscally-disciplined northern European nations such as Germany that seem to be trying to impose ownership of Europe through their banks and the Euro.
The Euro community, now more than $2 Trillion in debt, faces serious risk of dissolution and collapse.

# Europe Reawakens

Has Europe lost its vitality, identity and will to live, in part because of the addictive welfare state culture we enabled it to have?

Apparently not. While President Obama chose massive Keynesian stimulus in an effort to tax, spend and borrow America back to prosperity, key nations of Europe have turned right – inching back towards capitalism, reducing the size of government and the welfare state, and strengthening their economies through savings and austerity.

This rightward path briefly produced more than 8 percent economic growth in Germany, along with Keynes' economy-driving "animal spirits" of returning optimism and prosperity. That 2010 blip, alas, by May 2011 was slip-sliding away.

Germany understood firsthand the inflation nightmare of its Weimar Republic era and the role hyperinflation played in paving the way to Adolf Hitler.

German Chancellor Angela Merkel implored President Obama not to take the Weimar path of deliberately inflating the currency, but to join Europeans in a program of austerity. Mr. Obama rebuffed this plea from both Germany and the United Kingdom.

Under the Obama Administration, it appears that America is becoming infantile, as we see from the left's petulant political temper tantrums here.

Europe, meanwhile, is beginning to regain its adulthood after more than half a century of welfare state addiction, moral and physical disarmament, and dependency.

"Those who cannot remember the past," the philosopher George Santayana warned, "are condemned to repeat it."

# Chapter Six
# The Money Illusion

*"Of all the contrivances for
cheating the laboring classes of mankind,
none has been more effective than that
which deludes them with paper money."*

– Daniel Webster

Ben Bernanke's strange transformation reportedly happened while he was testifying before the Senate Finance Committee.

While reading from a prepared statement that The Fed was "unlikely" to raise interest rates, the Chairman of the Federal Reserve Board suddenly paused, then "shook his head in utter disbelief."

"It doesn't matter," he said. "'None of this – this so-called 'money' – really matters at all."

"It's just an illusion," the world's most powerful central banker reportedly said as he pulled paper dollars from his wallet and slowly spread them on the table in front of him. "Just look at it. Meaningless pieces of paper with numbers printed on them. Worthless."

"Oh my God, he's right," shouted Senator Orrin Hatch (R-UT). "It's all a mirage. All of it – the money, our whole economy – it's all a lie!"

As news of Bernanke's and Hatch's statements about our "collectively held delusion" spread, according to one story America's economy "ground to a halt, with dumbfounded citizens everywhere walking out on their jobs as they contemplated the little green drawings of buildings and dead white men they once used to measure their adequacy and importance as human beings."

As more and more Americans realized that their money was "just a symbolic, mutually shared illusion...a meaningless and intangible social construct," longtime trader Michael Palermo at a now-quiet New York Stock Exchange reportedly said: "I've spent 25 years in this room yelling 'Buy, buy! Sell, sell!' and for what? All I've done is move arbitrary designations of wealth from one column to another, wasting my life chasing this unattainable hallucination of wealth."

"What a cruel cosmic joke," added Palermo. "I'm going home to hug my daughter."

## Money's Mesmerism Ends?

"The realization that money is nothing more than an elaborate head game seems to have penetrated the entire country," recounted one report.

In Delaware one credit card collection agent reportedly "broke down in joyful sobs when he informed a woman on the other end of the phone that he had absolutely no reason to harass her anymore, as her Discover Card debt was no longer comprehensible."

At the White House the President's Press Secretary reportedly said that Mr. Obama would issue a statement soon, but that for now "his mind is just too blown to comment."

"It's back to basics for me," one Ohioan was quoted as saying. "I'm going to till the soil for my own sustenance and get anything else I need by bartering. If I want milk, I'll pay for it in tomatoes. If I need a new hoe, I'll pay for it in lettuce."

When a reporter asked how he might "pay for complicated life-saving surgery for a loved one," the man replied: "That's a lot of vegetables, isn't it?"

"For some Americans," said one story, "the fog of disbelief surrounding the nation's epiphany has begun to lift, with many building new lives free from the illusion of money."

## Money in Mind

As you probably guessed, this "news" story appeared in only one publication, the website of the online satire magazine *The Onion*. [88] The greatest satires and humor make us laugh precisely because they are rooted in elements of truth, as this is.

The whole truth is that the U.S. Dollar has no guaranteed exchange value or convertibility into anything. It actually *is* just pieces of paper that carry numbers and the words "This Note Is Legal Tender for All Debts Public and Private" on them....useful for debts that are denominated in dollars.

This is why John Exter, then a Fed board member and a Vice President of the Federal Reserve Bank of New York, once described today's U.S. Dollar as "an I.O.U. Nothing."

Like the world's other fiat – Latin for "let it be done," a decree based solely on governmental authority and power – paper monies, the dollar is a faith-based currency worth only what people are willing to swap for it on any given day.

So long as most of us believe in the value of these scraps of paper, the system of exchange based on them continues to function.

Belief is powerful, powerful enough to impart a placebo healing effect to sugar pills. What is history, said Napoleon, but a fable agreed upon...a fable that nowadays includes a constant stream of government and Fed statistics politically cooked up to calm down public concerns about the economy.

As the Cato Institute economist Steve Hanke recently observed, 98 percent of everything we know about the Fed comes from the Fed itself; we have access to few other sources of information about what this powerful entity is actually doing.

The ruling class knows that if people lose faith in the dollar's value, as in *The Onion's* fake news story or in the very real growing global reluctance to grant the U.S. Dollar its former purchasing power, these green pieces of paper for which we trade nearly one-third of our working lives can quickly lose their hypnotic attractiveness.

## Money Mysteries

At the heart of money's most fundamental dogmas – where the Law of Supply and Demand can no more be repealed than can the Law of Gravity – lay great mysteries about what drives demand and what persuades people that certain pieces of paper are worth exchanging for a large share of our short lives.

Economist Irving Fisher identified one of these mysteries in the title of his 1928 book *The Money Illusion*. Fisher's theory is that we tend to value paper currency not at its real purchasing power but at its numerical face value.

Fisher's theory holds that our economic decisions are not entirely rational, which runs counter to the Enlightenment view of how the marketplace works. Because of this, his theory was rejected for more than 60 years by most mainstream economists.

Today, however, new scientific research is finding evidence that the Money Illusion influences much of our economic behavior.

Which, for example, would you prefer – a two percent raise in an economy with one percent inflation, or a four percent raise in an economy with five percent inflation?

Oddly enough, researchers find that a major proportion of people tend to choose the bigger numerical raise even though even-higher inflation wipes it out.

The two percent raise would have been far more remunerative, in accord with the old principle: "It's not what you make; it's what you (in purchasing power) keep." Yet money illusion deludes our irrational minds with a larger number.

## Number Our Days

Writing about the pervasive power of "money illusion" in their book *Animal Spirits: How Human Psychology Drives the Economy, and Why It Matters for Global Capitalism*, University of California Berkeley Nobel laureate economist George A. Akerlof and Yale University economist Robert J. Schiller remind us that money is more than "a medium of exchange" and "a store of value."

Money, they write, is also a third thing, "a unit of account," meaning that "people think in terms of money" and the quality and quantity of its units. [89]

Our accustomed units of money such as U.S. Dollars or the Euro become the measure of our idea of value – in somewhat the same way that Americans think of distance in inches, feet and miles, while Europeans think in millimeters, meters and kilometers.

However, the units that both Americans and Europeans use for distance are fixed and unchanging. Miles can be converted into kilometers, or vice versa, by the same formulas today or 10 or 100 years from now.

Economists, according to Akerlof and Schiller, used to assume that money was merely a "veil," that "people saw through inflation and it had no effect on real transactions." New research suggests otherwise.

"We believe that, in going from nominal dollars to real dollars, something will be lost in translation," they write. "Such losses would be the consequences of money illusion."

## Casino Chips & Credit Cards

Our units of money, when under the influence of a variety of factors that include inflation and the psychologies of inflation expectation and money illusion, keep changing....shrinking or stretching like rubber in how our minds perceive and attach value to them.

Think of this as a variant of why gambling casinos have gamblers in their table games play with casino chips instead of actual money, or how banks provide credit cards that allow someone to spend and spend without needing to hand over even a single actual dollar bill. Both of these methods can distort a person's sense of reality and judgment about the transactions he or she is making.

Currency trading is an entire investment specialty based on wagering how one currency will rise or fall relative to another. We can use the objective, mechanical brain of a computer to calculate the results of such transactions.

Nevertheless, political human brains will manipulate the supply of dollars via inflation, and all-too-human emotional brains influenced by uncertainty and money illusion will respond with a subjective desire for greater numbers of dollars, even when inflation has made a larger number of dollars worth less. This is the psychological manipulation, the illusion, that has kept people working for the past 30 years with no increase in real, inflation-adjusted pay. They get more and more dollars that, because of deliberate inflation, each have less and less purchasing power.

Supply and demand is a natural law of economics, but this does not mean that either scientists or economists fully understand all the factors that give green pieces of paper their power to stir human demand. This power reaches beyond mere convertibility or exchange value.

## This Is Your Brain on Inflation

Researchers at California Institute of Technology and Stanford University in 2008 reported finding that the higher the price tag that tasters saw on a bottle of wine, the more "pleasantness" they experienced from drinking it.

People often respond better to a higher-priced product, expecting that the price is based on higher quality. What makes this research unusual was that its 20 participants responded while a sophisticated MRI monitored their brain activity.

The researchers identified more than half a dozen precise regions within the brain that seem to have a hedonic, a pleasure, response of "experienced pleasantness" to higher prices.

One of these same researchers, Antonio Rangel of Cal Tech, working with scientists at the University of Bonn in Germany, reported finding evidence that the brain's medial prefrontal cortex "exhibits money illusion."

Their study, published in 2009 in the *Proceedings of the National Academy of Sciences* of the United States of America, suggests "that money illusion is real in the sense that the level of reward-related brain activity [in this cortex] in response to monetary prizes increases with nominal changes that have no consequence for subjects' real purchasing power." [90]

If money illusion is real, these researchers write, then potentially "central banks can affect production, investment, and consumption through changes in monetary policy that have an impact on the inflation rate."

If the money illusion influences people to respond favorably to larger numeric quantities of money – even when that quantity has lower purchasing power – then, they note, this might be a possible cause of bubbles in markets such as housing.

If the money illusion exists, they write, this could become a factor in setting wages for workers. Employees under money illusion might care more about nominal wages (and promised future benefits) than about real wages.

"The existence of money illusion is important," they write, "for the understanding of the relation between income, inflation, and subjective well-being. Importantly, even small amounts of money illusion can have substantial effects...[in which] small deviations from rationality imply big and lasting effects in aggregate outcomes." [91]

Some researchers in this field call Money Illusion "the Inflation Illusion."

Such new scientific approaches, along with those from emerging disciplines such as neuroeconomics, are providing powerful new insights into money, inflation, and how we might be manipulated. These and other studies already suggest some disquieting realities.

## Addictive Dollars

The effects of money and the money illusion, and by extension an increase in the quantity of money as is seen in inflation or hyperinflation, vary widely from one individual to another – but research now suggests that in some people money apparently has the ability to:

– Cause changes within the brain and body, likely by stimulating the release of pleasure-inducing neurotransmitters. (Might this help explain why some people become shopaholics for certain high-priced merchandise?)

– Bypass or diminish our ability to think rationally, thereby subtly changing our perception of reality as well as our judgment and decision-making processes. (This effect in some cases could be akin to

the hallucinatory "high" caused by intoxicating alcohol or other per-
ception- and judgment-altering drugs.)

– Create cravings for ever-increasing quantities of money, a response
akin to addiction and chemical dependency.

Future scientific studies should pursue how far this parallel between
the mental and physiological effects of drugs and inflation goes.
From what the evidence already suggests, a few such questions
about inflation to consider are these:

– Does the diminishing value of money during inflation, or a person's inability to increase income as fast as prices rise, cause something akin to a drug user's withdrawal symptoms?

– Does inflation cause bipolar disorder, an emotional and physiological roller coaster ride of extreme ups and downs in which "irrational exhuberance" is followed by feelings of sickness, weakness,
disorientation, stress, anxiety and depression?

– Does a causal link exist between economic depressions and widespread emotional depression, and between the health of the economy and the physical and mental health of many people living in
that economy?

  Could this mean that by treating and curing a distorted economic
consciousness in individuals, we can cure economic problems in society – and vice versa?

## Inflaholics Anonymous

"Pecuniary [ *i.e., of, concerning or consisting of money* ] motives either do not act at all — or are of that class of stimulants which act
only as Narcotics," observed poet Samuel Taylor Coleridge.

"At Harvard Medical School, neuroscientist Hans Breiter has compared activity in the brains of cocaine addicts who are expecting to

get a fix and people who are expecting to make a profitable financial gamble," writes *Wall Street Journal* columnist Jason Zweig in his book *Your Money & Your Brain: How the New Science of Neuroeconomics Can Help Make You Rich.*

"The similarity isn't just striking," writes Zweig. "It's chilling."

Dr. Breiter's MRI brain images suggest, Zweig writes, that "once you score big on a few investments in a row, you may be the functional equivalent of an addict – except the substance you're hooked on isn't alcohol or cocaine, it's money." [92]

Both cash and cocaine can trigger release of the neurotransmitter dopamine in the brain, a chemical associated with excitement and pleasure that in tiny natural doses reinforces learning and memory when a person does something successful for the first time.

In unnaturally large amounts, things such as cocaine that elicit dopamine become addictive and destructive.

Perhaps this is one of the reasons why the Bible warns that "the *love of* money," an addictive, obsessive or near-idolatrous fixation on money, "is a root of all kinds of evil. It is through this craving that some have wandered away from the faith and pierced themselves with many griefs." (Emphasis added.)[93]

Society is more than the sum of its individual members, yet it embodies a kind of democracy of the prevalent values, habits, beliefs, strengths and weaknesses of a majority of its people. As the ancient Greek philosopher Plato said, society is "man writ large."

This may help explain why some societies are prosperous while others remain poor. [94]

## Drunk on Inflation

In 1992 the Nobel-prizewinning economist Milton Friedman drew what he called an "instructive analogy" between inflation and alcoholism. [95]

"When the alcoholic starts drinking, the good effects come first," wrote Friedman. "[T]he bad effects come only the next morning, when he wakes up with a hangover – and often cannot resist easing the hangover by taking 'the hair of the dog that bit him.'"

"The parallel with inflation is exact," continued Friedman. "When a country starts on an inflationary episode, the initial effects seem good. The increased quantity of money enables whoever has access to it – nowadays primarily governments – to spend more without anybody else having to spend less. Jobs become more plentiful, business is brisk, almost everybody is happy – at first. Those are the good effects."

"[T]hen the increased spending starts to raise prices," wrote Friedman. "Workers find that their wages, even if higher in dollars, will buy less; businesses find that their costs have risen, so that the higher sales are not as profitable as had been anticipated, unless prices can be raised even faster."

"The bad effects are emerging: higher prices, less buoyant demand, inflation combined with stagnation."

"As with the alcoholic," wrote Friedman, "the temptation is to increase the quantity of money still faster, which produces the kind of roller coaster the United States has been on."

"In both cases, it takes a larger and larger amount, of alcohol or of money, to give the alcoholic or the economy the same 'kick.'"

"The parallel between alcoholism and inflation carries over to the cure," wrote Friedman. "The cure for alcoholism is simple to state: stop drinking. But the cure is hard to take because this time the bad effects come first, the good effects later."

"The alcoholic who goes on the wagon suffers severe withdrawal pains before emerging in the happy state of no longer having that almost irresistible desire for another drink."

"So also with inflation," Friedman continued. The initial effects of a slower rate of monetary growth are painful: lower economic growth and temporarily higher unemployment without, for a time, much reduction in inflation."

"The benefits begin to appear only after one or two years or so, in the form of lower inflation, a healthier economy, [and] the potential for rapid noninflationary growth."

# Cold Turkey

In the early 1980s, noted Friedman, then-Fed Chair Paul Volker and President Ronald Reagan took the United States, cold turkey, off the insane, near-suicidal double-digit inflationary binge President Jimmy Carter's liberal policies unleashed.

Many of the evils threatening our world and economy today have their origins in the four-year ruinous reign of Mr. Carter, now second only to Mr. Obama as the least competent and most destructive president in American history.

President Carter, in effect, stole half the life savings' purchasing power of the American people. President Obama's policies are on track to steal every remaining penny of the life savings of Americans, to crash the U.S. Dollar and leave the U.S. economy wrecked beyond hope of repair or recovery.

It took great political and moral courage for President Reagan to restore sanity to the economy and soundness to the dollar. For millions of innocent Americans this wringing out of epidemic inflation caused pain, loss, temporary unemployment and hardship. He was detoxing America from getting hooked on President Carter's monetary morphine.

Millions of less innocent Americans, Friedman suggests, had "the absence of a real desire to end the addiction."

Inflation robs those who work hard, are thrifty and live sober, responsible lives. It punishes those who defer their pleasures and invest in building a better future.

Inflation rewards those who borrow and buy instead of saving, because it lets speculators repay their debts with debased, cheapened dollars.

"Many of us are not unhappy about inflation," wrote Friedman. "Naturally, we would like to see the prices of the things we *buy* go down, or at least stop going up. But we are glad to see the prices of the things we *sell* go up."

"One reason inflation is so destructive," Friedman continued, "is because some people benefit greatly and others suffer; society is divided into winners and losers."

"The winners regard the good things that happen to them as the natural result of their own foresight, prudence, and initiative. They regard the bad things – the rise in prices of the things they buy – as the fault of forces outside their control."

"Almost all of us will say that we are against inflation," wrote Friedman, when "what we generally mean is that we are against the bad things about it that have happened to us."

The drug of inflation, wrote Friedman, makes us "schizophrenic."

## Emotional Deflation

Does a causal link exist between economic depressions and widespread emotional depression, and between the health of the economy and the physical and mental health of many people living in that economy?

This question we raised earlier has an urgent importance.

Research by the Centers for Disease Control and Prevention published in 2011 has reportedly found evidence of a significant increase in suicides during past economic declines. [96]

Some of these suicides doubtless come from the outright despair of those who suddenly find themselves broke and deep in debt. Others probably happen because an unexpected decline in people's economic situations has brought other personal problems – fights with a spouse, eviction from a home, or other problems – that can turn economic depression into emotional depression.

Scientists frankly admit that they do not yet understand all the complex ways in which money and its loss might influence human psychology, identity, moods and neurochemistry.

The data in this 2011 CDC study clearly indicate, however, that when economic pressures push people to the edge, some will jump to their deaths from that edge.

Oddly, a few analysts point to a recent increase in divorces as evidence of an improving economy. They reason that in 2008-2010, economic uncertainties were so great that married couples who otherwise would have divorced stayed together to pool their incomes, homes and other resources that a separation would have shattered. As the economy slowly improves, these analysts say, two people no longer need to live as cheaply as one. [97]

## "Bernanke and Obama Lied. People Died."

Suffice it to say, paraphrasing leftist rhetoric about former President George W. Bush, that "Bernanke and Obama lied. People died."

When politicians and central bankers deliberately induce inflation and thereby cause severe economic hardships for vulnerable people, one of the results of such economic manipulation can be suicide.

Another is that Mr. Bernanke's and Mr. Obama's policies of exporting inflation to other countries have hit some countries where up to one billion poor people live on the edge of hunger all the time on incomes of only $100 or $200 per year.

The Bernanke-Obama deliberate inflation policies have sent food prices soaring for millions of the world's poorest people – and this has inevitably pushed many over the brink into malnutrition and starvation. [98]

Soaring food prices and the risk of future famine have also prompted rich neo-colonial nations such as Saudi Arabia and the People's Republic of China to buy up farmland across Africa and in Canada and the United States. As a result, while other real estate has been losing value in the U.S., prime farmland has risen in price. [99]

It is literally no exaggeration to say: "Bernanke and Obama lied. People died."

## The Obamanation's Empty Cradles

While some are killing themselves because of the Obama-Bernanke economy, others because of their inflationary policies are never born.

The Pew Research Center in 2010 reported that America's birth rate is in serious decline, and that this is apparently linked to our severe economic downturn. [100]

"The number of babies born in the United States dropped 2.6 percent last year...the latest in a long list of falling indicators," reported CNN in 2010. They cited a report by the National Center for Health Statistics showing that America's birth rate fell for a second year in tandem with the plunging economy. [101]

The declining birth rate did not surprise Johns Hopkins University sociologist Andrew Cherlin, who told CNN it was related to "the sad state of the American economy right now."

What CNN neglected to mention is that Obama-Bernanke economic policies have driven the United States to what might prove to be the lowest birthrate in our nation's history, only 13.5 births per year for every 1,000 people.

During the years Baby Boomers were being born – from 1946 until 1964 –America's total fertility rate never fell below an average of 3.0 children per woman. It peaked from 1955 to 1959 with an average of 3.7 children per woman.

By 1975-1979, at the height of the counterculture, it had plummeted to 1.8 children per American woman.

In 2010, following a large influx of Hispanics with a fertility rate higher than that of other Euro-Americans, this average rate had risen to an estimated 2.05 births per woman.

The implications of this birth dearth are terrifying, and not just because it means America might have far fewer taxpayers than expected to support the last wave of retired Baby Boomers on Social Security and Medicare/Obamacare.

This decline strongly suggests that the economy and President Obama's policies designed to turn the U.S. into a Eurosocialist welfare state are now giving us a sub-replacement fertility rate like that of Western Europe.

## The Magic Number 2.1

Because a small percentage of newborn babies die before they grow to child-bearing years, the married couples in a nation must have an average of 2.1 children to maintain their country's population.

Any total fertility rate below 2.1 means that a nation's indigenous population is in decline, that in effect it is committing slow suicide by failing to replenish itself.

With this in mind, consider the 2010 estimated average fertility numbers the Central Intelligence Agency (CIA) has compiled for some of Europe's socialist welfare states. [102]

As you read these, keep in mind that Europe has been turning into Londonistan and Eurabia.

Muslim immigrants from Europe's former colonies now comprise a significant percentage of the population in many European countries – especially in cities such as London, Paris and Amsterdam – and the average fertility rate is around 3.8 children per Muslim woman.

Many European politicians, fearful in places where Muslim voters are numerous enough to tip elections, have found it easier and easier to criticize Israel and Jews.

Other Europols are gaining support by criticizing easy immigration from Muslim countries; liberal multiculturalist acceptance of Islamic Sharia law in European countries; and the prospect of Europe, which once defeated Muslim invaders, now letting Muslims conquer Europe demographically by making love, not war.

The CIA numbers below include births to Muslim women in these countries, which increases the total fertility numbers.

The CIA estimates that the average fertility for all European Union nations combined is 1.5, far below replenishment rate.

| | | |
|---|---|---|
| Ireland 2.03 | Belgium 1.65 | Hungary 1.39 |
| France 1.97 | Liechtenstein 1.53 | Greece 1.37 |
| United Kingdom 1.92 | Malta 1.52 | Italy 1.32 |
| Iceland 1.90 | Monaco 1.50 | Latvia 1.31 |
| Luxembourg 1.78 | Portugal 1.50 | Poland 1.29 |
| Norway 1.77 | Spain 1.47 | Ukraine 1.27 |
| Denmark 1.74 | Switzerland 1.46 | Czech Republic 1.25 |
| Finland 1.73 | Estonia 1.43 | Lithuania 1.24 |
| Sweden 1.67 | Germany 1.42 | |
| Netherlands 1.66 | Austria 1.39 | |

# The Last Man

For comparison, the world's highest fertility rate is in the African nation Niger, where the average woman gives birth to 7.68 babies. The lowest are in Macau (.91), next door Hong Kong (1.04) and Singapore (1.10).

Japan's average fertility rate is only 1.20, South Korea's 1.22, and Taiwan's is 1.15. Mexico's is 2.31, and Canada's is 1.58. Australia's average fertility is 1.78, while cooler New Zealand's is 2.09

The People's Republic of China's, after several decades of restricting couples to one child, is 1.54, while rival India's is 2.68 and Muslim Pakistan's is 3.28.

Although Israel is a highly-advanced technological nation, its average fertility resembles that of several Muslim nations at 2.72 births per woman.

Among nations shaped by Marxism, North Korea's average fertility is 1.94. Vietnam's is 1.93. Cuba's is 1.61. And Russia's is only 1.54, far below the fertility needed to halt the rapid decline in its population.

What should we make of this information?

In 1992 scholar Francis Fukuyama, who helped found and later left the neoconservative movement, published a provocative book titled *The End of History and The Last Man*. In it he argued that the intellectual political arguments of recent centuries are now settled, that the world almost entirely agrees on a compromise.

Henceforth, Fukuyama proposed, our societies and the future global government will be based on high technology and highly-regulated liberal capitalism that includes a sizable social welfare state. [103]

The sub-replenishment birth rates of the world's advanced nations have made Fukuyama's title grimly ironic.

Unless current patterns change, the nations of high technology and the Western Enlightenment tradition seem trapped in a demographic death spiral, destined to end from our failure to reproduce. If this continues, we are indeed headed towards extinction – the end of at least our own history and our last men.

The meek of Africa and Latin America will inherit those parts of the Earth that we have depopulated.

## Infantile Economics

Scientists have endless speculations as to why fertility is declining in advanced nations. Is it electromagnetic radiation from our power lines? Or the estrogen-mimicking chemicals in hundreds of products we use that might be "feminizing" males?

We suspect that the Inflatocracy welfare states have something to do with this decline in the reproduction of humankind.

Life reasserted itself after World War II through a Greatest Generation that had fought and won a mighty conflict after suffering the privations of a Great Depression. Hardship had made them hard and upright

As happened six centuries earlier after the Black Plague cut down half of Europe's population almost overnight, love and faith rebuilt humankind within only a few generations. The post-World War II Baby Boom became another reassertion of life and love against the mass slaughter of war.

Did environmental chemicals neuter too many Boomers? Or did welfare statist values turn us fat, and produce an infantilized America of gimme pigs in the python dependent on a paternalistic government?

How else could the Democratic Party and President Obama recently create a healthcare law requiring that people up to age 26 remain covered as children on their parents' health insurance? Not that many centuries ago the average human lifespan was 25.

The Democratic Party's welfare state has largely been built on GARS, "Government Assuming the Role of Spouse" by providing free apartments and welfare checks for millions of young inner city teenagers seduced by such tawdry goodies into becoming pregnant and dropping out of school.

Like other entitlement programs, this was the left-liberals' Declaration of Dependence to create millions of Democratic voters hopelessly hooked on Big Government handouts.

For other Boomers, the welfare state seduction was a self-indulgent brew of available drugs, infantile sexual experimentation, and political tolerance for almost any degree of reckless irresponsibility and selfish expropriation of what others had earned.

America's culture during the 1960s was media-marinated in the "alternative lifestyles" that Bloomsbury Group Fabians like economist John Maynard Keynes, according to some provocative critics, had engaged in half a century earlier while moving Western culture one step at a time to embrace their values. [104]

Most of the Fabian socialists had few children, preferring to remain infantile and sexually licentious themselves while cheering the young Soviet Union and Communism as the way of the future.

# The Tytler Cycle

We might be experiencing the low points of a long cycle of civilizations attributed to Scottish historian Alexander Tytler, who wrote of it at the same time as the American Revolution.

The cycle begins with a people in bondage, wrote Tytler. From that bondage they turn to spiritual faith, which inspires them to courage, which moves them to take actions that win their liberty.

As the cycle continues, liberty and faith and courage guide this people to achieve material abundance.

What then has happened over and over throughout human history, wrote Tytler, is that abundance leads to selfishness, to feeling entitled to take more than they make, and to taking their freedom and success for granted.

As the downward cycle continues, selfishness begets complacency and apathy as people forget the values, work ethic and spiritual faith that led them to abundance and liberty.

Again and again, civilizations have tried to sustain their lifestyle and material wealth by going deep into debt in one way or another. This dependence soon returns a people to bondage, where centuries or millennia may pass before a new leader or generation finds the spiritual faith to begin the upward cycle anew.

It is not hard to see where many Americans are on Tytler's cycle. The challenge before us is to be a saving remnant, able to restore the up lifting values that move a people to greatness and renew the vision of America's Founders – for without vision the people perish. [105]

## American Exceptionalism

America is a special nation unlike any other, millions of us believe. How could we be brought down by cyclic forces that lifted up and then destroyed earlier nations and empires?

According to President Obama, the United States is exceptional only in the same way that Brits or Greeks see their countries as exceptional. He seems not to believe that America has any divine, special or manifest destiny or historic mission that makes our nation truly unique and important in the world. [106]

Yet even some scientists have put forth evidence that Americans are an exceptional people.

How can this be, since Americans have come from all over the world? That, it turns out, may be the answer. Our ancestors were the people who chose to come here rather than stay in their old country.

Only about 2 percent of people voluntarily leave the nation of their birth and move to another. What makes them different?

With the sole exception of those who were put in chains by Black Africans and Muslim traders and sold as slaves to visiting Europeans, the ancestors of nearly every American, including Native Americans, were part of a self-selected group of immigrants.

Through 400 years of generations in America, many have inherited the genes of parents who came by their free will. And African-Americans inherited the great strengths of ancestors strong and loving enough to endure slavery.

Ethnographer and economist Dr. Thomas Sowell has written that African-Americans who chose to move here from the Caribbean on average earn more than comparably-educated Caucasian Americans. Might this in part be because these self-selected immigrants brought with them the same questing hypomanic genes found disproportionately in many Americans descended from other immigrant groups?

UCLA Professor of Psychiatry Peter C. Whybrow and John D. Gartner of Johns Hopkins University Medical School have put forth their theories that for this reason a larger-than-elsewhere share of Americans carry genetic code that predisposes us to what *New York Times* reporter Emily Bazelon described as "restless curiosity, exuberance and competitive self-promotion – a combination known as hypomania." [107]

In his book *American Mania: When More Is Not Enough*, Dr. Whybrow suggests that many Americans carry what geneticists call D4-7 dopamine receptor alleles in their DNA. Such people may be genetically predisposed to novelty-seeking and other tendencies that might prompt a person to immigrate to a new land or seek out new opportunities. [108]

In his book *The Hypomanic Edge: The Link Between (A Little) Craziness and (A Lot of) Success in America*, Dr. Gartner defines "hypomanic" not as a clinical mental illness but as a mild form of mania, "a temperament, characterized by an elevated mood state that feels 'highly intoxicating, powerful, productive and desirable.'" [109]

Gartner suggests that Columbus, Founding Father Alexander Hamilton and steel tycoon Andrew Carnegie were probably hypomaniacs who felt this condition's restless energy, grand ambitions, tendency toward euphoria and feelings that one is destined to change the world.

## Green Genes

Both of these psychiatrists conclude that Americans carry traits of energy, enthusiasm and ambition that could help explain our nation's enormous success at business, entrepreneurship and innovation.

However, does carrying the genes of pioneers make Americans more susceptible to the emotional harm of inflation, money illusion and the welfare state than other peoples?

Our pioneer ancestors, as we read of them in antebellum America in Alexis de Tocqueville's volumes of *Democracy in America*, were hardworking, restless risk takers whose manic energy built and still can be felt in our country's culture, politics and marketplace.

The New World, as William Shakespeare wrote, is a "Brave New World."

America's National Anthem is unique among such songs because it ends not with a statement – but with a question: "Oh, Say, does that Star-Spangled Banner yet wave o'er the land of the free and the home of the brave?"

Well, does it? Each of us has a personal responsibility to answer this question, and if our answer is negative we have a patriotic duty to find within ourselves the bravery to reclaim, restore and revitalize America's lost freedom.

Thomas Jefferson believed that each generation is its own country and must keep liberty alive by creating its own cultural revolution, its own assertion of America's bedrock values against those who always try to make government bigger and more intrusive.

Has the drug of inflation changed from the occasional stimulant of our pioneer ancestors and today become the reality-altering, will-sapping, freedom-robbing mood- and mind-control drug Soma that Aldous Huxley described in his dystopian novel *Brave New World*?

The most frightening thing about Huxley's novel is that most of the people living in its carefully controlled society were so drugged and distracted by loose morals and "the feelies" – movies that electronically induced emotions into the audience – that they were almost all unthinking, unquestioning...and, in an artificially tranquilized way, happy.

Like Ryan and Peggy, we need to look deep into the mirror of our soul and honestly answer both the national anthem's and the *Brave New World* questions.

## Denaturing Our DNA?

Is our government's policy of creating unrelenting inflation changing what we are, and what it means to be an American? Is inflation somehow denaturing the DNA that helped make Americans exceptional?

For our pioneer ancestors America was a land of open frontiers that beckoned them, of freedom and opportunity. It was a great, expansive land perfectly suited to their nature and tendencies, a place where the biggest dreams could come true.

Today, however, the frontiers are closed.

(By President Obama's decision, we who were first to walk on the Moon soon will no longer have our own space shuttles to reach the International Space Station on President John F. Kennedy's "New Frontier." We will have to rely on Russian rockets to take our astronauts to the "High Frontier," the "new high ground" and commanding heights of outer space that will control Earth's future.)

Freedom is becoming more and more restricted and hedged in by government with each passing day. Achievement is taxed, ridiculed and otherwise punished by politicians who coercively take from the productive to reward the unproductive, who are systematically bleeding all the capital out of American capitalism.

Scientists used to believe that having a driven "Type A" personality was unhealthy, a source of stress and heart attacks.

Research later revealed that having such a personality was not a health problem as long as the "Type A" was successful.

## Blue Genes

The stress and heart attacks that occurred in "Type A" people happened in those who were thwarted and blocked from succeeding. When this happened, the result was as if the intense energy they had directed outward instead turned inward and produced stress and damage.

America used to be a land of free enterprise and opportunity. It drew to its shores the kind of energetic entrepreneurs who thrived in such an environment.

As America changes into the kind of oppressive European country most of our ancestors fled, what happens to the health and well-being of those with the pioneering and restless energy that built America still pulsing in their genes?

For these pioneer souls especially, today's left-liberal politicians are turning America into a prison colony in which what John Maynard Keynes called the "animal spirits," the optimism, vitality and hope that drives people to wager their savings on something new and improved in the marketplace, are being locked up and choked to death.

If people are genetically predisposed to free enterprise, we should recognize that discrimination against such entrepreneurs is just as racist and wrong as discrimination because of other inborn genetic traits such as skin color.

We should recognize that class warfare waged by the collectivist radical left is just another form of racism. [110]

# Chapter Seven
# Under Inflation's Spell

*"Civilizations die from suicide,
not murder."*

– Arnold J. Toynbee
Historian

"As inflation accelerates," wrote economist Milton Friedman, "sooner or later it does so much damage to the fabric of society, creates so much injustice and suffering, that a genuine public will develops to do something about it – as we saw happen in the United States in 1980."

"The level of inflation at which that may occur depends critically on the country in question and its history," he continued. "In Germany, the will to do something came at a low level of inflation because of Germany's terrible experiences after World Wars I and II...." [111]

As we discussed in great detail in our previous book *Crashing the Dollar: How to Survive a Global Currency Collapse*, all the great powers in World War I abandoned the gold standard and bankrolled their armies by printing money, taxing their people by thus inflating the currency.

No nation wants to risk losing a war because it bought anything less than the best, most expensive weapons and other tools. This is the rationalization politicians over thousands of years have invoked to remove constraints on wartime spending.

"War is the health of the state," wrote sociologist Randolph Bourne, because war rallies people around the flag and thereby vastly increases a state's internal power, authority and support. [112]

Indeed, this is why in recent times politicians and ideologues have framed almost everything as a war – such as the war on poverty, and the "hate the rich" class war promoted by today's left-liberals to win supporters by polarizing and Balkanizing our country.

Nations at war have often used a combination of rationing, patriotic peer pressure, and wage and price controls to reduce inflation's impact. And until the advent of today's high technology weapons that require highly-trained professional operators, governments since at least the Napoleonic era had cut costs by using conscription to supply human cannon fodder for their armies.

All the major nations involved in World War I chose to fight it on a credit card. All assumed that the war would be short. All assumed that they would be on the winning side and would have their war debts paid by reparations imposed on the losers.

Few reckoned that this War to End All Wars would drag on for half a decade, produce battles that claimed 100,000 lives a day, and kill 9.7 million soldiers and more than 6 million civilians. At its end the Great War had only losers.

At war's end most major nations returned to something like a gold standard to put the brakes on such inflation. This sent prices sharply upwards. The United States, at sacrifice to its own citizens, transferred part of its gold supply to Great Britain to facilitate John Bull's return to a gold standard.

The U.S. faced its own Depression in 1920-21, an event little noted in liberal history texts because it was quickly cured by Republican Presidents Warren G. Harding and Calvin Coolidge tightening the money supply and cutting the size of government by 25 percent to wring inflation out of the system – much as President Reagan did after the nightmare of President Carter's misrule.

Germany's currency, the Mark, by early 1920 had fallen to "only one-fortieth of its overseas purchasing power" back in 1914, wrote former European Parliament member Adam Fergusson in his 1975 book *When Money Dies: The Nightmare of the Weimar Collapse.*

Worth only pennies outside Germany, inside the country the Mark retained more than 10 percent of its 1914 purchasing power, and wages had increased to offset part of this loss by giving workers more Marks to spend.

Germany's newly-elected left liberal Weimar Republic made a fateful decision. Having lost the war, and burdened with crushing war reparation debt by the victors, the government had little foreign credit left to keep the German economy afloat.

Germany's gold reserves were largely depleted by foreign purchases during the war, and, if brought forth, its remaining gold would be demanded as payment by France and England. Returning to a gold standard under Germany's new democratic socialist regime was therefore unthinkable in 1920.

## Illusion of Prosperity

While other European nations and the United States slowed their printing of money, the Weimar government – eager for money not only to keep the economy running but also to expand its ambitious social welfare programs and the size of government – decided to continue printing paper fiat Marks at high speed.

Contrary to expectations, this flood of money at first was a tonic for the battered nation. While France, Great Britain and the United

States faced the shock of going cold turkey off their wartime addiction to inflated easy money, Germany simply kept injecting paper money for its stimulative effect.

"Everyone loves an early inflation," wrote economic historian Jens O. Parsson in his 1974 book *Dying of Money: Lessons of the Great German and American Inflations*. He makes many of the same points we saw earlier from economist Milton Friedman about the drug-like high-to-hangover cycle inflation causes.

"The effects at the beginning of inflation are all good," wrote Parsson. "There is steepened money expansion, rising government spending, increased government budget deficits, booming stock markets, and spectacular general prosperity, all in the midst of temporarily stable prices. Everyone benefits, and no one pays. That is the early part of the cycle."

This is precisely what happened during the early Weimar Republic. Factories were humming, and unemployment almost vanished. Food and beer were abundant, and incomes for a time rose faster than prices, which into 1921 were relatively stable.

As happens with all inflating fiat money, this was the illusion of prosperity bought on a credit card – and seemed almost miraculous, until the bills began coming due.

## The Hangover

"In the later inflation, on the other hand," wrote Parsson, "the effects are all bad. The government may steadily increase the money inflation in order to stave off the latter effects, but the latter effects patiently wait."

"In the terminal inflation," he wrote, "there is faltering prosperity, tightness of money, falling stock markets, rising taxes, still larger government deficits, and still roaring money expansion, now accompanied by soaring prices and ineffectiveness of all traditional remedies. Everyone pays and no one benefits. That is the full cycle of every inflation."

By late 1921 people began noticing that each Mark was losing value. The media acknowledged this, but blamed it on treachery and reparations paid to the French and English. Even much of Germany's financial world bought into this explanation for the weakening Mark, a confusion that would soon devastate the economy.

Looking back from what was becoming the "Great Inflation" of the 1970s during the presidencies of Richard Nixon, Gerald Ford and his WIN ("Whip Inflation Now") buttons, and Jimmy Carter, Fergusson wrote: "The most notable thing about the puzzlement of the financial world, not the least the writers of the *Frankfurter Zeitung*, was complete failure to consider the continuing flood of new banknotes as one of the reasons for the mark's behavior (depreciation)."

Major business people endorsed the government policy. Hugo Stinnes, then the richest and most powerful industrialist in Germany whose empire reached across one-sixth of its economy, "justifed inflation as the means of guaranteeing full employment....as the only course open to a benevolent government," wrote Fergusson. "It was, he maintained, the only way whereby the life of the people could be sustained."

But as Fergusson notes, Stinnes built his empire in an inflationary economy that let him acquire properties on the cheap. His wealth surged in an era of easy money and crony capitalism, not unlike General Electric's in our own time.

Later in the Weimar inflation, wrote Fergusson, the currency's "fall was reckoned disastrous for the finances both of the Reich and of the regional governments: all efforts to restore order in the federal budget had been rendered void. It meant the further impoverishment of the classes on fixed incomes, state officials included, and (as another newspaper feared) further recruits for the radical circles of the Right from the '*social declasses*.'"

"What impressed the ordinary politician," wrote Fergusson, "was the danger of social unrest which would...inevitably arise if there were any scarcity of currency."

## The Unseen Connection

But most Weimar citizens simply failed to notice any connection between printing vast quantities of money and its declining value, just as today few Americans are facing the inevitable inflationary consequences of multi-trillions of dollars being thrown into the economy via partisan cronies by President Obama and our own Weimar-like democratic socialist ruling party.

Why were people in the Weimar Republic blind to what was causing their accelerating inflation? And why did the early printing of vast quantities of paper fiat money not cause inflation instantly?

One answer is what economists call the velocity of money, the speed with which it moves from one hand to another. More money by itself will not necessarily cause inflation if that money has little or no velocity.

Another answer, reported by both Parsson and Fergusson, is that many of the German people "clung to the mark, the currency they knew and believed in," losing their faith in it slowly. While the inflation grew, many naively still thought of their money as reliable, as good as gold, the way it had been before the war.

"We used to say 'The dollar is going up again'," a small Hamburg businessman years later told journalist and novelist Pearl Buck, "while in reality the dollar remained stable but our mark was falling. But, you see, we could hardly say our mark was falling since in figures it was constantly going up – and so were the prices... It all seemed just madness, and it made the people mad."

Likewise, today the establishment's business journalists say that gold has surged above $1,500 per ounce, when in truth the U.S. Dollar has fallen so far and fast that it requires more than 1,500 of them to purchase the ounce of gold that used to cost $32 or less.

"The times made us cynical," the Hamburg businessman's daughter told Buck, referring to the wealth and opulent lifestyle of speculators and manipulators while middle-class people sold off their possessions to them to survive. "Everybody saw an enemy in everybody else."

For many, the hyperinflation created what University of Virginia English Professor Paul A. Cantor once called "hyperreality," a surreal, nightmare-like Weimar world that one can see reflected in the Oscar-winning 1972 movie *Cabaret* and in literature of the time such as poet T.S. Eliot's *The Waste Land*, Thomas Mann's novella *Disorder and Early Sorrow* and his autobiographical novel *Death in Venice*. [113]

"The young and quick-witted did well," wrote one such cynic, Sebastian Haffner, in 1939. "Overnight they became free, rich and independent. It was a situation in which mental inertia and reliance on past experience was punished by starvation and death."

## Shrugging Atlas

The first impulse for middle-class Germans in 1920 was to hold on to any Marks they did not immediately need to spend, and this slowed down the velocity of the outpouring of paper money.

"At the beginning of an inflationary cycle," wrote Parsson, "velocity declines while money quantity increases, thereby offsetting one another and masking the true inflationary potential."

Inflation's illusion of prosperity can at first make people feel better able, but less pressured, to spend immediately.

This happened "in Germany's prosperous expansion of 1920," wrote Parsson, "....because money holders were temporarily willing to hold their excess money, slowing down velocity and leaving prices unchanged."

Astute readers will notice that we today face a frighteningly similar situation. Vastly more money has been injected into the economies in both the United States and Europe, but the velocity of this money has been slowed almost to a crawl by businesses and banks stashing their cash and neither spending nor lending a crucial inflationary increment of the new currency.

At least part of this slowdown comes not just from uncertainty or fears about potential government policies, but also from growing anger over political left-wing redistribution of wealth that puts heavier and heavier taxes on those pulling the wagon while government encourages more and more people to ride for free in the wagon.

As mentioned earlier, have we since 2008 been witnessing what Ayn Rand depicted in her novel *Atlas Shrugged* – the productive people in effect going on strike, withholding a share of the fruits of their labor from an increasingly Eurosocialist American society, economy and government?

It is as if the private sector has tightened a temporary tourniquet to keep this dangerous inflationary drug from surging like snake venom through our economic bloodstream. But as with human beings, if the tourniquet is not soon loosened the tissues starved of blood will be injured or begin to die.

Today's fiat paper stimulus money soon will enter the economy, even though those who have studied the Weimar hyperinflation must know the terrible consequences of such reckless spending by President Obama and his party.

## The Money Delusion Shatters

The Mark's "Velocity started to rise with moderate vigor in the summer of 1921," wrote Parsson, "when Germans began to smell a government rat, and that signaled the gradual emergence of the latent price inflation."

Why a government rat? Parsson writes that he agrees with economist Milton Friedman that "inflation is always and everywhere a monetary phenomenon. No one can cause an inflation but the government, and neither more nor less is required to stop an inflation than that the government stop causing it."

"People's willingness to hold money can change suddenly for a 'psychological and spontaneous reason,' causing a spike in the velocity of money," wrote Ambrose Evans-Pritchard of the *London Telegraph* in an article about Parsson's newfound popularity with powerful bankers.

"Reichsbank officials were baffled," wrote Evans-Pritchard about Weimar. "They could not fathom why the German people had started to behave differently almost two years after the banks had already boosted the money supply."

The reason seems almost self-evident. If money is a reliable store of value, like gold, human beings tend to hang on to it. If money is unreliable as a store of value, then, wrote Parsson, "People naturally wish to hold money less and to spend it faster when they see its value falling."

As more Germans began to smell the socialist Weimar government rat, wrote Parsson, "Velocity took an almost right-angle turn upward in the summer of 1922," as people began spending their Marks faster and faster.

In Weimar as the inflation worsened, in part because of this accelerating money velocity, "Nobody wished to retain money," wrote Ludwig von Mises. "Everybody dropped it like a live coal."

Novelist Ernest Hemingway visited Weimar and witnessed the surreal re-valuing of society, both monetary and personal. He saw people rushing to stores with wheelbarrows of paper money that was losing its purchasing power by the hour.

"The first panacea for a misguided nation is inflation of the currency; the second is war," wrote Hemingway in 1935 as ominous clouds of an approaching World War II darkened the world.

"Both bring a temporary prosperity; both bring a permanent ruin," wrote Hemingway. And "both are the refuge of political and economic opportunists."

By shattering the work and thrift ethics of the German people and destroying the faith they had placed in their currency as a store of value, the left-liberal Weimar Government created a demoralizing reversal and vacuum of values that Adolf Hitler's demagoguery exploited to gain power.

## European Turnabout

After decades of preaching that the United States should imitate the Eurosocialist welfare states, it seems ironic that President Obama has flatly rejected Germany's suggestion that he follow Europe's new policy of austerity and capitalistic principles in these economic hard times.

Germany, remembering its Weimar nightmare, opted for austerity, smaller government, and lower tax policies akin to those adopted in 1981 by President Ronald Reagan. Having suffered under socialism from Weimar to Hitler to recent Social Democratic governments, Germany is inching back towards free market capitalism – and enjoyed some rapid economic growth and prosperity as a result.

President Obama and, until January 2011, a Congress dominated by his own left-liberal political party have chosen instead to turn America into Weimerica, to follow an economic policy of massively enlarging government, choking the private sector with more taxes and regulation, and printing, borrowing, and spending our way back to prosperity.

Socialism is fine, reputedly joked former pro-capitalism British Prime Minister Margaret Thatcher, "until you run out of other people's money."

In 2011, however, the largest independent buyer of American debt obligations, PIMCO, announced that it will no longer be purchasing U.S. Government debt.

The second largest foreign creditor buying our debt – holding nearly $900 Billion worth and thereby lending the U.S. money – is Japan. Devastated by massive earthquakes, a tsunami and the problems these natural disasters caused, Japan will require at least $300 Billion to rebuild. Analysts expect Japan for the next five years or more to be a seller, not buyer, of U.S. debt paper. It will likely also bring home some portion of its money invested in American enterprises, which will further weaken the U.S. economy.

## Dragon Down the Dollar

The biggest foreign buyer of American debt – more than $1.35 Trillion worth – is the People's Republic of China, now beginning to deal with high inflation and other serious internal economic problems of its own.

The old optimistic view advanced by those like Harvard University economic historian Niall Ferguson is that the convergence between crony state capitalistic Obamerica and crony state capitalistic Communist China is based on a mutually-beneficial relationship so tight and friendly that we are becoming one symbiotic entity that Ferguson calls "Chimerica." [114]

Is this view realistic, or is it another hallucination caused by Money Illusion and our growing dependence on Chinese products and credit?

The Chinese may hold a different view. They have moved on many fronts to undermine the U.S. Dollar and have it replaced as the world's Reserve Currency with a basket of currencies that includes the Chinese Reminbi/Yuan.

The Chinese are apparently doing this, in part, because our printing of trillions of paper dollars is drastically devaluing the dollars they hold in reserve and is, in effect, exporting our incipient inflation to them.

More sinister forces may be at work here. Consider an alternative scenario:

The People's Republic of China has long accused the West in general, and Great Britain in particular, of during the 19th Century imposing widespread, life-destroying drug addiction on the Chinese people.

British traders, according to this accusation, imported vast quantities of opium to China and sold it in defiance of China's imperial laws. It purportedly came from poppy plantations in British-ruled India.

Is America now the victim of China's revenge for what historians call the Opium Wars?

## China the Pusher

Americans in recent decades became spendaholics, addicted to inexpensive Chinese goods and to easy money and credit made possible in large measure by China buying up our debt.

The People's Republic of China became our "drug pusher," the enabler of our growing welfare state, knowing that this helps achieve two things its nominally Marxist regime very much wants:

(1) It is effecting the transfer of vast American wealth to China, much of which has been used to acquire weapons systems – enormously increasing both Beijing's economic and military strength in the Pacific and worldwide.

(2) By feeding America's spendaholism and bankrolling our welfare state, China is draining America's wealth, industrial capacity, moral fiber and, in the long run, our future standing as a global economic and military power.

China's ambitious leaders may be tempted to test President Obama's resolve by militarily attacking the free Chinese people of Taiwan sometime before the 2012 election.

This could prove unwise, because Mr. Obama, who seems occasionally decisive but often weak, might overreact in some unexpected ways.

China is an ancient culture that understands two things. First, from its ancient military General and theorist Sun Tzu, author of *The Art of War*, China knows that struggles are won not on battlefields alone, but on all fronts – including public psychology, patriotism, morality, and economics. [115]

Second, China is winning by the constant hemorrhage of wealth and moral strength from the U.S. to Beijing. Why confront a stumbling giant who is bleeding to death and self-destructing, when mere patience will bring him down and make you victorious?

The watching world is aware of credit-addicted America's rapid economic and moral decline, and is already showing signs of shifting allegiance towards the rising, increasingly-dominant great power of the East.

## Principles and Interest

Something every American should see and ponder is a video freely available on the Internet from the fiscal responsibility group Citizens Against Government Waste, whose web site is *CAGW.org*. [116]

This powerful 60 second video's drama opens on a "Chinese Professor" lecturing in a classroom alongside a huge banner of Chairman Mao Tse-dong, the founder of Communist China. The year is 2030, less than 20 years from today.

"Why do great nations fail?" the professor asks, speaking in Mandarin with English subtitles.

"The ancient Greeks, the Roman Empire, the British Empire and the United States of America. They all make the same mistakes, turning their back on the principles that made them great."

"America tried to spend and tax itself out of a great recession. Enormous so-called 'stimulus' spending, massive changes to health care, government takeovers of private industries, and crushing debt."

"Of course, we owned most of their debt," says the professor with a smile. "So now they work for us."

The Chinese students in this video burst into laughter, over which an announcer's voice says: "You *can* change the future. You have to. Join Citizens Against Government Waste to stop the spending that is bankrupting America."

We need to wake up a nation hypnotized by Money Illusion and the Inflation Deception.

# Part Three
# The Uses Of Inflation

# Chapter Eight
# Inflation as Taxation

*"Inflation is the one form of taxation
that can be imposed without legislation."*

– Milton Friedman
Nobel Laureate Economist

"The power of taxation by currency depreciation is one which has been inherent in the state since [ancient] Rome discovered it," wrote John Maynard Keynes in 1923. [117]

"The creation of legal tender has been and is a Government's ultimate reserve," Keynes continued, "and no State or Government is likely to decree its own bankruptcy or its own downfall so long as this instrument still lies at hand unused."

"The U.S. is bankrupt," wrote Boston University Professor of Economics Laurence J. Kotlikoff in August 2010.

The International Monetary Fund (IMF) announced that America is effectively bankrupt in a July 2010 *Selected Issues Paper.* Governments, of course, do not go bankrupt so long as they have citizens they can tax into individual bankruptcy. Inflation offers a way of "taxation" that governments can use to siphon off the earnings of those who think they pay no taxes, or who are secret tax evaders unknown to government agents.

"The U.S. fiscal gap associated with today's [U.S.] federal fiscal policy," wrote the IMF, "is huge for plausible discount rates" and "closing the fiscal gap requires a permanent fiscal adjustment equal to about 14 percent of U.S. GDP." [118]

"This fiscal gap," wrote Kotlikoff, "is the value today (the present value) of the difference between projected spending (including servicing official debt) and projected revenue in all future years."

Total government revenue today is approximately 14.9 percent of GDP.

## The Unsustainable Gap

"So the IMF is saying that closing the U.S. fiscal gap, from the revenue side, requires, roughly speaking, *an immediate and permanent doubling* of our personal, income, corporate and federal taxes as well as the payroll levy set down in the Federal Insurance Contribution Act." [*Emphasis added*]

This fiscal gap, writes Kotlikoff, "is the government's credit-card bill and each year's 14 percent of GDP is the interest on that bill. If it doesn't pay this year's interest, it will be added to the balance.... Our country is broke and can no longer afford no-pain, all-gain 'solutions'."

The non-partisan Congressional Budget Office (CBO) issued a report on July 27, 2010, titled "Federal Debt and the Risk of a Fiscal Crisis." The report's most likely fiscal scenario predicts that America's national debt was almost certain to rise above 62 percent of Gross Domestic Product expected by the end of 2010 and would certainly reach that level by 2020.

In February 2011 the *Washington Times* reported that President Obama's proposed budget would cause "the biggest one-year jump in debt in history...nearly $2 Trillion," increasing Federal debt to 102.6 percent of GDP by September 30, 2011. [119]

In their 2009 book *This Time Is Different: Eight Centuries of Financial Folly*, University of Maryland Economics Professor Carmen M. Reinhart and Harvard University Professor Kenneth S. Rogoff warn that debt reaching 90 percent of a nation's GDP is usually the point of no return for countries; those whose debt grows this large almost always see their currencies and economies crash and burn rather than regain health. [120]

CBO projects that if today's levels of government spending continue, the U.S. national debt will be close to 110 percent of GDP in 2025 and to 180 percent of GDP in 2035.

Such spending above and beyond national income, warned CBO, is simply "unsupportable....unsustainable."

And in January 2011 CBO projected that 2011's deficit will be an unexpectedly-high $1.48 Trillion, followed in 2012 by an additional shortfall of another $1 Trillion, with the possibility that our bar tab could add $1 Trillion or more each year for the next 10 years. [121]

## Debtor Superpower

Add to this another complication: approximately 42 percent of what the U.S. Congress has spent in recent years is borrowed money.

Our largest creditor is China, which buys roughly 21 percent of our foreign debt. And like other lenders, China is logically concerned that the United States appears unwilling either to double the tax burden on our citizens or to cut our government spending in half.

If our politicians dared do either of these things, Mu-Barack Obama might soon follow Egyptian President Hosni Mubarak into exile.

It is far easier for politicians to keep borrowing on the credit cards –
to "take the cash and let the credit go," as Persian poet Omar
Khayyam wrote – until lenders such as China take the credit cards
away.

China should require the United States to cut up its other credit
cards, its borrowing from other nations. This would collapse America's economy or force the government to do rapidly what it today is
doing a bit more slowly: printing all the money it needs.

The day China cuts off our credit, our last resort, short of declaring
bankruptcy, will be as John Maynard Keynes implied. Our politicians, including the politically-appointed head of the Federal Reserve, will switch on the printing presses and manufacture as much
"legal tender" paper money as needed to "monetize the debt," to pay
off our debt with nearly worthless pieces of debased currency.

Other countries, including Weimar Germany, destroyed their currency and economy by such acts.

## The Secret Tax

The United States has done a slow-motion version of using inflation
as a de facto tax for a long time.

In 1945 Beardsley Ruml, the Chairman of the Federal Reserve Bank
of New York, reportedly delivered a remarkable speech before the
American Bar Association in which he declared: "The necessity for a
government to tax in order to maintain both its independence and
its solvency is...not true for a national government." [122]

"Two changes of the greatest consequence have occurred in the last
twenty-five years which have substantially altered the position of the
national state with respect to the financing of its current requirements," said Ruml.

"The first of these changes is the gaining of vast new experience in the management of central banks," he said.

"The second change is the elimination, for domestic purposes, of the convertibility of the currency into gold."

FDR's prohibition of gold ownership by Americans meant that U.S. citizens could no longer seek a safe haven here against inflation by converting their paper dollars into gold bullion.

Ruml's speech, published in the January 1946 issue of the quarterly journal *American Affairs*, offered a surprising new vision of what taxes "are really for."

The primary purpose of Federal taxation listed by Ruml is "As an instrument of fiscal policy to help stabilize the purchasing power of the dollar."

The implication of Ruml's speech is that government can fund itself merely by printing as much money as needed. The new money produced out of thin air acquires its value, in effect, by devaluing the old dollars that productive people have earned and saved.

To prevent a blaze of high inflation or hyperinflation from burning up the entire value of every dollar in circulation, new and old, taxes will be used to selectively take back money from targeted individuals, groups and industries.

Tax policy, writes Ruml, will "express public policy in the distribution of wealth and of income, as in the case of the progressive income and estate taxes....[and] in penalizing various industries and economic groups...[and] to isolate and assess directly the costs of certain national benefits, such as highways and social security."

Inflation also carries the double whammy of boosting other taxes linked to prices. A 10 percent tax on a $5 product nets the government 50 cents. After inflation doubles that product's price to $10, however, this same tax snares $1 for the government's coffers. [123]

Thus inflation becomes a tax, a way to fund the government, while other modes of taxation can be targeted to prevent excessive inflation by picking the pockets of individuals and groups too small to threaten the ruling political elite with their votes.

# Declaration of Dependence

The central government can further punish or reward individuals and groups by how it shields them from the effects of inflation. If at the next election the ruling party needs the votes of senior citizens or specific minority groups, it can offer them special protection in the form of Cost-of-Living Adjustments (COLAs) or special payments to offset what inflation would otherwise drain from their government welfare or Social Security payments.

Such COLAs can be altered at any time, as President Obama has done by withdrawing them from Social Security recipients. Mr. Obama in fact made token payments to Social Security beneficiaries that he said were to help offset their loss of COLAs. Odds are that Social Security COLAs or their one-time payoff equivalent will be restored in 2012, when he is up for re-election.

Inflation measures such as the Consumer Price Index (CPI) have become a source of controversy because of which prices they choose to measure, and because they have been "adjusted" in ways that alter their findings. The "core inflation" index ignores food and energy costs, for example, while another gives weighted importance to housing costs.

# Deception by the Numbers

"[I]f we still calculated inflation the way we did when Jimmy Carter was president, the official inflation figures would look about as bad as they did when...Jimmy Carter was president," wrote *Wall Street Journal* financial columnist Brett Arends on January 26, 2011. [124]

"You Can't Trust the Inflation Numbers," Arends' column reported, based on data and analysis by economist John Williams at *Shadow-Stats.com* and other sources. [125]

Arends points to three major problems with the government's inflation statistics.

One is that the government has changed how it does its inflation analysis.

"Each change in methodology has come with plausible-sounding justifications," writes Arends. "But, as if by magic, each change has had the effect of flattering the numbers. Funny, that."

"According to Mr. Williams' calculations," writes Arends, "if we counted inflation under the old system the official rate wouldn't be 1.5%. It would be closer to 10%."

Government now assumes that if steak prices go up, you will switch to cheaper hamburger. "Presto – no inflation!" writes Arends.

If the price stays the same for, say, an Apple laptop computer, these same government inflation analysts calculate using "a piece of chicanery called 'hedonics....that the real price has actually fallen," writes Arends, because today's computers are better than a year ago so buyers get "more" for their money. In fact, the price has not fallen, he notes, so this inflation calculation is misleading.

"The second reason to treat the official inflation figures with some mistrust is that they look backward....not [at] what's about to happen," writes Arends. This, he notes, means that government is ignoring the cost of raw materials.

"Around the world prices are skyrocketing, from copper to cocoa. The United Nations Food Price Index has just hit a new record high. Oil's back near $90 a barrel. Wheat prices have nearly doubled since last summer," he writes, and nations have begun hoarding foodstuffs, making world supplies even tighter.

"Sooner or later this is going to show up in your supermarket, or at the mall, in higher prices," writes Arends. "How is this not inflation?" Yet the official backward-looking analysis continues to say that consumers face no inflation.

Arends' third reason to mistrust government inflation statistics is "economics." The government is printing vast quantities of paper dollars, far in excess of our nation's productivity. As said before, the Law of Supply and Demand can no more be repealed by the Fed and our politicians than can the Law of Gravity.

"[I]f you drastically increase the number of dollars without a commensurate increase in the number of goods and services, each dollar must, by definition, be worth less," Arends writes. "That's another way of describing inflation."

Arends could have gone even further. A fourth reason for skepticism is changes in how government does "weighting" of various inflation factors. [126]

China's government, for example, gives much more weight in its inflation calculations than our government now does to price increases for food and drink – and China has in 2010 and early 2011 raised its central bank lending rate three times to fight what it sees as dangerous inflation.

"So long as the Chinese tie themselves to the U.S. Dollar, they are importing our inflation," writes Arends. "[O]ne wonders how this can be called benign."

## Taxing the World

By using government's own manipulated inflation indexes, politicians and bureaucrats can avoid paying out hundreds of billions – even, over years, trillions – of dollars in Cost-of-Living Adjustments (COLAs) to senior citizens, welfare recipients, holders of TIPS government bonds that are supposedly protected against inflation, labor wage contracts, and others. Such manipulation is a kind of theft by fraud.

Senior citizens are now being triple-taxed, the head of one elder organization said. They were taxed as workers to pay for future Social Security. They must pay income taxes on the Social Security money they receive in retirement. And now, under President Obama, they are being taxed a third time through inflation stealing the purchasing power of their Social Security checks.

When the Obama Administration announced that Social Security recipients would receive no increase in 2010, 2011 and 2012, skeptics reasonably noted that CPI cannot reliably predict what inflation will be a year from now. Has Uncle Sam become Uncle Sham when claiming to predict future inflation? [127] No, the current Administration says, the COLA will vanish for millions in 2012 because of exotic juggling of benefits between Social Security and Medicare.

Or is this just a cynical and sneaky way to reduce Social Security benefits for seniors and all future beneficiaries so that no member of Congress has to vote on the record to cut this entitlement?

## The Vampire Tax

Meanwhile, the inflation tax is in many ways a dream for bureaucrats. It is dirt cheap to collect and requires no audits or enforcement agents. It simply sucks the lifeblood value out of everyone's dollars like an invisible vampire. And it derives vast revenue for the government even from those with off-the-books income and other tax evaders who remain undetected by the government.

"Inflation is a method of taxation which the government uses to secure the command of real resources; resources just as real as those obtained by ordinary taxation. What is raised by printing notes is just as much taken from the public as is income tax. A government can live by this means when it can live by no other. It is this form of taxation that the public finds hardest to evade, and even the weakest government can enforce it when it can enforce no other," wrote John Maynard Keynes.

"Inflation is the one form of taxation which even the weakest government can enforce, when it can enforce nothing else," said a League of Nations Report on European Inflations of the 1920s.

Everyone who uses the government's paper fiat money is taxed by its deliberate inflation.

This includes citizens and central banks of other countries who risk trusting the dollar as a reliable store of value.

Inflation has become the U.S. Government's way of taxing the world, not just its own citizens.

No wonder inflation has been called America's largest and most profitable export. [128]

## The Wheel of Inflation

Vladimir Lenin, founder of the Communist Soviet Union, said that the way to destroy the capitalist bourgeoisie was to "grind them down between the millstones of taxation and inflation."

Has deliberate inflation thus become a weapon of class warfare for President Obama and his political comrades?

This deliberate grinding by inflation is precisely what liberal presidents have done since Republican Richard Nixon in 1971 broke the U.S. Dollar's last anchor tying its value to gold.

In 1933 an earlier left-liberal Democrat, President Franklin Delano Roosevelt, made it illegal for Americans to own gold bullion and confiscated it. The Executive Orders outlawing and confiscating gold remained in effect until January 1975 – four years after Nixon killed the gold standard – when President Gerald Ford rescinded them.

FDR also destroyed by law something that was commonplace in major contracts when the American Dollar was backed by gold – a gold clause, which provided that if politicians destroyed the dollar, the person owed money could demand payment instead in a fixed quantity of gold. Such contract clauses impaired the ability of government to rob others by debasing the value of its currency.

FDR did not outlaw all gold. Those who used gold in certain professions, such as dentistry, were allowed to possess it through a special license. Numismatic gold coins were exempt from confiscation under FDR's Executive Orders, and those who owned them profited handsomely when gold's value jumped by approximately 60 percent immediately after gold bullion was confiscated.

FDR seized gold bullion using government's eminent domain power to acquire it at its old fixed price, thereby transferring to government the huge profit of gold's new, much higher market price.

FDR doubtless drove many Americans to drink by expropriating their gold. He soon facilitated this by supporting the 21st Amendment to the U.S. Constitution, which in December 1933 repealed the 18th Amendment – Prohibition of "intoxicating liquors," that had been the law of the land since January 1919.
The state whose legislature's vote repealed Prohibition was Utah.

The Kennedy Family, whose matriarch was daughter of the Democratic boss of Boston John "Honey Fitz" Fitzgerald, was probably heartbroken. Joseph Kennedy, Sr., during Prohibition reportedly had somehow been granted a special U.S. Government permit to legally import and lucratively sell "medicinal alcohol," which turned out to include three popular brands of Scotch whiskey.

## The Tax from Jekyll Island

The aim of left-liberals and so-called Progressives, with the 1913 establishment of the Federal Reserve Board and the income tax and continuing today, apparently has been to create disintegrating paper money....money with built-in obsolescence....all the better to tax you with.

Economic historian G. Edward Griffin explains this provocative idea in his history of the Federal Reserve Board *The Creature from Jekyll Island:*

"Inflation has now been institutionalized at a fairly constant 5% per year. This has been determined to be the optimum level for generating the most revenue without causing public alarm. A 5% devaluation applies, not only to the money earned this year, but to all that is left over from previous years. At the end of the first year, a dollar is worth 95 cents. At the end of the second year, the 95 cents is reduced again by 5%, leaving its worth at 90 cents, and so on. By the time a person has worked 20 years, the government will have confiscated 64% of every dollar he saved over those years. By the time he has worked 45 years, the hidden tax will be 90%. The government will take virtually everything a person saves over a lifetime." [129]

According to the government's official CPI index, inflation in December 2010 and January 2011 was running at 0.4 percent per month, which could average out to 4.8 percent per year, more than double Fed Chair Bernanke's 2 percent target but close to Griffin's 5 percent average, above. [130]

One way to escape this inflationary slavery is by studying and sharing this book and using what it and our previous book *Crashing the Dollar: How to Survive a Global Currency Collapse* teach about freeing yourself from the government's paper fiat money.

Our Nixonian no-longer-anchored-to-gold paper dollar continues to lose value every decade to inflation, and this is happening not by accident but by design.

Government tax and regulatory policies are snatching away our earnings, in part by making almost everything we buy more expensive in dollars.

Because of this, the American working class has scarcely increased its real purchasing power, its inflation-adjusted income in dollars, over almost 40 years.

And this grand paper dollar con game uses other tools as well.

## The "Tax the Rich" Deception

Liberals and progressives prey on human envy and covetousness. "Let's tax the rich who have more than you do," they have said for a century.

Are you "rich?" Most Americans think of themselves as middle class, but more than half of us now pay the "progressive" income tax that was supposed to hit only the rich.

This tax was originally proposed by Karl Marx and Friedrich Engels in 1848 in *The Communist Manifesto* as a way "to wrest, by degrees, all capital from the bourgeoisie," from business people and other capitalists. [131]

After many decades of letting inflation push people into higher and higher tax brackets, the income tax was supposedly "indexed" for inflation. However, we have already seen how deceptive inflation indexes can be, and how quickly greedy politicians eager for more revenue can manipulate the rules to squeeze money out of us.

Over and over, people have been conned into accepting taxes that were supposed to apply only to the wealthy. When the income tax was enacted in 1913, the "rich" included those making only $25,000 per year. How many realized that inflation would soon put a majority of us into this "rich" category subject to income taxation?

This same inflation deception that tricked people into accepting the so-called "progressive" income tax would later seduce Americans into swallowing the Alternative Minimum Tax (AMT) to catch "those rich people who avoid paying taxes." Thanks to inflation, a majority of Americans could soon be required to pay AMT.

This and a thousand other penalties and surcharges have been sold as targeting "only the rich." And thus today the successful Middle-Class American, whose dollar income (but not purchasing power) has risen mostly because of inflation, now pays a confiscatory tax rate that was originally supposed to rob only the rich.

Large parts of President Obama's new laws include tax and fee increases that are NOT indexed for inflation. Does anyone really believe this is accidental?

The coming hyperinflation will soon redefine almost all of us as "rich," just as the AMT has for millions of middle-class Americans, even though you will have less purchasing power than you did three decades ago.

Being fraudulently redefined as "rich" will subject you to an array of government money grabs.

## Waking Up to Inflation

What has really happened? An old joke makes it clear. A man falls asleep and, like fabled Rip Van Winkle, reawakens 20 years later. He promptly calls his broker to ask about his IBM stock.

"I have good news," his broker says. "Your $100,000 in IBM stock is now worth One Million Dollars."

The man starts to cheer, but is cut short by the pay telephone operator saying: "That will be $30,000 for the next three minutes, please."

The value of the U.S. Dollar is not what it used to be, but many government tax policies deliberately designed to use inflation as a way to tax ordinary income earners as if they were "rich" have not changed.

The capital gains tax, for example, is not indexed for inflation and will take a huge bite out of Rip Van Winkle's "gain" when he sells his almost-worthless IBM stock.

# Chapter Nine
# Inflatocracy: Inflation as Ideology and Power

*"The way to crush the bourgeoisie
is to grind them down between
the millstones of taxation and inflation."*

– Vladimir Lenin
Founder of the Soviet Union

Inflation can be extremely dangerous, so why do politicians and central bankers print reckless amounts of paper money, knowing the catastrophe this can cause?

The answer is that inflation is many things in addition to devaluation of the currency.

Inflation can be a tool, an ideology, a form of taxation that secretly extracts the earnings not only of Americans but also of unsuspecting people in other countries. It is also a means of wealth redistribution, a mode of social engineering, a device to weaken some and strengthen others both within a nation and in the global community of nations, and a way to seize and exercise power.

Inflation is being deliberately created and used to rob us of our money and property, our opportunities to pursue happiness, our independence, our security and peace of mind, our freedom and our rights, and our children's and grandchildren's future in what used to be a much freer America.

In Table One at the end of this chapter, we suggest ways that inflation has literally become a new kind of governance that imposes its own sinister rules and alternative values, values quite different from those of America's Founders.

Fed Chairman Ben Bernanke has long believed that by "inflation targeting," an approach that has spread to dozens of countries since New Zealand began practicing it in 1990, it is reliably possible to limit inflation to only two or three percent annually in our economy. [132]

Central bankers in recent years have boasted of the success of inflation targeting, but this, too, is part of the Inflation Deception.

As the Euro community and other currencies have all tried to lower their value – thereby making their exports cheaper and more successful abroad – the major currencies have increasingly moved in lock-step.

When the Fed cheapens the U.S. Dollar, it prompts trade competitors to likewise devalue their own currencies to avoid giving the dollar an advantage. This drives inflation in many places. The business networks then report this as a dramatic horse race between, e.g., dollar and Euro that take turns inching ahead of each other for a few days, then falling back.

## Currency Wars

The result of these "currency wars" has been a race to the bottom. However, as all currencies tend to lose value in tandem, they stay in roughly the same value relationship to one another. It's like several people who jump from a bridge together, staying side by side as they plummet towards a crash.

The major currencies therefore exhibit little inflation relative to each other.

When compared to commodities such as foodstuffs or gold, however, all these paper currencies have been rapidly losing value. Fiat dollars are now rapidly falling in value relative to real things, commodities, as every recent visitor to a supermarket or gas station can attest.

When a reporter says that gold has surged above $1,500 per ounce, the news you should hear is that the U.S. Dollar has fallen so far that it now takes 1,500 dollars to buy one ounce of gold. When the Fed was created in 1913, an ounce of gold cost only around $20.

The dollar back then was, of course, on the gold standard. While this anchor lasted, the U.S. Dollar was one of the world's most reliable stores of value. Inflation averaged one-quarter percent per year, so a dollar saved reliably retained its purchasing power for decades.

## Inflation's Winners and Losers

Inflation creates winners as well as losers, and those who advocate inflationary policy do so because they think of themselves as on the side of the winners.

Inflation favors debtors at the expense of creditors. It makes a nation's paper money worth less, which causes exports to be cheaper and more successful abroad while raising the price of imports (including oil) that compete with domestic products. Cheaper money attracts foreign tourists while making it more expensive for a nation's own citizens to travel abroad. [133]

And America, being the world's largest debtor, has the most of all to gain from inflation.

Inflation, as it did in Weimar, favors speculators over those who work hard, and the young at the expense of the elderly, the risk-averse, savers and those on fixed incomes whose life savings, pensions or Social Security checks may be rendered worthless by rapidly rising prices.

The majority of Americans – who play by the rules, work hard, live prudently and responsibly, strive to be self-reliant, reject theft and covetousness as the Bible's Ten Commandments say to do, and follow culturally conservative values – are the ones most injured and punished by high inflation.

## Inflation, Welfare and Values

Born in 1899 in Germany, Wilhelm Röpke experienced firsthand the horrors of World War I and the shattering of social values in the Weimar hyperinflation.

An economist and university professor, he fled the country after being targeted by the Nazis because he spoke out in public against Hitler and in defense of Jewish scholars.

After World War II Röpke served as an economic advisor to West German Chancellor Konrad Adenauer and was a prominent advocate for decentralized authority and local power – what in the United States we might call states' rights. He was one of the shapers of Germany's postwar "economic miracle."

In his 1958 book *A Humane Economy: The Social Framework of the Free Market*, Röpke looked with horror at the "Age of Inflation" that had taken over his nation's and much of the Western world's economies:

"It is the acute stage of a chronic pathological process fed by forces which are now permanently operative, and as such, it is not susceptible to any quick or lasting cure," wrote Röpke.

"The inflation of our time is intimately connected with some of its most obdurate ideas, forces, postulates, and institutions and can be overcome only by influencing these profound causes and conditions."

"It is not just a disorder of the monetary system which can be left to financial experts to redress, it is a moral disease, a disorder of society."

"This inflation, too, belongs to the things which can be understood and remedied only in the area beyond supply and demand." [134]

He saw this "moral disease" not only as a matter of economics and politics, but also as a problem with both psychological and spiritual dimensions. It represented a breakdown of values and human social relationships, symptoms of profound cultural and moral collapse.

American billionaire publisher Mortimer B. Zuckerman might agree. In April 2011 he wrote:

"Our national debt is literally an 'existential threat' to our finances. It suggests an erosion of the nation's character over the last 50 years. We have indulged ourselves for way too long, finding ways to extract money from future generations and leave them with the bill. We may have become a nation that is morally incapable of living within its means. This cannot continue *ad infinitum*." [135]

## Three Malignant Forces

Our modern widespread "chronic inflation," Röpke wrote, is the result of several negative new factors in society.

One cause is the rise of labor unions politically able to extract more money from companies than the free marketplace could afford without sending prices on an ever-upward spiral.

Another is politicians churning out tons of paper money to buy votes from a fast-growing welfare state population of beneficiaries.

"The blame for inflation," wrote Röpke, "must be laid at the door of the whole trend of postwar economic policy in most countries, that mixture of planning, welfare state, cheap money policy, fiscal socialism, and full-employment policy."

However, he wrote, "to understand this policy trend, we must go back to the revolution in economic theory which furnished the ideas and catchwords of inflationary policy and which is, above all, linked with the name of J.M. Keynes." [136]

The third malignant driver of inflation was the fashionable "new economics" theories of British economist John Maynard Keynes and his acolytes, who taught that injections of government stimulus money could somehow banish the capitalist economic cycle of boom and bust, and thereby allow a priesthood of elite economists and central bankers to conjure permanent prosperity and perpetual full employment.

## A New Economic Order

In past centuries the entire economy, including wages and charity, rose and fell with economic cycles, the heartbeat of a living modern paper economy.

With mass unionization, workers were less likely to be fired, and wages had only one direction – up. Union pay was determined not by voluntary negotiation and agreement in the free marketplace but by political clout and the willingness of unions to engage in acts of direct and indirect violence.

Union pay thus moved from the economic to the political sphere and became no longer determined by market forces such as supply and demand. (The same is true for government employees – nearly a third of whom in the U.S. are unionized – whose pay and benefits go up but rarely down.)

When competing goods of lower cost or higher quality began to draw customers away from union worker-made products, the response of unions is likewise political. It is to impose unionization on competing non-union companies, and to impose crushing tariffs, trade restrictions and the like on imported products.

The emergent welfare state likewise demands an ever-increasing supply of money, and pressures politicians not to cut welfare budgets during economic downturns. As with unionized workers, the economic cycle now has a ratchet that allows beneficiary income to go up, but not down.

Because in an Inflatocracy the supply of money keeps increasing, "cuts" are made by reducing the increases a person or group needs to "keep up" with inflation. President Obama's denial of three years of Cost-of-Living Adjustments for Social Security recipients is therefore a drastic "cut" in both their present benefits and – because it holds down their payment baseline – a huge cut in all future benefits.

Is President Obama's decision racist? By its "disparate impact," Mr. Obama's decision diverts money away from a group that is disproportionately (roughly 85 percent) Caucasian – current Social Security recipients.

These forces have drastically changed the economic relationships in society, ushering in a New Economic Order with new privileged classes.

Others would have to pay high prices for union-worker-made goods during recessions, and the government would have to collect ever-higher taxes during downturns to feed the always-growing welfare state apparatus.

Societies found harmony by sharing prosperity and sharing hardship as both the lower and middle classes rode the roller coaster of the economic cycle up and down in tandem.

Even the rich usually saw their fortunes rise and fall with this shared cycle as the economy moved from its own prosperous summers to recession winters and back again.

## New Privileged Classes

The emergence of politically powerful unions and the welfare state changed this. They created two large groups of people who, like the imagined rich, kept their high income in hard times at the expense of consumers, businesses and taxpayers.

Karl Marx had attempted to foment class warfare, but his ideas of revolution by an industrial proletariat took root mostly in unindustrialized lands of peasants and aristocrats such as Russia and China.

Socialists, however, created something akin to a class war that continues today by spawning newly-privileged groups – union workers, welfare recipients, and the ever-enlarging army of government employees – now increasingly seen to be robbing and exploiting the rest of us.

Gluttony, one of the deadly sins, is one way to describe the rapacious, ever-growing hunger of government to grab more and more of the wealth its citizens work to produce. Another is to evoke the title of William Voegeli's 2010 book *Never Enough: America's Limitless Welfare State*. [137]

## Never Enough

It is difficult to provide an always-increasing flow of money to pay these union workers, welfare recipients and welfare-state employees. Politicians cannot raise taxes to infinity – especially during the economic downturns that their Keynesian stimulus policies never really prevented.

The chief source of such ever-increasing money has become inflation

– simply printing more and more fiat paper, and letting the citizenry pay for the new economic order through the hidden tax of ever-rising prices.

Simply put, the very existence of a welfare state – and the political party elected by welfare beneficiaries – depend on inflation, on the power of government to keep welfare money coming and growing, whether the economy rains or shines.

This can be guaranteed only by politicians willing to print however much debased currency as they need to buy the votes to stay in power.

And this means that a symbiotic nexus exists between inflation and the modern welfare state.

Benjamin Franklin was right: "When the people find they can vote themselves money, that will herald the end of the republic."

Perhaps this is why British author Sylvia Townsend Warner wrote that "Inflation is the senility of democracies."

Implicit in Keynesianism is the unspoken idea that humans now have the power to play God, to repeal the Law of Supply and Demand and have a few superior unelected technocrats manipulate the entire economy in what they decide is our best interest.

Keynes and his disciples were elitists who deemed their rule over the economy superior to the free market ideal of separation of economy and state.

Today we have seen President Obama's Keynesian stimulus efforts produce anemic growth and longtime high unemployment, just like a European welfare state, despite the injection into the economy of trillions and trillions of dollars.

Today serious economists outside the liberal-left have become skeptical of Keynesian assumptions. One of many reasons for such doubt is that even inflated paper money printed from thin air comes from somewhere.

Even Keynesian convert and renowned judge Richard A. Posner in his 2010 book *The Crisis of Capitalist Democracy* admits that Keynes' "belief in the possibility of perpetual boom" is "an oddity" he finds difficult to swallow.

Even if Keynesian stimulus policy could create a "perpetual boom" – which it cannot – this would be like modifying the weather so that it is always springtime. It would be an unnatural economic Brave New World of government, an artificial garden of plastic plants based on elitist planning and control – not the free marketplace of the only natural economics that Michael Rothschild describes in his insightful 1990 book *Bionomics: The Inevitability of Capitalism.*

Stimulus money must either be taxed away from the economy before it is put back in – of course, always with a fat service charge subtracted for the government itself – or it must be "borrowed" in a way that sucks available credit and capital out of the productive private marketplace or kicks prices higher regressively for rich and poor alike.

## No Free Lunch

As the conservative-libertarian science fiction writer Robert A. Heinlein famously said: TANSTAAFL. This is an acronym for the truism "There Ain't No Such Thing As A Free Lunch."

You might be invited to an event where ham sandwiches are being given away, but somebody paid for them. Somebody grew the wheat and baked the bread, raised the pigs and milled the mustard, and paid for the gas to drive the completed sandwiches to this event.

Once upon a time almost all of us were producers. We understood by our calloused hands and the sweat of our brow the real cost of making what we consumed. We were in the world as makers, not just takers.

Today we live in a surreal American economy where more than 70 percent of our Gross Domestic Product comes not from production but consumption. We have grown fat, thanks to an obese government's largesse.

"If any man should continually sin against all the rules of reasonable living," wrote Röpke, "some organ of his body will slowly but surely suffer from the accumulation of his mistakes."

"The economy, too, has a very sensitive organ of this kind," he continued. "The organ is money; it softens and yields, and its softening is what we call inflation, a dilatation of money, as it were, a managerial disease of the economy." [138]

"Inflation is a disease, a dangerous and sometimes fatal disease," warned economist Milton Friedman, "a disease that, if not checked in time, can destroy a society...."

## The Psychology of Inflation

As author Gregory Wolfe noted in an essay about Röpke's moral vision and the psychology behind inflation, since World War II a large proportion of Americans have adopted new attitudes of dependency, self-centered morality, and a socialist-promoted psychology of entitlement. [139]

President Obama paternalistically reflected this infantilized America when he insisted that Obamacare keep "children" up to age 26 on their parents' health insurance policies.

Organized labor demonstrated a similar childish petulance by throwing a fit and threatening violence against Wisconsin lawmakers who wanted highly-paid union members to pay a far smaller fraction of their insurance costs than was routine for lower-paid private sector workers.

We demand the rights of adults while accepting no more responsibility for carrying our share of society's burdens than children. We behave as if others have a legal obligation to support us, and to let us ride for free in a wagon others are forced to pull.

To get all these free goodies we believe ourselves entitled to, a majority of voters in 2008 cast their ballots for an inexperienced presidential candidate who promised to "spread the wealth around," wealth that he announced would be confiscated from all who earned more than $250,000 per year.

We have become the decadent modern people playwright Oscar Wilde described as knowing "the price of everything and the value of nothing."

Millions of us are literally dying of consumption, and from living as vampire parasites on the tree of liberty our infantile selfishness is killing. This may be the "giant sucking sound" former presidential candidate and billionaire Ross Perot claimed to hear.

"If we want to go to the roots of the chronic inflation of our times," wrote Röpke, "then we must recognize that the mental attitude which generates inflation, tolerates it, resists it but feebly, or defends it cynically is the monetary aspect of the general decline of the rule of law and of respect for the law."

"Democracy," he wrote, "...degenerates into arbitrariness, state omnipotence, and disintegration whenever the decisions of government, as determined by universal suffrage, are not contained by the ultimate limits of natural law, firm norms, and tradition."

"It is not enough that these should be laid down in constitutions," Röpke wrote. "They must be so firmly lodged in the hearts and minds of men that they can withstand all onslaughts."

"One of the most important of these norms," he wrote, "is the inviolability of money. Today its very foundations are shaken, and this is one of the gravest danger signals for our society and state." [140]

For a time prior to World War I, wrote Röpke, the gold standard among nations prevented the deadly spider of inflation from poisoning society. The removal of the gold standard allowed politicians to print paper money with little restraint, spend wildly, and again release the deadly spider of inflation and all its attendant evils into our society.

## Inflationism

An economic and political ideology called "inflationism" promotes deliberate inflationary government policies (which it calls "expansionism") to increase the supply of money. It was widely held and advocated as good for society less than a century ago. Even Ben Franklin, who as we noted earlier profited from printing Pennsylvania's paper money, supported the creation of ample paper currency.

"The popularity of inflationism is in great part due to deep-rooted hatred of creditors," wrote famed Austrian economist Ludwig von Mises in *Human Action*. "Inflation is considered just because it favors debtors at the expense of creditors." [141]

America's Civil War spawned its own early inflationists. To fund the war, the North issued $450 Million "Greenbacks," paper fiat money not backed by gold or silver.

After the war President Andrew Johnson authorized the Treasury to pay gold for Greenbacks. This was a boon to creditors, but a burden to those who hoped to repay their debts with cheap Greenbacks.

A movement arose, mostly among Western Democrat farmers, that advocated "inflating the Greenback" to ease their debt and thereby redistribute more of the nation's wealth from East to West. [142]

In 1874 President Ulysses Grant vetoed the "Inflation Bill" that would have issued another $14 Million in Greenbacks, four years after a U.S. Supreme Court ruling declared such unbacked paper fiat money to be constitutional.

# Inflationism, Capitalism and Revolution

Some "naïve inflationists" do not understand that inflation dimin-
ishes the purchasing power of money, wrote Mises in *The Theory of
Money and Credit*, while other inflationists see its problems yet believe inflation can serve higher values, including in time of war the
survival of the state. [143]

Inflation can also be an ideological weapon to overthrow nations and
economic systems, at least according to liberal economist John Maynard Keynes in his 1919 book *The Economic Consequences of the
Peace*.

"Lenin is said to have declared that the best way to destroy the Capitalist System was to debauch the currency," wrote Keynes. "By a continuing process of inflation, governments can confiscate, secretly
and unobserved, an important part of the wealth of their citizens...."

"As the inflation proceeds and the real value of the currency fluctu-
ates wildly from month to month," Keynes continued, "all permanent relations between debtors and creditors, which form the
ultimate foundation of capitalism, become so utterly disordered as
to be almost meaningless; and the process of wealth-getting degenerates into a gamble and a lottery."

"Lenin was certainly right," Keynes concluded. "There is no subtler,
no surer means of overturning the existing basis of society than to
debauch the currency. The process engages all the hidden forces of
economic law on the side of destruction, and does it in a manner
which not one man in a million is able to diagnose." [144]

Inflation makes a nation's currency and economy weaker, and it also
makes that nation's individual citizens weaker, less self-reliant and
independent, more insecure, and more willing to surrender their
rights to a protective, paternalistic government.

Honest money, in addition to being a monetary unit of account, serves
two functions: as a medium of exchange, and as a store of value.

Inflation destroys a currency's ability to be a reliable store of value. Having no intrinsic value of its own, a fiat paper currency such as the U.S. Dollar can be made worthless almost overnight merely by government printing and tossing from a helicopter or hot-air balloon 120 trillion paper dollar bills.

## Insecurity Deposits

When a nation's money is always losing value through inflation, as the U.S. Dollar is, a constant psychological pressure exists to spend instead of save. In this way inflation acts like a Keynesian prod to stimulate spending.

In individuals, this psychological pressure of constantly-rising prices can prompt more spending on marginal and frivolous purchases.

In businesses this pressure, like that caused by income tax deductibility, encourages spending on marginally-useful supplies and equipment because prices will increase.

This, economist John Maynard Keynes argued in what he called "the paradox of thrift," is good because spending rather than saving increases stimulus in the overall economy.

Such spending, however, is all too often malinvestment that is not the best or wisest use of an enterprise's limited capital. The line blurs between spending money and squandering it, and the society experiences an artificial "high," a kind of pseudo-prosperity that is far from the best, most efficient use of financial resources.

If government and the Fed hold down interest rates, the resulting easy money flows from smart investment to speculative bubbles and herd-mentality booms that go bust.

(To see two hilarious-yet-educational videos about this from George Mason University that feature Economics Professor Russ Roberts and media producer John Papola rapping as John Maynard Keynes confronting Friedrich A. Hayek, go to *http://www.swissamerica.com/ media.php* and scroll down to "Fear the Boom and Bust" and "Fight of The Century." Check other features there, too.

## Inflation and Power

Inflation means that no citizen who holds his or her life savings in the form of paper dollars can ever be secure – can never rest easy with confidence that he or she has earned and saved "enough" money to meet all basic needs in old age.

In a fiat currency society, therefore, citizens are more inclined to look to government as a source of security and for favors such as selective Cost-of-Living Adjustments (COLAs).

The essence of the welfare state is that "they break your legs, then offer you crutches."

High taxes and government-caused inflation leave millions unable to earn or save enough to be self-reliant. This forces many into a dependence on government that would have been unnecessary had they been allowed to keep and save what they earned.

This same pattern plays out in many other ways – e.g., government makes it illegal for you to build a high wall around your property, own a firearm, or defend yourself, then offers to protect you in exchange for a sizable piece of your earnings and freedom.

## Inflatocracy

In Table One at the end of this chapter, we lay out some of the implications of our theory that inflation has expanded from an economic policy into a ruling ideology, a mode of governance we call "Inflatocracy" that is now emerging in the United States.

Inflatocracy is political rule of, by and for the elite that controls inflation and its political constituency groups that benefit in one way or another from inflation.

Like other styles of government, Inflatocracy reshapes the values of the people it needs in order to retain and expand its power. It uses inflation to encourage and to buy their loyalty, support and votes.

This new mode of governance has turned us into an "Inflation Nation" largely ruled by the unelected Federal Reserve, whose Chairman, as head of the Central Bank of the World, has arguably become more powerful than the President of the United States.

"I doubt...the autonomy of the Federal Reserve," wrote Carnegie Mellon University political economist Allan Meltzer, author of a history of the Federal Reserve, in 2009.

"[U]nder Mr. Bernanke, the Fed has sacrificed its independence and become the monetary arm of the Treasury," complete with bailouts and the bankrolling of government projects. [134]

## Conflicting Mandates

The Fed purportedly began with a simple purpose – to keep the U.S. Dollar stable. The ongoing devaluing of the dollar by inflation shows that at this – its original and primary responsibility – the Fed has failed.

Under President Carter the Fed was given a second mandate that often conflicts with the first: to adjust economic policy to produce full employment, even though this can mean debasing the dollar through recklessly low interest rates and inflation that harms savers and those on fixed incomes.

Current Fed Chairman Ben Bernanke appears to have taken on a third role – defender and booster – or "levitator," as one financial analyst calls him – of equity values and the stock market. Nothing in its enabling legislation gives the Fed this job or authority, but

Mr. Bernanke apparently has claimed it. [146]

As we suggested earlier and explored in our book *Crashing the Dollar*, this means that Fed money may have been used, openly or secretly through third parties, to help rally the market.

(As we also noted earlier, some wonder if Chairman Bernanke has also embraced a fourth mandate, to do everything necessary even if temporary to create a favorable economic environment to help reelect President Obama in November 2012.)

Such Fed activities distort the free marketplace and give unrealistic signals to investors – which, indeed, may be the Fed's way to "nudge" – as Mr. Obama's regulatory czar Cass Sunstein might describe it – misled investors back into buying stocks.

Along the way, today's Fed has driven interest rates close to zero. This might be good for borrowers if economic and legal uncertainties and higher interest rates had made banks more willing to lend.

Alas, rock-bottom interest rates also determine what banks pay to savers, who today have little incentive to have a bank account that pays one-tenth the real, concealed rate of inflation. Whatever interest they earn will be taxed as income while losing value to a higher inflation rate.

We shall never know how much money, foreign and domestic, was not invested in either U.S. Treasuries or U.S. banks because the Fed's policy made interest rates more attractive in other countries.

## Helicopter Ben

We are being turned into a Euro-Socialist welfare state with near-double-digit unemployment and inflation as our normal state of affairs.

Those who share President Obama's ideology have long argued that the United States should become more like democratic-socialist Western Europe.

Ironically, this is happening at the same time that some of the biggest Euro-Socialist nations – Germany, France and Great Britain – have chosen to fight today's economic difficulties with austerity measures and by shrinking the size of their governments. They are becoming more capitalistic.

President Obama by contrast, as we noted earlier, has taken the opposite path that led to Weimar – heavy borrowing, astronomically-increased debt, and paper-money printing to create Keynesian stimulus. His old belief that the United States should become more like France has suddenly fallen silent, now that France is moving to the right.

Fed Chair Bernanke – sometimes called "Helicopter Ben" because in 2002 he said that it could be effective economic stimulus to throw money out of a helicopter – nowadays is expressing genuine worry.

A February 9, 2011, CNBC story quoting the Fed Chairman was headlined "Bernanke to Congress: We're much Closer to Total Destruction Than You Think." [147]

"By definition, the unsustainable trajectories of deficits and debt that the CBO outlines cannot actually happen, because creditors would never be willing to lend to a government with debt, relative to national income, that is rising without limit," Bernanke told a congressional committee.

"One way or the other, fiscal adjustments sufficient to stabilize the federal budget must occur at some point," Bernanke continued.

"The question is whether these adjustments will take place through a careful and deliberative process...or whether the needed fiscal adjustments will come as a rapid and painful response to a looming or actual fiscal crisis."

Now you can understand why the cover of our book *Crashing the Dollar: How to Survive a Global Currency Collapse*, features President Obama piloting a giant paper dollar airplane...and why Fed Chair Bernanke is shown as his praying co-pilot. To see this cover, go to *http://www.crashingthedollar.com*.

See Table One for examples of how the emerging Inflatocracy promotes values that are the opposite of what America's Founders believed in.

## Table One

| "Capitalist Paradigm-America's Founders" | "Inflationist/Inflatocracy Paradigm" |
|---|---|
| 1. A penny saved is a penny earned, as Benjamin Franklin wrote. | 1. A penny saved is a penny lost to inflation. Saving money is foolish. You should spend it immediately. |
| 2. Saving is wise, good and responsible. | 2. Saving is anti-social. It takes money out of the high velocity exchange needed for a prosperous economy, which is what Keynes meant by the "paradox of thrift." |
| 3. Individualism and self-reliance are good. | 3. Almost nobody can be independent of the collective, which protects and cares for us all, so all should support the ruling elite. Individualism is selfish. |
| 4. Wealth is usually an achievement earned by hard work and ability. | 4. The rich are just "winners in life's lottery" who should share their luck-caused wealth equally with everyone by giving it to the government. |
| 5. Able-bodied welfare recipients are parasites and should feel ashamed. | 5. Welfare recipients are better than the wealthy because they recognize their dependence on the collective dispenser of wealth and justice. |
| 6. Inflation is theft, a policy created to steal purchasing power from those who earned it. | 6. Inflation is redistribution of wealth, and the government thus balances society as its collective dispenser of wealth and social justice. |
| 7. Taxes are to fund the government. | 7. Government is funded by the "tax" of inflation, the printing of money as government needs it. Other taxes are imposed to take back surplus wealth from those who do not deserve it in order to regulate the economy and prevent prices from exploding. |
| 8. Inflation is regressive, hurting most the poor and those on fixed incomes. | 8. Inflation is a necessary social control that equalizes unfair income disparities. Government can give special exemptions and cost of living increases to shelter its favorites against the ravages of inflation. |
| 9. Families should save and accumulate wealth to pass on to their offspring. | 9. Inflation retards the accumulation of wealth in families because what they try to save is always losing value. This is just, because one family should not be richer than another, and wealthy families can become power centers critical of the collective and immune to its peer pressure. |
| 10. Money should be a stable and reliable store of value, and people should save as much of it as they can. | 10. 71 percent of America's Gross Domestic Product (GDP) comes from consumer spending, so anything such as saving that slows consumer spending hurts the economy on which we all depend. |
| 11. You can rely on your savings, private insurance and neighbors, just as our pioneer ancestors did. | 11. Only government can protect you against the declining value of your savings, the collapse of private insurance, the decline of property values, and other problems. Your neighbors are as helpless as you are. |
| 12. Debt is often bad, and people should avoid shopping with credit cards that, like colorful gambling casino chips, help them forget that they are spending real money. | 12. Debt is good because it fuels prosperity for all by driving our overconsuming society. |
| 13. Government is constrained by its need to tax the same people to whom its politicians offer "free" goodies. | 13. Government is now totally unconstrained because it can fund itself merely by printing money. This invisible form of mass taxation breaks the last link between collecting taxes and unlimited government revenue. Inflation is a cunning way of taxing the 47 percent of Americans who now think they pay no taxes.<br>— by Lowell Ponte |

# Part Four
# Arresting Inflation

# Chapter Ten

# Three Political Ways
# to Rein in Inflation

*"The national budget must be balanced.*
*The public debt must be reduced;*
*the arrogance of the authorities*
*must be moderated and controlled.*

*Payments to foreign governments*
*must be reduced.*

*If the nation doesn't want to go bankrupt,*
*people must again learn to work,*
*instead of living on public assistance."*

– Cicero
Roman Republic statesman
55 B.C.

Inflation has become a ruling ideology in its own right in the United States and in several other nations. It will be difficult to slow, reverse, dismantle or escape.

Today's Inflatocracy could be slowed or halted by any or a combination of the approaches below.

We can readily agree, as the mice did in one of the ancient Greek storyteller Aesop's fables, that their world would be better if they put a bell around the neck of the local cat so it could never sneak up on them. The challenge, then as now, is to muster the will and skill to bell the inflation cat.

In this and the following two chapters are seven approaches that could help end the Inflatocracy and restore America's democratic republic, now on the verge of being snuffed out and replaced with an imperial government, as was Cicero's Roman Republic.

## #1 Vote Inflation out by electing honest lawmakers.

*We can attack Inflatocracy with democracy.*

**Chance of success: 20 percent.  Odds: Five to One**

In today's Inflatocracy we have not yet lost our right to vote. Why not just elect lawmakers and presidents who have sworn to cut spending and taxes?

In theory this can, of course, happen in our democratic republic.

In practice, however, the chance of rolling back inflation by this method is at best a long shot.

As we discussed earlier, the entrenched and enthroned ruling ideology, Inflatocracy, has a huge constituency.

Inflation is an essential part of the modern welfare state, so those who benefit from government transfer payments can readily be recruited to oppose a change that threatens to reduce or end their free ride on the gravy train.

As the grim Obama-era joke goes, the Clinton pretense of "Big Government being Over" is over. Big Government is back, greedier and hungrier than ever.

At present more than 44 percent of American households include at least one person who receives some kind of government check.

If present welfare and entitlement program expansion continues, by 2020 this proportion of households receiving government checks could exceed 60 percent – a supermajority so large that almost no politician would dare try to roll these programs back.

If and when that happens, we can kiss democracy goodbye.

The welfare state will be able to buy all the votes it needs to stay in power forever...at least, as we noted earlier, until – in former British Prime Minister Margaret Thatcher's phrase – it runs out of other people's money.

## Point of No Return

Politically, we may already have passed this tipping point of no return in many congressional districts.

Twice as many Americans now work for government than are employed in all of manufacturing. Ending inflation would threaten their government paychecks and pension checks.

Nearly 44 million Americans currently receive Food Stamps. Millions more receive welfare and other forms of government assistance, including unemployment checks that can now continue for 99 weeks, nearly two years, or more.

If welfare and wealth transfer programs continue their current skyrocketing upward trajectory, writes Peter Ferrara last April (2011) in *Forbes* Magazine, then by 2013 the welfare programs alone will be spending approximately $1 Trillion annually. [148]

In addition to these, Social Security and Medicare by 2010 had already reached $1.179 Trillion in annual spending just prior to Baby Boomers reaching full retirement age to begin benefitting from Medicare.

Put these together, as Ferrara does in his 2011 book *America's Ticking Bankruptcy Bomb*, and we find that in 2010 welfare, Social Security and Medicare added up to $1.879 Trillion, more than half of the entire Federal budget spending of $3.720 Trillion. [149]

Today more than half of every tax dollar is "transfer payments," snatching the money you have earned or will pay in direct or hidden taxes such as rising prices from inflation, and putting the fruits of your labor into someone else's pocket.

## Borrowed Prosperity

Remember that nearly 42 percent of the operating 2010 budget – approximately $1.562 Trillion – is *borrowed* money on which you and other taxpayers – and probably your children and grandchildren – will be paying interest for decades to come.

If you thought receiving compound interest on your bank account was amazing and enriching, imagine your excitement at the moment you recognize how amazing and impoverishing a lifetime of compound *inflation* can be as prices soar higher year after year, usually outpacing any increase in consumer income or increase you can earn on your savings.

As economist Milton Friedman once argued, a new government program costs the average taxpayer 50 cents, but to those who get a check or a job from that new program it is worth many thousands of dollars. Who do you think has the greater incentive to fight for or against each new government program?

In passing Obamacare, Democrats cunningly – and in violation of customary congressional procedures – included $105 Billion of automatic funding in its thousands of pages of fine print.

This provided seed money to rapidly build a giant constituency of people getting government checks from Obamacare – and hence a very selfish incentive to defend the new law – without lawmakers needing to take another controversial vote to fund it.

Whether voting can roll back inflation or not, Americans can and should use the ballot box for an additional purpose: restoring economic growth.

A one percent increase in economic growth can add approximately $1.75 Trillion to reduce our debts over 10 years. A four percent increase in real growth (that is, 4 percent *above* the all-devouring rate of inflation) might be enough to start reversing America's runaway train to national insolvency. [150]

Such growth would generate prosperity much faster than it expands government. If the full growth potential of our great nation were unleashed in a free enterprise environment, we might have a chance to turn even today's enormous economic problems around.

## The Donkey Effect

One of the biggest factors limiting and strangling growth in America is the presence of an openly-socialist political party within striking distance of taking power in every election. We call this political drag on our economy and prosperity "The Donkey Effect."

Since its methodical internal takeover by so-called "progressives" and radicals, the Democratic Party has become a party controlled by ideologues so extreme that today they scarcely even bother to conceal their hatred for free enterprise, private property, individualism, the Founders of our country and the limits on government power that the Founders wrote into our Constitution.

Many, and perhaps still a majority, of rank and file Democrats think of their party founded by Presidents Thomas Jefferson and Andrew Jackson as a party of working people, rural America and states' rights. They regard themselves as Democrats because this was the party of their parents and grandparents.

This, alas, is no longer what today's Democratic Party is. Voters in recent elections who elected moderate or "Blue Dog" Democrats merely put those with the ideology of San Francisco radical Nancy Pelosi and other extremist Democratic bosses in seats of power.

(We find it interesting that the mainstream media refers to Republican lawmakers who vote like Democrats as "moderate," but Democratic lawmakers who vote like Republicans as "conservatives" or blue-colored "dogs.")

Ms. Pelosi, after she was made Speaker of the House of Representatives by the election of a few dozen "moderate" Democrats, proceeded to appoint hardcore left-liberals and members of Congress's openly socialist "Progressive Caucus" to chair key committees. Ms. Pelosi planned and rammed through a de facto government expropriation of much of America's banking, automotive and healthcare industries.

## Climate of Fear

Our point here is not to debate each policy decision, nor the relative merits of free market capitalism versus Eurosocialism.

Our point is merely that putting the ideological enemies of private property, business, and free markets in control of, or even close to, the levers of power has profound and predictable negative economic consequences.

Real unemployment plus underemployment and discouraged job seekers have been frozen at a combined nearly 20 percent of American workers.

For the first time since the Great Depression, one in five adult American men in their working years has no job, a problem that David Brooks of the *New York Times* describes as "structural" and therefore difficult to change in today's economy.

Why do people not understand that this has been the pattern of un-employment in the European welfare states? This is no accident or coincidence.

This is the logical consequence of government making it too risky and too costly for investors and private companies to hire more peo-ple, and too easy for people to turn our welfare state's lavish social safety net into a hammock.

Why do people not see that American companies continue to move off-shore and to keep hundreds of billions of dollars of their income out-side the United States?

Companies are doing this, and holding back on more investment in-side the United States that would grow their companies here, be-cause our government imposes the heaviest business taxes in the world.

Companies are also doing this because one of our two major politi-cal parties is now openly hostile to business and free enterprise. Democratic Party leaders demand even more taxation and regulation on companies.

Investors saw the crazed grab for private companies that President Obama and Speaker Pelosi carried out during their two years of unchecked power.

## Intimidation Nation

If you were a businessperson, how much would you invest in a United States where one of the two major ruling parties is increas-ingly obsessed with expropriation of private enterprises – by confiscation, forced unionization, ever-higher taxation and penalties, regulation and other means, including inflation?

The British economy has never fully recovered from decades during which an openly-socialist Labour Party made investors afraid to commit their savings where each election could mean they faced expropriation or bankruptcy. After the huge investor losses caused by John Law's schemes, it took the French more than 100 years to again begin trusting banks.

American businesspeople now face a similar threat in an economy where a company's survival may require government favors bought with endlessly demanded campaign contributions – in effect, coerced bribes – to politicians.

As of April 2011 President Obama had already announced that he would raise $1 Billion for his 2012 re-election campaign – and was arm-twisting Wall Streeters to pay $35,800 per seat to attend his fund raisers. [151]

We have always found it odd that the same liberals who regard businesspeople as greedy and grasping are quick to believe that businesspeople are eager to offer tens of thousands of their dollars to politicians, as if the businesspeople are the ones initiating a payoff to otherwise-virtuous politicians.

Think about this logically, based on the idea that businesspeople want to hold on to their money. It is obvious that politicians' operatives come to businesses asking for money. Tight-fisted businesspeople give in to such pressure by paying what amounts to "protection money."

Their concern was summed up years ago by a partisan money raiser member of Congress telling a crowd of businesspeople: "We hope you will take a big interest in donating to the Democratic Party, because if you don't I guarantee you that the government can take a very big interest in your business."

# Free Market Politics

The bigger and more intrusive government becomes, the more powers it has to harass businesses. This gives businesspeople more reasons to bow to the money demands of the very politicians who keep making government bigger.

Would you invest your life savings in a business in America's current political environment, knowing that the natural cycles of politics and Republican vacillation could soon bring the Democratic Party back into political power?

How does such a destructive party win elections? Some cynics have said that half the citizens of this country have an I.Q. of 100 or less, which explains why Democratic politicians can campaign successfully using so much illogical nonsense and class warfare hate speech.

Others vote for the Big Government Party because they directly or indirectly benefit from a government check. Who they vote for is often not even a matter of policies or ideology. It is simply greed and their own self-interest. Unfortunately, their selfish votes are destroying the United States for their children and grandchildren as well as ours.

If all those who receive a government welfare check or paycheck were removed from voter rolls because all have a conflict of interest when voting, the Democratic Party would shrink overnight to a fifth tier very minor political party.

As its socialist ideology stands today, the mere existence of this political party within striking distance of power is probably costing America 25 percent or more of the greater prosperity, jobs and opportunity we could have if people had no political fear of investing and of growing new companies.

The drag that the Democratic Party puts on investment may be as damaging to the American economy as inflation, unemployment and our weakening dollar. It certainly makes all three of these problems much, much worse.

America craves political leaders who stand up consistently for free markets and will not compromise with Democrats on fundamental issues of economic liberty. What this meant in a recent Gallup Poll is that nearly half of Americans have lost faith in the two major political parties and want a third alternative choice on their ballots.

## #2 A Balanced Budget Amendment

*We can amend the Constitution to prevent the deficit spending and borrowing that drive inflation.*

**Chance of Genuine Success: 15 percent.  Odds: About seven to one.
Chance of Sham Success: 25 percent.  Odds: One in Four.**

Except for Vermont, every state in the United States requires its legislature to produce some sort of balanced budget.

Why not simply amend the U.S. Constitution to require this of the Federal Government? This in theory would limit the ability of the Congress to borrow money and run the nation into debt.

Those with faith in this idea have never studied the bookkeeping gimmicks, loopholes and chicanery some state legislatures use to "balance" their budgets.

This is why rating service Standard & Poor's California Analyst Gabe Petek diplomatically told *cnbc.com* that a Balanced-Budget state's "budget is a political and legal document, and may not always equal fiscal reality..." [152]

## Two Left Hands

In New York, for example, the Democratic Governor recently proposed a way that various levels of government could meet the legal requirement to fund public employee retirement funds. How? By borrowing almost $6 Billion to make current payments to the state pension fund – from the same state pension fund. [153]

You can't make up stuff this surreal, irrational and deceptive, yet this is a typical example of why you cannot trust a balanced budget requirement in New York State or in the U.S. Constitution to remedy the greed, guile and brazenness of today's politicians.

Perhaps 75 percent of everything the Federal Government does today, including its massive coerced redistribution of wealth among citizens, is in violation of the enumerated powers clause of Article I Section 8 of the Constitution....and why each new bill should be required to state in writing why it is constitutional under Article I Section 8.

The legal requirement for budget balancing in many cases does force state lawmakers to trim, at least a bit, their boundless ambitions and bottomless appetites for borrowing and spending. State lawmakers, of course, lack the Federal Government's constitutional power to create money.

Truth be told, a Balanced Budget Amendment could be a rope thrown to a drowning economy – or could become a noose around the necks of the most productive people and entities in society.

To balance its budget, government is not limited to two options – cut spending or raise taxes...with higher taxes usually the path chosen. A third way exists, in theory albeit seldom in practice.

## Land Lords

Government could pay many debts simply by selling off government property, as Arizona has done in recent years by selling, then leasing back, even its Capitol and other government buildings. [154]

Other states have allowed foreign entities to purchase government prerogatives, e.g., the power to collect tolls for years or decades on government toll roads. This is akin to the tax farming policies in an-

cient Rome, when the empire sold to the highest private bidders the
authority to squeeze whatever tax money they could from the people.

Government effectively owns nearly 40 percent of all land in the
United States.

In our country, nominally dedicated to free enterprise and private
property, fully 28 percent (635 million acres) of American land is
owned by the Federal Government; 9 percent (195 million acres) is
owned by state and local governments; and over 2 percent (56 million acres) is held "in trust" by the Bureau of Indian Affairs. [155]

The Federal Government owns 65 percent of all American land west
of Denver, but only 2 percent of the land east of Denver.

The Federal Government owns so much of the property in some
states as to make a mockery of state sovereignty – Nevada, for example, being 86 percent Federal property. [156]

Most politicians, however, and especially those whose long-term socialist aim is government expropriation of all private property by
taxation and other means, have the attitude that private property
and wealth can always be taken for government purposes – yet government property is sacrosanct and must never be sold back to private owners.

One of the most famous Supreme Court cases in American history,
*McCullough v. Maryland* in 1819, blocked Maryland's attempt to impose state taxes on an office of the Second Bank of the United States.
In this decision, Chief Justice John Marshall ruled that state taxation
of Federal Government property is unconstitutional, writing that
"the power to tax involves the power to destroy."

## The Seduction of Power

Apart from selling government property, a legislative budget can
honestly be balanced in only two ways:

(1) Spending can be confined to a level no greater than existing government revenues, or

(2) Government can increase its taxes and other revenues.

Politicians generally for the past half-century or more have preferred to increase spending, and inflation has given them both a means and a reason to seek ever-larger government revenues.

"The natural progress of things is for liberty to yield and government to gain ground," warned Thomas Jefferson.

Some reasons for this are self-evident. Even those who enter politics out of pure idealism are eager to change things, and change usually involves the enlargement of government power and spending.

Most of those who enter politics have an all-too-human nature that combines idealism with ego – a craving for recognition and power. For a lawmaker, the easiest path to recognition and power is to spend money on things that carry his or her name.

After being elected, most young lawmakers quickly discover that power comes from compromise of the "go along to get along" variety. The deal that one fellow lawmaker wants in exchange for supporting your piece of legislation may be your vote for a new road or bridge in his district. The favor asked by another for her vote is that you support funding for a welfare center in her district.

Political purity for most young lawmakers is quickly replaced by "pragmatism," by what advances their own career and prospects for re-election. With each vote they become more compromised and compromising.

Germans call this *realpolitik*. The founding father of the German welfare state, Otto von Bismarck, more than a century ago purportedly said that one should never watch two things being made – sausages and laws.

## Down the Food Chain

Governments in our time have found ways to "tax" one another. In California, as we noted earlier, the state government has expropriated property tax revenues that used to provide the main source of revenue for city and county governments. The state is also greedily planning to confiscate the huge pools of money held by special taxing districts.

In San Diego County, California, voters democratically elect a Board of Supervisors to govern their county, but the state and Federal governments mandate how and where 95 cents of every county government dollar must be spent.

The Federal Government likewise imposes hundreds – indeed, thousands – of its mandates onto California and every other state government.

In today's America at least 11 rules are created by unelected bureaucrats for every one law passed by our elected representatives. Bureaucrat mandates shape everything from highway speed limits to the content of local public school lunches. [157]

Like the Bill Clinton Administration, President Barack Obama's Administration eagerly invokes bureaucratic rules in lieu of law. Mr. Obama's Environmental Protection Agency (EPA), for example, asserted that it has regulatory power over all emissions of carbon dioxide – a gas you naturally exhale with every breath – after his attempt to enact this into law was rejected as extremist even by Democratic legislators.

Alas, the view of many politicians is that what government has expropriated belongs to government forever, but what private citizens own is always subject to expropriation via taxation, regulation and eminent domain.

With governments now expropriating each other's claim on your wallet and mandating where money must be spent, a Federal balanced budget amendment would have to be just that – a Constitutional amendment.

Passing a Constitutional amendment requires a two-thirds vote of both houses of Congress and an approving vote of three-quarters of the states.

## Red Welfare States

As if this hurdle were not high enough, some states, including ones we think of as culturally conservative, have for decades gotten back more money – in some instances at least twice as much money – in Federal spending than their citizens have paid in taxes to Washington, D.C.

Call them "welfare states," and do not hold your breath expecting them to sign on to a Federal Balanced Budget Amendment that might end their ride on this gravy train.

The politicians of such states might be like students at the left-liberal University of California Berkeley who were recently asked by an interviewer if they would be willing to pay their $47,000 per citizen share of the National Debt.

A selection of their answers can be seen on YouTube.com. [158]

According to this video, the "vast majority" of these students refused to sign an agreement to pay their equal share, even though as university graduates they are likely to earn a much higher than average lifetime income.

Several of these students on the famously left-liberal campus suggested that the national debt should be paid by "the rich."

President Obama has described himself as a "citizen of the world" and is apparently eager to strengthen global governance.

Perhaps these students should consider that when a progressive world government rules, they will be classed among "the rich" to pay a disproportionately heavy and redistributive share of global taxes so that America's wealth gets "spread around," in Mr. Obama's words, to the poorer nations of the Earth.

## #3 Enact a Better, More Egalitarian Tax System.

*We must find a way for most citizens to become taxpayers as well as tax takers so that all have an incentive to rein in inflation and government.*

**Chance of Success: 5 percent. Odds: One in 20.**

America's Founders believed that to keep government limited, those who vote should also be those who pay taxes.

Their reasoning is clear: those who pay government's bills have the most incentive to keep government frugal and small, because a wasteful and overgrown government will cost these same taxpayers more of the money that they could instead spend on themselves.

Today 47 percent of Americans pay no direct income tax at all, yet their vote can cancel out the vote of someone who pays 40 percent or more of his or her income in Federal, state and local taxes.

This 47 percent believes (wrongly) that government has become a giant machine that gives them free goodies and costs them nothing.

This near-majority of the population, therefore, has no incentive to make government smaller.

On the contrary, many swallow hook, line and sinker the promises of politicians that bigger government will be able to give them even more freebies.

# Invisible Taxes

These suckers, truth be told, pay lots of taxes – taxes on cigarettes, alcoholic beverages, sales taxes, gasoline taxes, tariffs on imported materials, and many more.

The same President Obama who promised that he would never add "even a nickel of tax on anyone making less than $250,000 a year," has in 2011 proposed a per-mile tax on cars and trucks that will plunder middle-class pocketbooks and violate privacy.

President Ronald Reagan had his economists document how many hidden taxes are passed on to consumers in the form of higher prices.

As a staple food, bread is exempted from most states' sales taxes. Yet as President Reagan reported, the price of a typical loaf of supermarket bread includes a concealed share of the property tax of the wheat farmer, the Social Security tax of the baker, the road use tax and tire excise tax of the trucker, the corporate tax of the supermarket, and more.

In all, the price of that loaf of bread is higher because, according to President Reagan, it includes at least 135 invisible taxes. He did not mention the most secretive and regressive tax of all – inflation.

# Stake Through the Heart

A national sales tax such as the Fair Tax advocated by national radio talk star Neal Boortz and others would restore equity and the Founders' check-and-balance on government expansion by making a large majority of Americans think of themselves as taxpayers again, as citizens who will pay in taxes for the things government "gives them" and millions of others "for free." [159]

One precondition of considering one or another form of the Fair Tax is that its adoption must irrevocably be preceded by repeal of the Constitution's 16th Amendment – driving a stake through the heart of the blood-sucking vampire "Progressive" income tax.

If the income tax is not thus "terminated with extreme prejudice," Americans will soon find themselves paying both a national sales tax AND an income tax.

A "Flat Tax" in which everyone paid roughly the same share of their income would likewise redistribute the tax burden and give most of us more reason to keep government small and "frugal," as Thomas Jefferson intended.

One could think of the flat tax merely as an "unprogressive" income tax that treats all taxpayers semi-equally. It is an income tax without the confiscatory "progressive" high rates for the "rich" that Karl Marx and Friedrich Engels proposed in *The Communist Manifesto* as one of several ways to destroy capitalism.

## Taxing Your "Imputed" Income

Libertarian economist Murray Rothbard argued against the Flat Tax.

"The flat tax," wrote Rothbard, "proposes that every individual and every organization be subjected to the same, uniform proportional income tax. To achieve that uniformity, the flat-taxers propose the ruthless suppression of all credits, deductions, exemptions, and shelters, all of which are sneered at as 'loopholes' in the tax system."

"In the flat-taxers' pure theory," Rothbard continued, "the proportional income tax would apply to everyone [except the poor] regardless of income....Every homeowner is going to get it, but good, under the flat-tax regime."

Homeowners under a flat tax might lose their mortgage interest tax deduction, their ability to defer capital gains on a home sale if they buy another home within two years, and their one-time exemption of a large share of the proceeds from selling their home.

Rothbard raised another concern for homeowners.

"The flat-taxers," he wrote, "have figured out that homeowners benefit, in a real though non-monetary way, by not having to pay rent. And so the flat-taxers propose to tax every homeowner on the 'imputed rent' they are earning by not having to pay rent to a landlord." [160]

Left-liberals for decades have quietly been investigating how to tax the "imputed income" of many things. Do you get a parking space at work? They are planning someday soon to make you pay taxes on the rental value of this parking space as if it were part of your paycheck.

## "I'll Tax Your Feet"

To paraphrase Beatle George Harrison's song "Taxman": "If you drive a car I'll tax the street... If you take a walk, I'll tax your feet....'Cause I'm the tax man...and you're working for no one but me...."

In this song Harrison wrote "If you're overweight, I'll tax your fat," anticipating the kinds of taxation that some Nanny State leftists now openly advocate.

Harrison wrote this song for the Beatles' 1966 *Revolver* album after learning that the band's income was being expropriated by a 95 percent "Supertax" in Great Britain imposed by Labour Party Prime Minister Harold Wilson – the same kind of confiscatory soak-the-rich tax dreamed of by President Obama.

The greed and rapacity of politicians simply have no limit. The question Americans ought to contemplate is: at what level of taxation are we turned from citizens into slaves?

What is this turning point into servitude between zero percent and 100 percent taxation?

President Richard Nixon was once asked at what average rate of taxation a country ceases to be free. Having apparently thought deeply about this, Nixon instantly answered "35 percent."

Many working Americans who live in high-tax states such as California and New York – states dominated by Democrats – already face a combined burden of Federal, state and local taxes significantly higher than 35 percent.

If we factor in taxes hidden and passed on in higher prices and inflation, the tax burden for a majority of Americans probably exceeds 35 percent.

Where would this stop? Since each of these three government levels can in theory tax you 100 percent of your income and wealth, it would probably stop even for the "rich" at around 300 percent of income.

## Point of No Return

Chances are that our democratic republic has already passed the tipping point of no return to enact a Flat Tax reform that would give everybody a reason to reduce the size and spending of government.

The majority of Americans, who pay little or no personal income tax, have a powerful incentive to vote to keep things as they are, with the playing field tilted in what they see as their favor. In a sense, they mistakenly believe they are supporting a system in which taxpayers are their slaves, and they are the masters. Election after election, they vote for politicians who oppose equal protection under the law.

They do not comprehend that high taxes on corporations and businesspeople are passed on to them concealed as higher prices.

We are not professional psychologists, but we suspect that when one person exploits others, he subconsciously feels guilty. To cope with this guilt he creates a rationale for his exploitation. Such are the roots of anti-Semitism and anti-capitalism.

Our society would be healthier and happier if the near-half of our population riding in the wagon started helping to pull the wagon by paying "their fair share" of taxes.

We recommend that you not hold your breath waiting for these free-riders and the class-warfare politicians they elect to embrace equality of taxation.

Until they do, the politicians these "takers" vote into office will continue to enlarge the welfare state, run America deeper into debt to buy votes, and increase the most regressive tax of all, inflation.

# Chapter Eleven

# Three Ways Alternative Money Can Handcuff Inflation

*"The return to sound money policies
is of utmost importance. Without sound money
there can be no economic recovery, no prosperity....
Sound money is the cornerstone of individual liberty.
Sound money is metallic money.
It is the gold standard."*

– Hans Sennholz
Economist

You have choices in almost everything, but when it comes to currency the government largely insists that transactions be carried out only in its monopoly money. Anything else is to be taxed as a barter transaction.

Maybe that's why our cash has lost 98 percent of its purchasing power since the Federal Reserve Board took it over in 1913.

Uncle Sam took away our gold and silver, and in their place gave us pieces of paper like those used in the board game Monopoly.

Restoring citizen choice in money could put an end to the inflation game our politicians are using against us.

Here are three ways to restore choice and competition to the money we use.

# #1 Allow alternative currencies... governmental and private.

*Why not let Americans buy and sell in Euros? In British Pounds? In Canadian "Loonies"? Or even in private precious metal "barter currency?" Let a variety of currencies compete.*

**Chance of Success: 40 percent. Odds: two in five.**

Americans could embrace a new Global or Regional Currency such as the widely-speculated potential currency the Amero, North America's potential answer to Europe's Euro.

We could try the International Monetary Fund's Special Drawing Rights (SDRs) based on a "basket of currencies," or a similar variant such as the "dey" (a basket based on dollars, Euros and Japanese Yen).

Or we could launch and use various global currencies such as economist John Maynard Keynes' proposed "bancor" or the *Economist* Magazine's proposed "phoenix." [161]

At this moment of global economic change, would any other currency be better than today's shrinking and weakening U.S. Dollar? Our dollar remains the world's official "reserve currency," but might soon lose or have to share this now-exclusive status.

Some economic experts already describe gold as the world's new real reserve currency.

# Just Say Noah

It makes sense to remember Noah, who brought two of every creature on board the Ark. You should not have to limit your savings or your spending to only one national currency.

The dollar's status as "global reserve currency" – what former French President Charles De Gaulle called America's "exorbitant privilege" – means that we control the supply and distribution of the world's official exchange medium for oil and other key commodities. When Japan buys a barrel of oil from Saudi Arabia, the price is set and payment is made in U.S. Dollars.

Without this special status, the United States would have to pay a premium price to buy whatever other currency is used to price and purchase oil. Today other nations must buy our dollars to purchase oil, which gives us a significant advantage in global credit and trade.

This, of course, gives others gas pains when the U.S. Government and Federal Reserve inflate our currency by running trillions off the printing press – thereby exporting our inflation to them and taxing them to enrich ourselves.

"There could be no more effective check against the abuse of money by the government than if people were free to refuse any money they distrusted and to prefer money in which they had confidence," wrote Nobel laureate economist Friedrich A. Hayek.

"Nor could there be a stronger inducement to governments to ensure the stability of their money than the knowledge that, so long as they kept the supply below the demand for it, that demand would tend to grow."

"Therefore," wrote Hayek, "let us deprive governments (or their monetary authorities) of all power to protect their money against competition: if they can no longer conceal that their money is becoming bad, they will have to restrict the issue." [162]

Or pass laws that end the U.S. Dollar monopoly as "legal tender" in

America that require dollar payment of taxes and goods priced in dollars. Change the "legal tender" laws so that no one is forced to accept anything as payment for debts, public or private, except as a contract specifies – the way pre-1933 American contracts had "gold clauses" giving the creditor the choice of being paid in dollars or in units of gold.

## Separation of Money and State

Hayek laid out his argument for the separation of money and state in the 1990 third edition of his brilliant book *Denationalisation of Money: The Argument Refined: An Analysis of the Theory and Practice of Concurrent Currencies.*

In earlier times, he argued, governments claimed that their monopoly over a nation's money provided a convenient, consistent currency for its citizens.

Today, wrote Hayek, national (and nationalized) money "has the defects of all monopolies: one must use their product even if it is unsatisfactory, and above all, it prevents the discovery of better methods of satisfying a need for which the monopolist has no incentive."

"If the public understood what price in periodic inflation and instability it pays for the convenience of having to deal with only one kind of money in ordinary transactions...," wrote Hayek, "it would probably find it very excessive." [163]

Hayek envisioned a society in which people could choose to make transactions in many kinds of currency, as well as in silver and gold.

## "We Don't Care. We Don't Have to..."

Older citizens will remember when each community had only one telephone company that, being a monopoly, charged high rates for often-poor service and even charged customers for connecting their telephone to their own answering machine.

Comedienne Lily Tomlin back then played as one of her stock characters "Ernestine," a telephone operator. "We don't care. We don't have to," Ernestine would tell irate customers. "We're the phone company."

The much more controversial comic Lenny Bruce used to say that, even at its best, "socialism is like one big telephone company," a government monopoly that felt free to ride roughshod over people who had no other choice.

Hayek wanted people to have choice in the currencies they can use. We see the remarkable innovations, benefits and savings that breaking the telephone monopoly and introducing a little free market competition have produced.

Imagine what a country of currencies, each competing for customers, could produce.

The government could also allow private currency. In some ways we already do. The store coupon that is worth $1 if used to buy a particular product on or before a particular date is, arguably, a kind of currency. Some cities and localities issue their own local or regional scrip "money," just as many did during the Great Depression. [164]

When the U.S. Dollar was strong, our Federal Government showed little concern with such marginal "competitors" to its money monopoly.

As the dollar grows weaker and becomes more debased by reckless, uncontrolled government spending and the printing of trillions of paper fiat dollars by the Fed, the Obama Administration has begun going to wild extremes to crush competing currencies.

## "A Unique Form of Domestic Terrorism"

In March 2011 Mr. Bernard von NotHaus, 67, a resident of North Carolina, was convicted of minting and circulating "Liberty Dollars" and "Ron Paul Dollars," which without the permission of the Texas Congressman bear his name and likeness.

NotHaus now faces up to 25 years in prison, fines of up to $750,000, and the forfeiture of 16,000 pounds of "Liberty Dollars" and of nearly $7 Million worth of gold and silver that Federal authorities seized in a raid.

NotHaus has produced items such as "Ron Paul Dollars" – which he calls "a functioning currency...a barter currency" – for approximately 10 years.

According to NotHaus, "we've never said [these items are] legal tender." They are used to trade for things based on their weight in pure gold or silver.

Anne M. Tompkins, the U.S. Attorney for the Western District of North Carolina who prosecuted this case, declared:

"It is a violation of federal law...to create private coin or currency systems to compete with the official coinage and currency of the United States." [165]

"What's wrong with competition?" asks Fox Business Channel libertarian host John Stossel. "As long as there's no fraud or counterfeiting – which NotHaus has not been convicted of – I would think that individuals should be allowed to use whatever currency they want." [166]

We have no such freedom here, said U.S. Attorney Tompkins:

"Attempts to undermine the legitimate currency of this country are simply *a unique form of domestic terrorism*. While these forms of anti-government activities do not involve violence, they are every bit as insidious and represent a clear and present danger to the economic stability of this country."

"We are determined," U.S. Attorney Tompkins continued, "to meet these threats through infiltration, *disruption*, and dismantling of organizations which seek to challenge the legitimacy of our democratic form of government." (*Emphasis added.*)

## Obamite Standards

Let's ponder this.

The Obama Administration refused to prosecute Black Panther Party radicals who used a weapon to intimidate elderly Jews at a Philadelphia polling place to prevent them from voting, while verbally assaulting them with racist slurs.

The Obama Administration refused to pursue or prosecute organized labor goons who severely beat a peaceful African-American Tea Party activist in St. Louis while assaulting him with racist epithets and violating his civil rights. The Obama Administration has not lifted a finger to track down and prosecute union thug terrorists who literally threatened the lives of Wisconsin state lawmakers and their families, thereby directly assaulting the people's elected representatives and "our democratic form of government."

Oh, and President Obama has not arrested himself or the Federal Reserve for involvement in the issuing of more than $4 Trillion in fiat dollars unbacked by either precious metals or economic productivity – dollars that, therefore, are already robbing all Americans through inflation in exactly the same way outright counterfeit dollars would do.

Yet an Obama-appointed U.S. Attorney eagerly brought a zealous prosecution against a man whose only crime was to mint a private "barter currency" with a precious metal value at least comparable to United States coinage, and to accuse this peaceful senior citizen of being engaged in "domestic terrorism."

Is the U.S. Dollar now so shaky that the highest priority of law enforcement must be devoted to protecting government's money monopoly, and to prosecuting those who dare to mint a tiny quantity of their own gold and silver coins?

# # 2 Restore a Gold Standard

*Gold – the world standard of value since Biblical times – restored stability, reliability and trust in the money of the most advanced nations during the 19ᵗʰ and early 20ᵗʰ Centuries, so why not let it do so again?*

**Chance of Success: 20 percent. Odds: One in Five.**

Influential economist John Maynard Keynes called gold "a barbarous relic," but as paper currencies keep sinking in value from inflation, a growing number of voices have started saying good things about the merits of gold.

In January 2011, the President of the Kansas City Federal Reserve Thomas Hoenig said that the gold standard is "a very legitimate monetary system" that could help create price stability. [167]

In February 2011, J.P. Morgan Chase announced that its clients were now able to use gold as collateral for some loans. [168]

In late 2010 the President of the World Bank Robert Zoellick made headlines by suggesting that countries consider "employing gold as an international reference point of market expectations about inflation, deflation and future currency values" to create a more stable and cooperative international system of trade and finance. [169]

In May 2011 former GOP presidential candidate and publisher of *Forbes* Magazine Steve Forbes predicted that the United States would restore a gold standard within five years.

"What seems astonishing today could become conventional wisdom in a short period of time," Forbes told the conservative newspaper *Human Events*. "People know that something is wrong with the dollar. You cannot trash your money without repercussions." [170]

Congressman Paul was a member of the U.S. Gold Commission created by President Ronald Reagan, and has co-authored *The Case for Gold*, a book about what it documented. [171]

"Reagan was open to [restoring the gold standard] – He told me, 'A country doesn't remain great if it gets off the gold standard. But his advisors wouldn't let him," Rep. Paul told Joshua Green of *The Atlantic* Magazine in 2010. [172]

Dr. Paul is one of at least two prominent Republican presidential candidates as of May 2011 who support returning to a gold standard. The other is business executive Herman Cain.

The University of Texas recently converted somewhere between $750 Million and one billion of its endowment from dollars to gold, and Mexico's Central Bank followed the gold rush of several Asian nations by buying 100 tons of gold. [173]

Left-liberal central bankers and politicians happily quote economist John Maynard Keynes' view that gold is a "barbarious relic." But when we look at their actions, not their words, the bankers have been acquiring gold – in some cases urgently. China is stockpiling gold at the rate of 400 tons annually. [174]

And when analysts from free enterprise organizations such as the Cato Institute point out that the United States could sell off at least half a trillion dollars of its gold to pay down our national debt, liberal lawmakers suddenly offer an encyclopedia of excuses why this would destabilize the world economy, cause chaos, and so forth. [175]

Bottom line: Even politicians who cheer paper fiat money and the politically useful inflation it allows them to create know that when monetary and financial stability must be restored, the world will ask one question – Got Gold?

We recommend that you remember the advice of a teacher from Galilee: recognize a tree by its fruits, not what words are attached to it. Do what the big powers do by converting part of your nest egg out of unreliable paper dollars and into something solid that the politicians and central bankers cannot print.

Why are so many turning to gold, specified as money in the Bible, while the value of paper fiat currencies keeps falling?

Under a metal-backed currency, the Dollar on average actually gained value from 1823 until 1913. What cost $100 in 1823 would have cost only $63.02 in 1913. [176]

This is deflation, the boogey man Fed Chairman Ben Bernanke fears most. Deflation is the reverse of inflation. In Deflation money gains value.

## The Biggest Borrower

This means that borrowers – including the biggest borrower of all, the government and its free-spending politicians who therefore gain more than anyone else from deliberate inflation – cannot repay their debts with inflation-devalued money. This is therefore the biggest nightmare of those who want a welfare state whose cost is concealed and funded by inflation.

Gold makes a welfare state's spending harder, yet it also makes a warfare state less likely. The gold standard is a powerful restraint on extreme government spending, whether for welfare or war.

It tells politicians that they can only do what they have enough gold already saved to pay for.

This is why governments usually abandon or put in abeyance their gold standards at the start of major wars – as both sides did at the start of WWI.

As we noted earlier, President Richard Nixon severed the last bit of convertibility between gold and the dollar in 1971. The gusher of paper fiat money printed to bankroll the Vietnam War, Nixon knew, if redeemed for gold by European central banks as the Bretton Woods agreement allowed, would have drained America's gold reserves at Ft. Knox.

Gold is sober money for responsible grown-ups. Incorruptible by rust or tarnish, gold always shines through when fiat paper currencies are collapsing.

The trouble is, our wild-spending politicians might not be responsible grown-ups. They might prefer to go on freely spending trillions in fiat paper money, and not be seen for what they are when reflected in a mirror of gold.

Under a properly-functioning national and international gold standard, the Federal Reserve would be unnecessary and could be closed down.

*Forbes* Magazine columnist Bill Frezza in May 2011 suggested that the sole positive legacy of Fed Chair Ben Bernanke could be his policies that drove the United States back to the gold standard. [177]

The closing of the Fed would lead to the curtailing of inflation.

## #3 Encourage States to Authorize Gold and Silver As Legal Tender, and Urge the Federal Government To Accept Its Own Gold and Silver Coins as Legal Tender at Face Value.

*Why not let Americans use existing gold and silver coins as money?*

**Chance of Success: 25 percent. (100 percent in Utah).
Odds: One in Four**

Fourteen states are considering or have recently considered whether to make gold and silver coins a form of legal tender within their borders.

These states are Colorado, Georgia, Idaho, Indiana, Minnesota, Missouri, Montana, New Hampshire, North Carolina, South Carolina, Tennessee, Vermont, Virginia and Washington State.

Specific details and proposed legislation in these states is available on the website *http://www.constitutionaltender.com*.

A fifteenth state, Utah, passed such a measure, and Utah Governor Gary Herbert signed it into law on March 25, 2011.

This law, which went into effect throughout Utah on May 10, 2011, "recognizes gold and silver coins that are issued by the federal government as legal tender in the state and exempts the exchange of the coins from certain types of state tax liability."

"These actions by state legislatures are mostly symbolic," said George Mason University Economics Professor Lawrence H. White.

"Declaring that people can use a one-ounce federally-minted gold coin at its face value of $50 doesn't really give people a reason to do that," he told ABC News. "But it's a statement by the state legislators that they are concerned by the state of the dollar." [178]

## Coin of the Realm

According to longtime Galveston-area Texas Congressman Ron Paul, a Republican who in 1988 was the presidential candidate of the Libertarian Party, America needs "to legalize competition. Restore to Americans their right to use precious metals as a medium of exchange – a simple and reasonable initial step if we believe in freedom."

"It is essential," wrote Rep. Paul in his 2008 book *The Revolution: A Manifesto*, "that Americans be given the chance to escape from this system and protect themselves from possible financial ruin, by being able to use gold and silver if they so desire."

"If anyone would rather continue to transact in the depreciating dollar, he would be free to do so," wrote Paul, now Chairman of the House Financial Services Subcommittee on Domestic Monetary Policy and Technology and a member of the Joint Economic

Committee and House Committee on Financial Services.

With gold available as money, says Dr. Paul, "anyone who prefers a currency that holds its value and won't become worthless before his eyes just because his government ran the printing press one too many times would have real options." [179]

"Right now, various disabilities make it difficult for gold to be used in market transactions," wrote Rep. Paul. "Sales and capital gains taxes on precious metals should be promptly repealed, and the enforceability of gold clauses in private contracts definitively reaffirmed."

## Taxable Events

Such new state laws could mean that the buying and selling of gold or silver coins can no longer be treated as a "taxable event," and that therefore no state or Federal sales tax and no capital gains tax on sil ver or gold coin appreciation can be collected.

This is a grand opportunity for the states to act as the laboratories of democracy, as America's Founders intended.

Chances are that states allowing gold coins as currency would profit from having the most honest money in America. Such states would probably lure investors and successful home buyers.

Would this violate the U.S. Constitution? Presumably not, because the Constitution limits states to the use of gold and silver coins (Article I Section 10), as James Madison discussed in Federalist Paper No. 44. But the use of established gold and silver coins as money is precisely what these proposed laws would allow.

These proposed laws would let Americans once again buy and sell using a variety of precious metal coins, as was routinely done in colonial times and in the early days of the American Republic.

Using gold and silver coins – not the states' paper fiat currency –

worked well way back then and, with modern instant global communications and readily-available market information from around the planet, would work even better today.

## Gimme Shelter

"What other policy for sheltering Americans from the collapse of the dollar is being advanced?" asked Rep. Ron Paul.

"Is there any, apart from the comforting delusions that the Federal Reserve, which is itself responsible for our financial mess, can be trusted to put everything right?" wrote Paul.

"How can we be expected to place so much trust in a Federal Reserve System we're not even allowed to audit?" [180]

As Chairman of a powerful congressional subcommittee, Congressman Paul continues to press for impartial audits of the Fed. Fed Chairman Ben Bernanke and the Obama Administration continue to resist Paul's efforts, even though Mr. Bernanke has now held his first press conference in what he says should persuade the public that the Fed is open and above board.

"The Federal Reserve now no longer reports the figures on M3, the total money supply," wrote Paul, who contends that "the real reason we don't get these figures anymore, I am certain, is that they are too revealing. They tell us more about what the Fed has been up to and the damage it has been doing to our dollar than they care for us to know." [181]

If other states follow Utah's lead and begin enacting laws that make gold coins legal tender, will these coins' value be established by their face value or their gold content?

## Unintendered Consequences

Suppose Professor White is correct and their legal tender value is set at, for example, a gold coin's face value of $50 when its one ounce of gold has a market value of $1,500.

Let's say that the Federal Government accepts, either by its action or inaction, that $50 is the tender value of such U.S. coins.

Would you be foolish to use such coins?

None of what follows is to be taken as legal or financial advice. It is merely hypothetical speculation based on how future courts and government agencies might interpret hypothetical future laws defining U.S. gold coins as legal tender in all or parts of the United States.

To the best of our knowledge, the U.S. Government has never renounced the legal tender status of its historic numismatic gold and silver coins. In 1933 President Franklin D. Roosevelt's notorious executive order that made it illegal for most Americans to own gold bullion exempted numismatic gold coins, which remained legal to own and trade.

Consider just a few of the hypothetical possibilities they could create: What if in 2015, Jack and Jill wish to purchase Ryan and Peggy's home for a never-advertised $300,000?

If this transaction is made in fiat paper U.S. Dollars, with government's lust for taxes having grown, this might subject Ryan and Peggy to a 25 percent capital gains tax of $75,000.

It could force Jack and Jill to pay a 10 percent sales tax of $30,000, as well as lifelong property tax on the value of the property of 6 percent – $18,000 year after year, and increasing from this purchase price baseline forever.

What, however, if this home were purchased using $50 U.S. gold coins as legal tender, the transaction could be done with only 200 gold coins whose market value is $300,000 – but whose face value is $10,000?

If a court ever ruled that this set the legal tender price of the house at $10,000, then the capital gains tax on its sale would be $2,500 instead of $75,000.

The sales tax on its sale would be $1,000 instead of $30,000.

The baseline annual property tax would be $600 instead of $18,000.

If that happened, then both buyer and seller could gain significant benefits by conducting such a transaction in gold coins.

## Long Ago Prices

Some senior citizens reading this might notice that, even with government having imposed new taxes, the costs in such a transaction seem nostalgic.

These price tags reflect what homes and taxes *used to* cost before the huge Inflation Deception that government cunningly created during the last half-century and more, and continues to use to rob us today.

Imagine some other instances where money changes hands in either paper fiat money or legal tender gold coins:

What, hypothetically, might happen if a dying parent converts his $10 Million estate into 6,667 $50 gold coins having a legal tender face value of $333,350?

In dollars, such a transfer might have cost up to half of his estate – his son's or daughter's inheritance – via the Death Tax, the so-called Estate Tax.

If instead, however, government recognized his Will and Trust as transferring only a third of a million dollars of face value in gold coins, the inheritance for his family might then no longer be subject to the Death Tax. Even if it were, this tax might be on a much smaller gold face value amount.

# Bordering on Freedom

Or imagine restrictions placed on an American citizen carrying $10,000 when crossing the U.S. border, whether coming or departing.

This hypothetically could someday mean that a citizen could carry 200 one Troy ounce U.S. gold coins – having a combined weight of 13.714 conventional (Avoirdupois) pounds – with a combined legal tender face value of $10,000 into or out of the United States and be in total compliance with this restriction.

The market value of the gold in such coins, however, would be approximately $300,000, and if these are high quality numismatic coins their value would be significantly higher than this plain gold bullion amount.

What would a Utah citizen whose wages are paid only in $50 U.S. numismatic gold coins owe in income taxes now that the Utah law has declared such coins to be legal tender and not mere objects of barter or sale?

As an unintended consequence of new state legal tender laws, these and other financial transactions, transfers and activities might someday soon bring hypothetical tax or regulatory benefits if carried out via legal tender U.S. coins.

Unless you live in Utah, no legislated legal tender state benefits yet exist. In any event, you should consult with your tax attorney, Certified Public Accountant and other specialists to learn how the governments with which you deal define and view these issues.

Nothing we hypothesize here should be taken as legal, financial or investment advice; we merely offer ideas about what in future legislatures, courts and government agencies might want to consider.

Would government surrender such huge tax revenues if people bought, sold and otherwise used U.S. gold coins as legal tender?

Our elected public servants might have to, because ultimately our government is supposed to serve the people and do what voters demand.

This is what government teachers have always taught to children in government schools, right?

# Chapter Twelve

# How to Escape from the Inflatocracy

*"This is the shabby secret of the welfare statists'*
*tirades against gold. Deficit spending is simply*
*a scheme for the 'hidden confiscation' of wealth.*
*Gold stands in the way of this insidious process."*

– Alan Greenspan
1966, 21 years before President
Ronald Reagan appointed him as
Chairman of the Federal Reserve

The Bible's Gospel of Matthew tells of an attempt by opponents to "entangle [Jesus] in his talk" by asking whether it was legal to give tribute to Caesar.

If Jesus approved paying such tribute, he would violate Jewish law and lose the support of many devout fellow Jews. If he told listeners not to pay the tribute, he could be arrested for violating the law of the Roman Empire.

"Shew me the tribute money," said Jesus, who then asked his interrogators: "Whose is this image and superscription?" on the coin. They replied: "Caesar's."

"Render therefore unto Caesar the things which are Caesar's," said Jesus, "and unto God the things that are God's." [182]

Those who hold their savings and bank accounts denominated in the paper fiat money of the Inflatocracy – U.S. Dollars – are holding promissory notes from an entity that, as we mentioned earlier, according to the International Monetary Fund is already effectively bankrupt.

Would you invest in the stock of a company whose financial chart looked like this?

That is what you are doing whenever you collect your pay or keep your savings in paper fiat U.S. Dollars. This is like investing in the stock of a company fast approaching insolvency, bankruptcy.

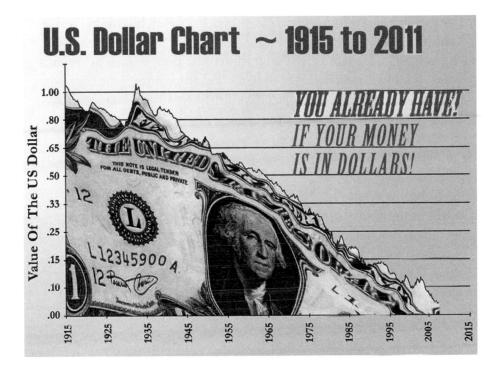

# U.S. Dollar Chart ~ 1915 to 2011

*YOU ALREADY HAVE! IF YOUR MONEY IS IN DOLLARS!*

A share of this stock, which we can call one dollar, has since the creation of the Federal Reserve lost 98 percent of its previous value in purchasing power, and continues to fall.

We really should not call this stock share a Dollar. It's really now a "penny stock," so debased that today it is worth only two cents of its former 100 penny value.

Is the dollar likely to recover its previous value? We report. You decide.

U.S. debts today are in excess of $120 Trillion in unfunded liabilities, an amount so large that a 100 percent tax on the income of all U.S. citizens would be insufficient to pay it off.

The politicized Federal Reserve Board is already monetizing this debt with devalued paper currency run off the electronic printing press as rapidly as Mr. Bernanke dares, as he takes care to avoid causing a panicked flight of people out of U.S. Dollars.

We are only one bad newspaper headline from such a mass panic.

The Fed is moving carefully to avoid driving people into other currencies, tangible commodities that politicians cannot print, or what
since Biblical times has been accepted universally as intrinsically
valuable money that needs no government endorsement: silver and gold.

## Gold Versus The Welfare State

A silver bullet is widely believed to have the power to kill a were-
wolf, if such a creature exists.

Gold is the bullet that, without doubt, can kill the very real monster
of inflation, which is almost entirely a creature of government paper
fiat currency printing.

This is why economist Alan Greenspan, later to chair the Federal
Reserve Board, wrote in 1966 about why so many "welfare-state advocates" have "An almost hysterical antagonism toward the gold
standard," which anchors a currency to gold convertibility and
thereby handcuffs politicians eager to run the Mint's printing presses.

Welfare-statists, Greenspan wrote, realize that "the gold standard is
incompatible with chronic deficit-spending (the hallmark of the welfare state).... [T]he welfare state is nothing more than a mechanism
by which governments confiscate the wealth of the productive members of a society to support a wide variety of welfare schemes."

"In the absence of the gold standard," wrote Greenspan, "there is no
way to protect savings from confiscation through inflation. There is
no safe store of value.... The financial policy of the welfare state requires that there be no way for the owners of wealth to protect
themselves."

"Deficit spending is simply a scheme for the 'hidden' confiscation of
wealth," Greenspan continued. "Gold stands in the way of the insidious process. It stands as a protector of property rights. If one grasps

this, one has no difficulty in understanding the statists' antagonism toward the gold standard." [183]

## Safety in Diversity

If inflation worries you, as it does Ryan and Peggy, isn't it time to diversify a portion of your paper dollar savings into something secure that politically-created inflation cannot devalue and politicians cannot run off a printing press?

The politicians are unlikely to restore a government gold standard. Their power, after all, comes from the Inflatocracy, a political system based on the deceptive printing of paper fiat money and the dependency it creates.

Now you understand why welfarists from FDR to Fed banker Beardsley Ruml saw the end of the gold standard as key to expanding the government and welfare state.

"Gold and economic freedom are inseparable," wrote Greenspan. "[T]he gold standard is an instrument of *laissez-faire* and...each implies and requires the other."

And the reverse side of this coin is equally true: a gold standard makes it almost impossible politically to sustain a welfare state and to deny citizens economic freedom.

No Inflatocracy can exist where honest money prevents inflation and restricts the printing of more paper fiat currency.

## Creating Your Own Gold Standard

If everyone decided to convert his and her paper money bank deposits into metal with intrinsic value and stopped accepting government paper money, wrote Greenspan, then "government-created bank credit would be worthless as a claim on goods." Government fiat money, in other words, could no longer buy anything.

The highway to the socialist welfare state, and to serfdom, is a carpet of government paper fiat money.

The path back to the practical and moral values of America's Founders requires us to restore the precious metal they constitutionally specified as real money.

This is the philosophical difference between a society built on paper promises and a society built on a solid foundation of integrity and gold.

# A Fable for Our Times

Children have always learned values from stories they are told. We can learn from the traditional and, thanks to Ethel C. Fenig at *AmericanThinker.com*, from the modern, politically-correct versions of one such story:

Once upon a time a Little Red Hen found several grains of wheat in the farmyard. Instead of eating them, she gathered them and then went to her neighbors.

"If we plant this wheat, we shall have bread to eat," she told them. "Who will help me plant it?"

"Not I," the cow and duck and pig and goose all told her.

"Then I will do it myself," said the Little Red Hen, and she did. The wheat soon grew and ripened into golden grain.

"Who will help me harvest the wheat?" asked the Little Red Hen.

Again the other animals refused to help.

"I'd lose my unemployment compensation," the goose told her.

The Little Red Hen herself harvested the wheat, ground it into flour, and then asked who would help her bake it into bread.

The other animals again refused, with excuses.

"I'd lose my welfare benefits," said the duck.

"Then I will do it myself," said the Little Red Hen, who baked five loaves and then showed them to the others.

"And who will help me eat this bread?" asked the Little Red Hen.

"I will," they all replied.

"If you don't give me any bread," added the goose, "that's discrimination."

"No," replied the Little Red Hen. "I made the bread and I shall eat all five loaves." And she did.

The more-or-less traditional children's story ends here, and Ms. Fenig's modern, politically-correct version kicks into high gear:

"Excess profits!" cried the cow.

"Capitalist leech!" screamed the duck.

"And they all painted 'Unfair!' picket signs and marched around and around the Little Red Hen, shouting obscenities."

"Then Farmer Obama came. He said to the Little Red Hen, 'You must not be so greedy.'"

"'But I worked hard and earned the bread,' protested the Little Red Hen."

"'Exactly,' said Barack the farmer. 'That is what makes our free enter-prise system so wonderful. Anyone in the barnyard can earn as much as he wants. But under our modern government system, the productive workers must divide the fruits of their labor with those who are not productive. It is only fair.'"

"The Little Red Hen smiled and clucked, 'I am grateful, for now I truly understand.'"

"The Little Red Hen never again baked bread but signed up for all the free stimulus bread, joining her friends the cow, the duck, the pig and the goose."

"And one by one all the bread bakers stopped baking bread, follow-ing the example of their friend, the Little Red Hen."

"And soon there was no more bread and everyone was hungry."

"And all the Democrats smiled. Fairness and equality had been es-tablished and ruled the land." [184]

America's Founders and modern wise men and women understood this.

"Were we directed from Washington when to sow and when to reap," wrote Thomas Jefferson, "we should soon want bread."

"If you put the federal government in charge of the Sahara Desert," wrote economist Milton Friedman, "in 5 years there'd be a shortage of sand."

Why would any sane person put government politicians or bureau-crats in charge of anything?

If we want something done and done correctly, as the Little Red Hen discovered, we must do it for ourselves.

## Render Unto the Inflationistas

The good news is that we Americans can be the traditional Little Red Hens with the pluck to take charge and not wait for others to rescue us.

We can each choose to create our own gold standard, our own store of dependable value that inflation and politicians cannot steal.

Gold can be your and your family's own Declaration of Independence from the Inflatocracy, its invisible taxes and its welfare state.

Render unto the Inflationistas their paper inflat-a-money, and render unto yourself and your family a solid financial foundation of real money such as gold that is inflation-proof and whose value cannot be stolen by the Inflation Deception.

*Like gold, U.S. dollars have value only
to the extent that they are strictly limited in supply.
But the U.S. government has a technology, called a printing press
(or, today, its electronic equivalent), that allows it to produce
as many U.S. dollars as it wishes at essentially no cost.
By increasing the number of U.S. dollars in circulation,
or even by credibly threatening to do so, the
U.S. government can also reduce the value of a dollar
in terms of goods and services, which is equivalent
to raising the prices in dollars of those goods and services.
We conclude that, under a paper-money system,
a determined government can always generate
higher spending and hence positive inflation.*

– Ben S. Bernanke
Member, Board of Governors
Federal Reserve Board
(and now Fed Chairman)
November 21, 2002

# Sources

As indicated herein, many of the books and articles cited here and in our Additional Background Sources can be downloaded at no cost from the Internet, usually to a computer and in a few instances to book reader devices such as the Amazon Kindle and Apple ipad. We have provided many URLs for those wishing to do this.

We encourage you to consider making a donation to entities providing these resources, such as the Ludwig Von Mises Institute, the Foundation for Economic Education, the Cato Institute, the Heritage Foundation, the Competitive Enterprise Institute, Swiss America Trading Corporation, Great Britain's Institute of Economic Affairs in London, and other organizations that make such materials available to advance the world's education about economics.

[1] Mia Lamar, "US Family Income Down 18% Post-Crisis: Fed," cnbc.com, March 24, 2011. URL: http://www.cnbc.com/id/42253012/US_Family_Income_Down_18_Post_Crisis_Fed

[2] Mortimer B. Zuckerman, "3 Reasons the U.S. Economy Remains in a Coma," U.S. News & World Report, March 25, 2011. URL: http://www.usnews.com/opinion/mzuckerman /articles/2011/03/25/3-reasons-the-us-economy-remains-in-a-coma

[3] Tamar Lewin, "Burden of College Loans on Graduates Grows," New York Times, April 11, 2011. URL: http://www.nytimes.com/2011/04/12/education/12college.html

[4] "A Dozen Shocking Personal Finance Statistics," EconomyWatch.com, April 23, 2011. URL: http://www.economywatch.com/personal-finance/a-dozen-shocking-personal-finance-statistics.23-04.html

[5] Craig R. Smith and Lowell Ponte, Crashing the Dollar: How to Survive a Global Currency Collapse. Phoenix: Idea Factory Press, 2010. For its two chapters on the housing crisis as trigger for the Great Recession, see pages 39-70. This book is available from Swiss America Trading Corporation.

[6] Hans F. Sennholz, "Inflation Is Theft," LewRockwell.com, June 24, 2005. See also Hans F. Sennholz (Editor), Inflation Is Theft. Irvington-on-Hudson, New York: Foundation for Economic Education, 1994. A copy of this book may be downloaded at no cost from FEE's website at http://fee.org/wp-content/uploads/2009/11/InflationisTheft.pdf

[7] Lowell Ponte, "Building Your Own Home Makes Sense," Reader's Digest, March 1982.

[8] "Gallup Finds U.S. Unemployment Up Slightly in January to 9.8%," Gallup.com, February 3, 2011. URL: http://www.gallup.com/poll/145922/gallup-finds-unemployment-slightly-january.aspx

[9] For an up-to-date compilation and overview of such statistics, go to http://www.usdebtclock.org.

[10] "Cokie Roberts Says Government Accounts for 40 percent of GDP," PolitiFact.com/St. Petersburg Times [Florida], October 4, 2009. URL: http://www.politifact.com/truth-o-meter/statements/2009/oct/06/cokie-roberts/cokie-roberts-says-government-accounts-40-percent-/

[11] Steven Pearlstein, "Much of Nation's Recent Growth May Have Been a Mirage," Washington Post, February 1, 2011. URL:http://www.washingtonpost.com/wp-dyn/content/article/2011/02/01/AR201102010 6617.html

[12] Jeffrey H. Anderson, "Mandatory Spending to Exceed all Federal Revenues – 50 Years Ahead of Schedule," The Weekly Standard, March 16, 2011. URL:http://www.weeklystandard. com

*/blogs/mandatory-spending-exceed-all-federal-revenues-fiscal-year-2011_554659.html*

[13] Pete Kasperowicz, "'$58,000 per Second,': Member Wants Debt Clock Displayed in House Chamber," *The Hill*, April 18, 2011. URL: *http://thehill.com/blogs/floor-action/house/156469-new-york-rep-wants-debt-clock-displayed-in-house-of-representatives*

[14] Jill Schlesinger, "18 Scary US Debt Facts," *CBSMoneyWatch.com*, November 18, 2010. URL: *http://moneywatch.bnet.com/economic-news/blog/financial-decoder/18-scary-us-debt-facts /2824/*

[15] Emily Stephenson, "Pile of Debt Would Stretch Beyond Stratosphere," *Reuters*, May 19, 2011. URL: *http://www.reuters.com/article/2011/05/19/us-usa-debt-size-idUSTRE74 I5TL201 10519*

[16] Mortimer B. Zuckerman, "The National Debt Crisis Is an Existential Threat," *U.S. News & World Report*, April 26, 2011.

[17] "Vampire Economics," *FrontPageMagazine*.com, May 12, 2011. URL: *http://frontpagemag .com/2011/05/12/vampire-economics-2/print/*

[18] Stephen Moore, "We've Become a Nation of Takers, Not Makers," *Wall Street Journal*, April 1, 2011.URL: *http://online.wsj.com/article/SB100014240527487040502045762190738 67182108.html*

[19] Kevin D. Freeman, *Economic Warfare: Risks and Responses: Analysis of Twenty-First Century Risks in Light of the Recent Market Collapse* (Monograph). Cross Consulting and Services, 2009. This can be downloaded from the Internet at no cost from URLs:*http://av.r.ftdata.co .uk/files/2011/03/49755779-Economic-Warfare-Risks-and-Responses-by-Kevin-D-Freeman.pdf*

or, also at no cost, from *http://www.freemanglobal.com/uploads/Economic_Warfare_Risks_and_ Re-sponses.pdf*

[20] Rachel Ehrenfeld and Alyssa A. Lappen, "The Fifth Generation Warfare," *Front-PageMagazine.com*, June 20, 2008.URL: *http://acdemocracy.org/viewarticle.cfm?category=Eco-nomic%20Warfare&id= 611*

[21] Eamon Javers, "Pentagon Preps for Economic Warfare," *Politico*, April 9, 2009. URL: *http://www.politico.com/news/stories/0409/21053.html*

[22] Jonathon M. Seidl, "Pentagon Has Been 'War Gaming' for Economic Disaster Since Early '09," *TheBlaze.com*, December 7, 2010. URL: *http://www.theblaze.com/stories/pentagon-has-been-war-gaming-for-economic-disaster-since-early-09/*

[23] Jim Kouri, "$1 Trillion Lost Annually to Cyber Crime, Say U.S. Senators," *Examiner.com*, May 24, 2011. URL: *http://www.examiner.com/public-safety-in-national/1-trillion-lost-annually-to-cyber-crime-say-u-s-senators*

[24] Ibid.

[25] Olga Belogolova, "Mullen Addresses Debt, New National Security Team," *National Journal*, April 28, 2011. URL: *http://www.nationaljournal.com/nationalsecurity/mullen-addresses-debt-new-national-security-team-20110428*

[26] Michael MacKenzie and Telis Demos, "Fears Linger of a New 'Flash Crash,'" *Financial Times*, May 5, 2011. URL: *http://www.ft.com/intl/cms/s/0/d18f3d28-7735-11e0-aed6-00144feabdc 0.html#axzz1NMV 0d14H*

See also John Melloy, "Year After May 6 'Flash Crash,' Rumblings of a Stock Correction," *cnbc.com*, May 4, 2011. URL: *http://www.cnbc.com/id/42899594/Year_After_May_6_Flash_ Crash_Ru mblings_of_a_Stock_Correction*

[27] Lowell Ponte, "Terrorism Central?" *FrontPageMagazine*.com, August 18, 2003. URL:

*http://archive.frontpagemag.com/readArticle.aspx?ARTID=16740*

[28] Jeff Cox, "$6 Gas? Could Happen if Dollar Keeps Getting Weaker," *cnbc.com*, April 20, 2011. URL: *http://www.cnbc.com/id/42683030/6_Gas_Could_Happen_if_Dollar_Keep s_Getting_ Weaker*

[29] J. Kevin Meaders, "Charting the Course to $7 Gas," *Mises Daily*, April 25, 2011. URL: *http://mises.org/daily/5223/Charting-the-Course-to-7-Gas*

[30] Dennis Cauchon, "Federal Workers Earning Double Their Private Counterparts," *USA Today*, August 13, 2010. URL: *http://www.usatoday.com/money/economy/income/2010-08-10-1Afed-pay 10_ST_N.htm? csp=hf*

*Apparently unable to dispute the total compensation disparity Cauchon found between Federal and private sector employees in Department of Commerce Bureau of Economic Analysis (BEA) data, liberal media voices have argued that the average Federal employee is a better, "higher-skilled" person who deserves to be paid even more than twice as much as the average private sector worker.*

*See, for example,* E.S.S., "Fox Continues to Push False Federal vs. Private Pay Comparison," *Media Matters for America*, December 1, 2010.URL: *http://mediamatters.org/iphone/research/201 012010020*

[31] Liz Alderman, "Why Denmark Is Shrinking Its Social Safety Net," *New York Times*, August 16, 2010. URL: *http://economix.blogs.nytimes.com/2010/08/16/why-denmark-is-shrinking-its-social-safety-net/*

[32] Elizabeth MacDonald, "Government Cash Handouts Now Top Tax Revenues," *FoxBusiness.com*, April 20, 2011. URL: *http://www.foxbusiness.com/markets/2011/04/20/government-cash-handouts-exceed-tax-revenues/*

[33] Daniel Indiviglio, "Is the U.S. Becoming a Welfare State?" *TheAtlantic.com*, March 9, 2011. URL: *http://www.theatlantic.com/business/archive/2011/03/is-the-us-becoming-a-welfare-state/72 217/*

[34] For Adams' self-described background, see URL: *http://www.gerardadams.com*

[35] "NIA Responds to Harvard Economics Professor About Inflation," (Press Release), March 29, 2011. URL: *http://inflation.us/harvardeconomics html*

[36] Daniel Indiviglio, "Is the U.S. Becoming a Welfare State?" *TheAtlantic.com*, March 9, 2011. URL: *http://www.theatlantic.com/business/archive/2011/03/is-the-us-becoming-a-welfare-state/ 72217/*

[37] Kimberley A. Strassel, "Obama's 'Gangster Politics'," *Wall Street Journal*, May 5, 2011. URL:*http://online.wsj.com/article/SB10001424052748703992704576305414137806694.html*

See also "The IRS Gets Political" (Editorial), *Wall Street Journal*, May 18, 2011. URL: *http://online.wsj.com/article/SB10001424052748703730804576321090737945116.html? mod=WSJ_newsreel_opinion*

[38] Shahien Nasiripour, "Financial System Riskier, Next Bailout Will Be Costlier, S&P Says," *Huffington Post*, April 19, 2011. URL: *http://www.huffingtonpost.com/2011/04/19/financial-system-riskier-_n_ 851122.html*

[39] Peter J. Tanous and Jeff Cox, *Debt, Deficits and the Demise of the American Economy*. Hoboken, New Jersey: John Wiley & Sons, 2011.

[40] See "Geithner Gone Wild: Treasury Entertains 100 Year and GDP-Linked Bonds to Fill New $2.4 Trillion 'Demand,'" *ZeroHedge.com*, February 4, 2011. URL: *http://www.zerohedge .com/article/geithner-gone-wild-treasury-entertains-100-year-and-gdp-linked-bonds-fill-new-24-trillion-de* ; Rebecca Christie and Liz Capo McCormick, "Treasury Advisory Panel Suggests 'Ultra-Long' Debt," *Businessweek/Bloomberg*, February 2, 2011. URL: *http://www.businessweek. com/news /2011-02-02/treasury-advisory-panel-suggests-ultra-long-debt.html*

[41] Michael F. Bryan, "On the Origin and Evolution of the Word *Inflation*," (Monograph). Cleveland, Ohio: Federal Reserve Bank of Cleveland, October 15, 1997. URL: *http://www.cleveland fed.org/research/commentary/1997/1015.pdf*

[42] Ronald McKinnon, "The Return of Stagflation," *Wall Street Journal*, May 23, 2011. URL: *http://online.wsj.com/article/SB10001424052702304066504576341211971664684.html*

[43] Craig R. Smith and Lowell Ponte, *Crashing the Dollar: How to Survive a Global Currency Collapse*. Phoenix: Idea Factory Press, 2010. Pages 157-158.

[44] Murray N. Rothbard, "Taking Money Back," *Mises Daily*, June 14, 2008. URL: *http://mises.org/daily/2882*

[45] David von Drehle, "The Man Who Said No to Easy Money," *Time* Magazine, February 14, 2011.

[46] Ron Paul, *End the Fed*. New York: Grand Central Publishing, 2009. Page 181.

[47] George A. Akerlof and Robert J. Schiller, *Animal Spirits: How Human Psychology Drives the Economy, and Why It Matters for Global Capitalism*. Princeton, NJ: Princeton University Press, 2009.

[48] Senator Tom Coburn, *Wastebook 2010: A Guide to Some of the Most Wasteful Government Spending of 2010*. (Monograph.) URL: *http://coburn.senate.gov/public/index.cfm?a=Files.Serve&File_i d=774a6cca-18fa-4619-987b-a15eb44e7f18*

[49] "The Economic Stimulus That Wasn't" (Editorial), *Investor's Business Daily*, January 25, 2011. URL: *http://www.investors.com/NewsAndAnalysis/Article/560910/201101251850/The-Economic-Stimulus-That-Wasnt.aspx*

[50] Robert J. Barro, "Government Spending Is No Free Lunch," *Wall Street Journal*, January 22, 2009. URL: *http://online.wsj.com/article/SB123258618204604599.html*

[51] Ethan Ilzetzki and others, "How Big (Small?) are Fiscal Multipliers?" *NBER* (National Bureau of Economic Research) Working Paper No. 16479 (October 2010). URL: *http://www.nber.org/papers/w16479.pdf*. For a slightly earlier version of this paper available on the Internet, go to: URL: *http://econweb .umd.edu/~vegh/papers/multipliers.pdf*

See also David Brooks, "The Two Cultures," *New York Times*, November 15, 2010. URL: *http://www.nytimes.com/2010/11/16/opinion/16brooks.html?_r= 1&ref= davidbrooks*

[52] Craig R. Smith and Lowell Ponte, *Crashing the Dollar: How to Survive a Global Currency Collapse*. Phoenix: Idea Factory Press, 2010. Pages 80-81.

[53] Diana Olick, "Negative Home Equity Surges, Weighing on Housing Recovery," *cnbc.com*, February 9, 2011. URL: *http://www.cnbc.com/id/41483676/print/1/displaymode/1098/*

[54] John Crudele, "Tricks But No Miracles in Recent Jobs Report," *New York Post*, February 8, 2011. URL: *http://www.nypost.com/p/news/business/tricks_but_no_miracles_in_recent _5BVccbpjg-GSJR4cvIzr54N*

[55] _____, "Another View on Why There is No Robust Job Growth," *New York Post*, February 10, 2011. URL: *http://www.nypost.com/p/news/business/another_view_on_why_there_is_ no_4hr26jGyaVVNP8zVsCA23L*

[56] _____, "The Super Bowl of Jobs Reports is Out Tomorrow," *New York Post*, February 3, 2011. URL: *http://www.nypost.com/p/news/business/the_super_bowl_of_jobs_reports_is_ dBjG6Ut UNOplnuUjZs24VL*

[57] John Crudele, "On Jobs, President Clueless Really Doesn't Get It," *New York Post*, January 11, 2011. URL: *http://www.nypost.com/p/news/business/on_jobs_president_clueless_really_oOM-cwNZUA vvDnxSj7ughgL*

[58] "Gallup Finds U.S. Unemployment Up Slightly in January to 9.8%," *Gallup.com*, February 3, 2011. URL: *http://www.gallup.com/poll/145922/gallup-finds-unemployment-slightly-january.aspx*

[59] "Bernanke, BLS Lie About Inflation: Dr. Doom Faber," *cnbc.com*, February 2, 2011. URL: *http://www.cnbc.com/id/41385143/Bernanke_BLS_Lie_About_Inflation _Dr_Doom_Faber*

[60] Richard A. Posner, *The Crisis of Capitalist Democracy*. Cambridge, Massachusetts: Harvard University Press, 2010.

[61] Matt Cover, "Hoyer Says Federal Budget May Not Be Balanced for 20 Years," CNSnews.com, March 8, 2011. URL: *http://cnsnews.com/print/82375*

[62] Rohini Chowdhury, "'Eureka!' - The Story of Archimedes and the Golden Crown," *Stories Behind Great Discoveries* (2002). URL: *http://www.longlongtimeago.com/llta_greatdiscoveries_archimedes_eureka.html*

[63] Murray N. Rothbard, *What Has Government Done to Our Money?* Auburn, Alabama: Ludwig von Mises Institute, 2008. Page 74. This book can be downloaded from the Internet at no cost from *http://mises.org/Books/Whathasgovernmentdone.pdf*

[64] Murray N. Rothbard, "Taking Money Back," *Mises Daily*, June 14, 2008. URL: *http://mises.org/daily/2882*

[65] Robert L. Schuettinger and Eamonn F. Butler, *Forty Centuries of Wage and Price Controls: How NOT to Fight Inflation*. Washington, D.C.: Heritage Foundation, 1979. This can be downloaded from the Internet at no cost from *http://mises.org/books/fortycenturies.pdf*

[66] Naphtali Lewis and Meyer Reinhold (Editors), *Roman Civilization: Sourcebook II: The Empire*. New York: Harper Torchbooks, 1966. Pages 440-445.

[67] Ibid. Pages 463-473; see also Robert L. Schuettinger and Eamonn F. Butler, *Forty Centuries of Wage and Price Controls: How NOT to Fight Inflation*. Washington, D.C.: Heritage Foundation, 1979. Pages 20-27.

[68] URL: *http://www.merriam-webster.com/dictionary/soldier*

[69] Jonathan Williams (Editor), *Money: A History*. New York: St. Martin's Press, 1997. Page 155.

[70] Jack Weatherford, *The History of Money: From Sandstone to Cyberspace*. New York: Crown Publishers, 1997. Pages 126-127.

[71] Louise Levathes, *When China Ruled the Seas: The Treasure Fleet of the Dragon Throne, 1405-1433*. Oxford: Oxford University Press, 1997.

[72] Gavin Menzies, *1421: The Year China Discovered America*. New York: Harper Perennial, 2002, and *1434: The Year a Magnificent Chinese Fleet Sailed to Italy and Ignited the Renaissance*. New York: Harper Perennial, 2009.

[73] To learn more about John Law, see Niall Ferguson, *The Ascent of Money: A Financial History of the World*. New York: Penguin Press, 2008. Pages 137-157.

[74] F.A. Hayek, *Choice in Currency: A Way to Stop Inflation* (Monograph). London: Institute of Economic Affairs, 1976. URL: *http://www.iea.org.uk/sites/default/files/publications/files/upld book409.pdf*

[75] Murray N. Rothbard, "Commodity Money in Colonial America," *Mises.org*, February 22, 2011. URL: *http://mises.org/daily/5020/Commodity-Money-in-Colonial-America*

This is an excerpt from Murray N. Rothbard, *A History of Money and Banking in the United States: The Colonial Era to World War II*. Auburn, Alabama: Ludwig von Mises Institute, 2002. This can be downloaded from the Internet at no cost from *http://mises.org/Books/HistoryofMoney.pdf*

[76] Benjamin Franklin, *A Modest Enquiry into the Nature and Necessity of a Paper-Currency.* (Monograph). Philadelphia: Franklin Printery, 1729. To retrieve it from the University of Virginia Electronic Text Center: URL: *http://etext.virginia.edu/users/brock/webdoc6.html*

[77] Ibid.

[78] "Continental Currency Featured in Heritage Boston ANA Auction," Heritage Auctions, *CoinNews.com*, August 2, 2010. URL: *http://www.coinnews.net/2010/08/02/continental-currency-featured-in-heritage-boston-ana-auction/*

[79] Alexander Hamilton, James Madison and John Jay, *The Federalist Papers.* New York: Mentor / New American Library, 1961. Pages 280-288. For an online version of James Madison's Federalist Paper No. 44, go to this URL: *http://www.constitution.org/fed/federa44.htm*

[80] George Selgin and Larry White, "How Would the Invisible Hand Handle Money?" *Journal of Economic Literature.* Vol. 32 No. 4 (1994). Pages 1718-1749.

[81] Robert P. Murphy, *The Politically Incorrect Guide to Capitalism.* Washington, D.C.: Regnery, 2007. Pages 94-95.

[82] "'Dixie' Originated from Name 'Dix,' An Old Currency," *Louisiana Works Progress Administration Collection*, Vol. 2 No. 150 Page 3 Col. 1. Document dated May 29, 1916. URL: *http://louisdl.louislibraries.org/cdm4/document.php?CISOROOT=/LWP&CISOPTR=1384 &CISOSHOW=1382*

[83] Pallavi Gogol and Barbara Hagenbaugh, "Billions of AIG's Federal Aid Went to Foreign Banks," *USA Today*, March 17, 2009. URL: *http://www.usatoday.com/money/companies/management/2009-03-16-some-aig-billions-went-to-banks_N.htm*

See also Donal Griffin and Bob Ivry, "Libya-Owned Bank Got 73 Loans From Fed Discount Window After Lehman Fell," *Bloomberg/Business Week*, April 1, 2011. URL: *http://www.business week.com/news/2011-04-01/libya-owned-bank-got-73-loans-from-fed-window-after-lehman.html*

[84] Charles August Lindbergh, *Banking and Currency and the Money Trust.* Washington, D.C.: National Capital Press, 1913. Google books reading copy: URL: *http://books.google.com /books?id=B9IZAAAAYAAJ&printsec=frontcover&source=gbs_ge_summary_r&cad=0#v= onepage &q&f=false*

[85] Charles August Lindbergh, *Why Is Your Country At War and What Happens to You After the War and Related Subjects.* Washington, D.C.: National Capital Press, 1917. Google books reading copy: URL: *http://books.google.com/books?id=qzAWAAAAYAAJ&printsec=frontcover&source=gbs_ ge_summary_r&cad=0#v=onepage&q&f=false*

[86] Friedrich A. Hayek, *Denationalisation of Money: The Argument Refined: An Analysis of the Theory and Practice of Concurrent Currencies. Third Edition.* London: Institute of Economic Affairs, 1990. This can be downloaded from the Internet at no cost from *http://mises.org/books/denationalisation.pdf*

[87] Patrick Allen, "The Fed Will Make Sure Obama Wins in 2012: Strategist," cnbc.com, April 28, 2011. URL: *http://www.cnbc.com/id/42794512/The_Fed_Will_Make_Sure_Obama_ Wins_in_ 2012_Strategist*

[88] "U.S. Economy Grinds To Halt As Nation Realizes Money Just A Symbolic, Mutually Shared Illusion," *The Onion*, February 16, 2010. URL: *http://www.theonion.com/articles/us-economy-grinds-to-halt-as-nation-realizes-money,2912/*

[89] George A. Akerlof and Robert J. Schiller, *Animal Spirits: How Human Psychology Drives the Economy, and Why It Matters for Global Capitalism.* Princeton, NJ: Princeton University Press, 2009. Page 47; for perspective on today's money as a unit of account, see Richard W. Rahn, "A Constant Unit of Account," *Cato Journal*, Vol. 30 No. 3 (Fall 2010). Pages 521-533.

[90] Hilke Plassmann, John O'Doherty, Baba Shiv, and Antonio Rangel, "Marketing actions can modulate neural representations of experienced pleasantness," *PNAS* (*Proceedings of the National Academy of Sciences of the United States of America*), Vol. 105 No. 3 (January 22, 2008). pp. 1050-1054. URL: *http://www.pnas.org/content/105/3/1050.full.pdf+html*

[91] Bernd Weber, Antonio Rangel, Matthias Wibral, and Armin Falk, "The medial prefrontal cortex exhibits money illusion," *PNAS* (*Proceedings of the National Academy of Sciences of the United States of America*), Vol. 106 No. 13 (March 31, 2009). pp. 5025-5028. URL: *http://www. pnas.org/content/106/13/5025.full.pdf+html*

See also Jianjun Miao and Danyang Xie, "*Monetary Policy and Economic Growth Under Money Illusion*," Boston University Department of Economics Working Papers Series # wp2007-045. October 29, 2009.

See also Markus K. Brunnermeier and Christian Julliard, "Money Illusion and Housing Frenzies," *Review of Financial Studies*, Volume 21 #1 (January 2008). Pages 135-180. NBER Working Papers 12810.

[92] Jason Zweig, *Your Money & Your Brain: How the New Science of Neuroeconomics Can Help Make You Rich*. New York: Simon & Schuster, 2007.Page 53.

[93] I Timothy 6:10 (English Standard Version).

[94] Among the many books on this topic, see George Gilder, *Wealth and Poverty*. New York: Basic Books, 1981; David S. Landes, *The Wealth and Poverty of Nations: Why Some Are So Rich and Some So Poor*. New York: W.W. Norton, 1998; Jared Diamond, *Collapse: How Societies Choose to Fail or Succeed*. New York: Viking / Penguin, 2005; and Hernando de Soto, *The Mystery of Capital: Why Capitalism Triumphs in the West and Fails Everywhere Else*. New York: Basic Books, 2000.

[95] "The Cause and Cure of Inflation," in Milton Friedman, *Money Mischief: Episodes in Monetary History*. New York: Harcourt Brace, 1992. Pages 214-219.

[96] Feijun Luo and others, "Impact of Business Cycles on US Suicide Rates, 1928-2007," *American Journal of Public Health*. April 14, 2011. Advance look abstract citation: 10.2105/AJPH.2010.300010. URL: *http://ajph.aphapublications.org/cgi/content/abstract/AJPH .2010.300010v1*

See also Molly Peterson, "Suicide Rates in U.S. Increase as Economy Declines, CDC Researchers Find," *Bloomberg*, April 14, 2011; Sara Murray and Betsy McKay, "Early Data Suggest Suicides Are Rising," *Wall Street Journal*, November 23, 2009; "Suicide Rates Spike During Recessions," *Wall Street Journal*, April 18, 2011; Benedict Carey, "Study Ties Suicide Rate in Work Force to Economy," *New York Times*, April 14, 2011; Edward Tenner, "Does the Economy Predict Suicides?" *The Atlantic* Magazine online, April 18, 2011; Bill Hendrick, "Suicides Go Up When Economy Goes Down: Since the Great Depression, Hard Economic Times Have Driven Up Suicide Rates, Study Finds," *WebMD Health News*, April 14, 2011.

[97] Virginie Montet, "Rising US Divorce Rate Signals Economic Recovery," *Agence France Presse* (AFP), April 28, 2011. URL: *http://news.yahoo.com/s/afp/20110428/ts_alt_afp/usaeconomysociety-divo rce_201104282 02945*

[98] Richard Blackden and Harry Wilson, "Fed Chief Ben Bernanke Denies US Policy Behind Record Global Food Prices," *London Telegraph*, February 3, 2011; Abhijit Banerjee and Esther Duflo, "More Than One Billion People Are Hungry in the World: But What If the Experts Are Wrong?" *Foreign Policy*, May/June 2011; Frederick Kaufman, "How Goldman Sachs Created the Food Crisis," *Foreign Policy*, April 27, 2011; Lucas Van Praag, "Don't Blame Goldman Sachs for the Food Crisis," *Foreign Policy*, May 3, 2011.

[99] Lester R. Brown, "The New Geopolitics of Food," *Foreign Policy*, May/June 2011; Brian Louis, "Farmland Boom Provides Boost to Slumping U.S. Midwest Real Estate Market," *Bloomberg*, February 16, 2011; Augustino Fontevecchia, "Why World Food Prices Will Keep

Climbing," *Forbes.com*, March 9, 2011; Addison Wiggin, "The Food Crisis of 2011," *Forbes.com*, October 27, 2010.

[100] Gretchen Livingston and D'Vera Cohn, "U.S. Birth Rate Decline Linked to Recession," Pew Research Center/Pew Social and Demographic Trends, April 6, 2010. URL: *http://pewsocial-trends.org/2010/04/06/us-birth-rate-decline-linked-to-recession/*

[101] "U.S. Birth Rate Falls for Second Year in Midst of Recession," *CNN.com*, August 28, 2010.

[102] Central Intelligence Agency, *The World Factbook 2009*. Washington, D.C.: Central Intelligence Agency, 2009.

[103] Francis Fukuyama, *The End of History and The Last Man*. New York: Free Press, 1992.

[104] Zygmund Dobbs, "The Social Consequences of Moral Depravity," Chapter Nine of his provocative book *Keynes at Harvard: Economic Deception as a Political Credo*. West Sayville, New York: Probe Research, Inc., 1969. URL: *http://www.keynesatharvard.org/book/KeynesatHarvard-ch09.html*

[105] John Eberhard, "The Tytler Cycle," *CommonSenseGovernment.com*, September 15, 2003. URL: *http://commonsensegovernment.com/article-09-15-03.html*

See also Proverbs 29:18 — "Where there is no vision, the people perish: but he that keepeth the law, happy is he." (The Bible, KJV)

[106] Steve Benen, "Political Animal," *Washington Monthly*, April 5, 2009. URL: *http://www.washingtonmonthly.com/archives/individual/2009_04/0176 14.php*

[107] Emily Bazelon, "Hypomanic American, The," *New York Times*, December 11, 2005. URL:*http://www.nytimes.com/2005/12/11/magazine/11ideas_section2-7.html*

[108] Peter C. Whybrow, *American Mania: When More Is Not Enough*. New York: W.W. Norton, 2005.

[109] John D. Gartner, *The Hypomanic Edge: The Link Between (A Little) Craziness and (A Lot of) Success in America*. New York: Simon & Schuster, 2005.

[110] Lowell Ponte, "Protect the Overprivileged," *Wall Street Journal*, November 14, 1997.

[111] "The Cause and Cure of Inflation," in Milton Friedman, *Money Mischief: Episodes in Monetary History*. New York: Harcourt Brace, 1992.

[112] "The State" in Randolph Bourne, *Untimely Papers*. 1919. Reissued in 2010 by Nabu Press in Charleston, South Carolina. Text of this essay can be found at URL: *http://fair-use.org/randolph-bourne/the-state/*

[113] Paul A. Cantor, "Hyperinflation and Hyperreality: Thomas Mann in Light of Austrian Economics," *The Review of Austrian Economics*, Vol. 7 No. 1 (1994). Pages 3-29. URL: *http://mises.org/journals/rae/pdf/RAE7_1_1.pdf*

[114] Niall Ferguson, *The Ascent of Money: A Financial History of the World*. New York: Penguin Press, 2008. Pages 283-340.

[115] Sun Tzu, *The Art of War*. (Samuel B. Griffith translation, Foreword by B.H. Liddell Hart). London: Oxford University Press, 1963. See also J.H. Huang, *Sun Tzu: The New Translation*. New York: Quill / William Morrow, 1993.

[116] To see this video go either to *CAGW.org* or *http://swineline.org/media/*

[117] John Maynard Keynes, *Essays in Persuasion*. New York: W.W. Norton, 1963. Pages 86-87.

[118] Craig R. Smith and Lowell Ponte, *Crashing the Dollar: How to Survive a Global Currency Collapse*. Phoenix: Idea Factory Press, 2010. Pages 76-77.

[119] Stephen Dinan, "Debt Now Equals Total U.S. Economy," *Washington Times*, February 14, 2011. URL: *http://www.washingtontimes.com/news/2011/feb/14/debt-now-equals-total-us-economy/*

[120] Quoted in Craig R. Smith and Lowell Ponte, *Crashing the Dollar: How to Survive a Global Currency Collapse. Phoenix: Idea Factory Press, 2010. Page 77-78.*

[121] Congressional Budget Office, *The Budget and Economic Outlook: Fiscal Years 2011 to 2021.* Washington, D.C.: U.S. Government Printing Office, January 2011. URL: *http:www.cbo. gov/ftp-docs/120xx/doc12039/01-26_FY2011Outlook.pdf*

[122] Beardsley Ruml, "Taxes for Revenue Are Obsolete," *American Affairs*, Vol. VIII No. 1 (January 1946). Pages 35-39. URL: *http://www.constitution.org/tax/us-ic/cmt/ruml_obsolete.pdf*

[123] See "Government Revenue from Inflation" in Milton Friedman, *On Economics: Selected Papers.* Chicago: University of Chicago Press, 2007. Pages 135-145.

[124] Brett Arends, "Why You Can't Trust the Inflation Numbers," *Wall Street Journal*, January 26, 2011. URL: *http://online.wsj.com/article/SB100014240527487040136045761043510 50317610.html*

[125] John Williams, "Hyperinflation Special Report (Update 2010)" [Monograph], *shadowstats.com*, December 2, 2009. URL: *http://www.shadowstats.com/article/hyperinflation-2010* Pdf version: *http://www.shadowstats.com/article/hyperinflation-2010.pdf*

The Shadow Government Statistics website offers this independent economist's analysis and alternative charting of the inflation rate, unemployment, the money supply, Gross Domestic Product and more. URL: *http://www.shadowstats.com/*

[126] Daniel Indiviglio, "Should the Government Reform How It Measures Inflation?" *The Atlantic* Magazine. January 26, 2011. URL: *http://www.theatlantic.com/business/archive/2011/ 01/should-the-government-reform-how-it-measures-inflation/70292/*

[127] "Top Investor: 'U.S. Government's Inflation Data Is a Sham'" and "What Is the Real Inflation Rate?" *Whistleblower* Magazine, January 2011; see also the CPI vs. Shadow Government Statistics graph showing a divergence in data after the Clinton Administration changed CPI methodology and sampling, *Whistleblower* Magazine, January 2011, page 5.

[128] Ronald McKinnon, "The Latest American Export: Inflation," *Wall Street Journal*, January 18, 2011. URL: *http://online.wsj.com/article/SB10001424052748704405704576064252782421930.html*

See also Ronald McKinnon, "The Return of Stagflation," *Wall Street Journal*, May 23, 2011. URL: *http://online.wsj.com/article/SB10001424052702304066504576341211971664684.html*

[129] G. Edward Griffin, *The Creature from Jekyll Island: A Second Look at the Federal Reserve*, Third Edition. Westlake Village, California: American Media, 1998. Pages 550-553.

[130] "Economic News Release: Consumer Price Index Summary," Washington, D.C.: U.S. Bureau of Labor Statistics, February 17, 2011. URL: *http://www.bls.gov/news.release/cpi.nr0.htm*

[131] Karl Marx and Friedrich Engels, *The Communist Manifesto.* London: Penguin Classics, 1985. Page 104.

[132] Ben S. Bernanke and others, *Inflation Targeting: Lessons from the International Experience.* Princeton, NJ: Princeton University Press, 1999. For a contrarian view, see Columbia University economist and Nobel Laureate Joseph E. Stiglitz, "The Failure of Inflation Targeting," *Project Syndicate*, May 6, 2008. URL: *http://www.project-syndicate.org/commentary/stiglitz99/ English*

[133] Ludwig von Mises, *Human Action: A Treatise on Economics*, Third Revised Edition. Chicago: Contemporary Books, 1966. Pages 789-790.

[134] Wilhelm Röpke, *A Humane Economy: The Social Framework of the Free Market*. Chicago: Henry Regnery Company, 1960. Page 192. [The German edition was published in 1958.] This book can be downloaded without charge from the the Ludwig von Mises Institute at URL: *http://mises.org/books/ Human_Economy_Ropke.pdf*

[135] Mortimer B. Zuckerman, "The National Debt Crisis Is an Existential Threat," *U.S. News & World Report*, April 26, 2011.

[136] Wilhelm Röpke, *A Humane Economy: The Social Framework of the Free Market*. Chicago: Henry Regnery Company, 1960. Page 192. [The German edition was published in 1958.] This book can be downloaded without charge from the the Ludwig von Mises Institute at URL: *http://mises.org/books/ Human_Economy_Ropke.pdf*

[137] William Voegeli, *Never Enough: America's Limitless Welfare State*. New York: Encounter Books, 2010.

[138] Wilhelm Röpke, *A Humane Economy: The Social Framework of the Free Market*. Chicago: Henry Regnery Company, 1960. Page 217. [The German edition was published in 1958.] This book can be downloaded without charge from the the Ludwig von Mises Institute at URL: *http://mises.org/books /Human_Economy_Ropke.pdf*

[139] Gregory Wolfe, "Beyond Supply and Demand: The Psychology of Inflation," *The Freeman*, Volume 29 Issue 2 (February 1979).

[140] Wilhelm Röpke, *A Humane Economy: The Social Framework of the Free Market*. Chicago: Henry Regnery Company, 1960. Page 220. [The German edition was published in 1958.] This book can be downloaded without charge from the the Ludwig von Mises Institute at URL: *http://mises.org/books/ Human_Economy_Ropke.pdf*

[141] Ludwig von Mises, *Human Action: A Treatise on Economics*, Third Revised Edition. Chicago: Contemporary Books, 1966. Pages 789-790, pages 466-471.

[142] Michael F. Bryan, "On the Origin and Evolution of the Word *Inflation*," (Monograph). Cleveland, Ohio: Federal Reserve Bank of Cleveland, October 15, 1997. URL: *http://www.cleveland fed.org/research/commentary/1997/1015.pdf*

[143] Ludwig von Mises, *The Theory of Money and Credit*, New Edition. Irvington-on-Hudson, NY: Foundation for Economic Education, 1971. Pages 219-231.

[144] John Maynard Keynes, *Essays in Persuasion*. New York: W.W. Norton, 1963. Pages 86-87.

[145] Allan H. Meltzer, "Inflation Nation," *New York Times*, May 4, 2009. URL: *http://www.nytimes.com/2009/05/04/opinion/04meltzer.html*

[146] Jeff Cox, "Is the Fed's Real Target 1,755 for the S&P?" *cnbc.com*, February 4, 2011. URL: *http://www.cnbc.com/id/41426974/Is_the_Fed_s_Real_Target_1_755_for_ the_S_P*

[147] John Carney, "Bernanke to Congress: We're Much Closer to Total Destruction Than You Think," *cnbc.com*, February 9, 2011.URL: *http://www.cnbc.com/id/41491193/Bernanke_to_Congress_We_re_Much_ Closer_to_Total_Destruction_Than_You_Think*

[148] Peter Ferrara, "America's Ever Expanding Welfare Empire," *Forbes* Magazine, April 22, 2011. URL: *http://blogs.forbes.com/peterferrara/2011/04/22/americas-ever-expanding-welfare-empire/*

[149] Peter Ferrara, *America's Ticking Bankruptcy Bomb: How the Looming Debt Crisis Threatens the American Dream – and How We Can Turn the Tide Before It's Too Late*. New York: Broadside Books, 2011.

[150] James K. Glassman, "The 4 percent Solution," *National Review*, May 2, 2011. URL: *http://www.nationalreview.com/articles/266128/4-percent-solution-james-k-glassman*

[151] John Carney, "Wall Streeters Paying $35,800 to Dine with Obama," *cnbc.com*, April 27, 2011. URL: *http://www.cnbc.com/id/42780381/Wall_Streeters_Paying_35_800_to_Dine_With_Obama*

[152] _____, "S&P: Passed 'Balanced' State Budgets May Not Always Equal Fiscal Reality," *cnbc.com*, May 6, 2011.

[153] Danny Hakim, "State Plan Makes Fund Both Borrower and Lender," *New York Times*, June 11, 2010. URL: *http://www.nytimes.com/2010/06/12/nyregion/12pension.html*

[154] Allison Bennett and Brendan A. McGrail, "Arizona Sells Supreme Court Building to Raise $300 Million for Schoolkids," *Bloomberg*, June 7, 2010. URL: *http://www.bloomberg.com/news/2010-06-08/arizona-sells-supreme-court-building-to-raise-300-million-for-schoolkids.html*

[155] Rubin S. Lubowski and others, *Major Uses of Land in the United States, 2002*. (Monograph). Washington, D.C.: Economic Research Service Report Summary/U.S. Department of Agriculture, May 2006. URL: *http://www.ers.usda.gov/publications/ EIB14/eib14_reportsummary.pdf*

[156] Henry Lamb, "The Fight Against Government Land Ownership," *WorldNetDaily.com*, April 16, 2005. URL: *http://www.wnd.com/news/article.asp?ARTICLE_ID=43824*

[157] Clyde Wayne Crews, Jr., *Ten Thousand Commandments: An Annual Snapshot of the Federal Regulatory State*. 2011 Edition. (Monograph). Washington, D.C.: Competitive Enterprise Institute, 2011.

[158] To see this unscientific survey of University of California Berkeley student responses, on the Internet go to: *http://www.youtube.com/watch?v=4rDahs4cmuc*

[159] Neal Boortz and John Linder, *The FairTax Book: Saying Goodbye to the Income Tax and the IRS....* New York: Regan Books / HarperCollins, 2005. See also Neal Boortz, John Linder and Rob Woodall, *FairTax: The Truth: Answering the Critics*. New York: Harper, 2008.

[160] Murray N. Rothbard, "The Case Against the Flat Tax" in L.H. Rockwell (Editor), *The Free Market Reader*. Auburn, Alabama: Ludwig von Mises Institute, 1988. URL: *http://mises. org/rothbard/flattax.pdf*

[161] Llewellyn H. Rockwell, Jr., "The Inflationist Dream," *The Free Market*, Volume 23, Number 9 (September 2003). URL: *http://mises.org/freemarket_detail.aspx?control=455*

[162] F.A. Hayek, *Choice in Currency: A Way to Stop Inflation* (Monograph). London: Institute of Economic Affairs, 1976. URL: *http://www.iea.org.uk/sites/default/files/publications/files/upldbook409.pdf*

[163] Friedrich A. Hayek, *Denationalisation of Money: The Argument Refined: An Analysis of the Theory and Practice of Concurrent Currencies*. Third Edition. London: Institute of Economic Affairs, 1990. Pages 27-28. This can be downloaded from the Internet at no cost from *http://mises. org/books/denationalisation.pdf*

[164] Clifford F. Thies, "The Economics of Depression Scrip," *Mises Daily*, June 30, 2010. URL: *http://mises.org/daily/4521*

[165] "Defendant Convicted of Minting His Own Currency," (Department of Justice Press Release), Charlotte, North Carolina: U.S. Federal Bureau of Investigation, March 18, 2011. URL: *http://charlotte.fbi.gov/dojpressrel/pressrel11/ce031811.htm*

[166] John Stossel, "Starting A New Currency is 'Domestic Terrorism"? *FoxBusiness.com*, March 22, 2011. URL: *http://stossel.blogs.foxbusiness.com/2011/03/22/starting-a-new-currency-is-"domestic-terrorism"/print/*

See also Seth Lipsky, "When Private Money Becomes a Felony Offense," *Wall Street Journal*, March 31, 2011. URL: *http://online.wsj.com/article/SB10001424052748704425804576220383 67360 8952.html*

[167] Huma Khan, "States Look to Bring Gold Standard Back: Utah is First State to Recognize Gold and Silver as Legal Tender; Inflation Worries Loom," *ABC News*, April 15, 2011. URL: *http://abcnews.go.com/Politics/tea-party-momentum-utah-bill-brings-gold-standard/story?id=13377409*

[168] Ibid.

[169] Ibid.

[170] Forrest Jones, "Steve Forbes: Gold Standard to Return in Five Years," *Moneynews.com*, May 11, 2011. URL: *http://www.moneynews.com/StreetTalk/Steve-Forbes-Gold-Standard/2011/05/11 /id/395 949*

[171] Ron Paul and Lewis Lehrman, *The Case for Gold: A Minority Report of the U.S. Gold Commission*. Auburn, Alabama: Ludwig von Mises Institute, 2007. This can be downloaded from the Internet at no cost from *http://mises .org/books/caseforgold.pdf*

[172] Joshua Green, "The Tea Party's Brain," *The Atlantic* Magazine, November 2010. URL: *http://www.theatlantic.com/magazine/archive/2010/11/the-tea-party-8217-s-brain/8280/*

[173] "Mexican Central Bank Quietly Buys 100 Tons of Gold," *cnbc.com*, May 5, 2011. This story appeared originally in *The Financial Times*. URL: *http://www.cnbc.com/id/42909399/Mexican_Central_Bank_Quietly_Buys _100_Tons_of_Gold*

[174] Robert Lenzner, "Central Banks Leading New Gold Rush," *Forbes* Magazine, September 10, 2010. URL: *http://www.forbes.com/2010/09/10/barrick-gold-mining-markets-china-india.html*

[175] David Pietrusza, "Selling Gold at Fort Knox Emerges as Next Big Question in Debate on Federal Debt Limit," *New York Sun*, May 17, 2011. URL: *http://www.nysun.com/national/selling-gold-at-fort-knox-emerges-as-next-big/87350/*

[176] Ron Paul, *The Revolution: A Manifesto*. New York: Grand Central Publishing / Hachette, 2008. Page 150.

[177] Bill Frezza, "Ben Bernanke's Lone Positive Legacy: A Return To The Gold Standard," *Forbes* Magazine, May 3, 2011. URL: *http://blogs.forbes.com/billfrezza/2011/05/03/ben-bernankes -lone-positive-legacy-a-return-to-the-gold-standard/*

[178] Huma Khan, "States Look to Bring Gold Standard Back: Utah is First State to Recognize Gold and Silver as Legal Tender; Inflation Worries Loom," *ABC News*, April 15, 2011. URL: *http://abcnews.go.com/Politics/tea-party-momentum-utah-bill-brings-gold-standard/story?id=13377409*

[179] Ron Paul, *The Revolution: A Manifesto*. New York: Grand Central Publishing / Hachette, 2008. Pages 154-155.

[180] Ron Paul, *The Revolution: A Manifesto*. New York: Grand Central Publishing / Hachette, 2008. Page 155. See also Arnold Kling, *The Case for Auditing the Fed Is Obvious* (Monograph). Washington, D.C.: Cato Institute, April 27, 2010. URL: *http://www.cato.org/pubs/bp/bp118.pdf*

[181] Ron Paul, *The Revolution: A Manifesto*. New York: Grand Central Publishing / Hachette, 2008. Page 150.

[182] Book of Matthew 22:15-21, The Holy Bible (King James Version). URL: *http://www.bible-gateway.com/passage/?search=Matthew+22%3A15-21& version=KJV*

[183] Ayn Rand, *Capitalism: The Unknown Ideal*. New York: Signet Books, 1967. Greenspan's essay appears on pages 96-101. An online text of Greenspan's essay "Gold and Economic Freedom" can be found at: URL: *http://www.constitution.org/mon/greenspan_gold.html*

[184] Ethel C. Fenig, "An Updated Version of 'The Little Red Hen," *American Thinker*, February 24, 2009. URL: *http://www.americanthinker.com/blog/2009/02/an_updated_version_of_ the_litt.html*

# Additional Background Sources

Liaquat Ahamed, *Lords of Finance: The Bankers Who Broke the World*. New York: Penguin Books, 2009.

George A. Akerlof and Robert J. Schiller, *Animal Spirits: How Human Psychology Drives the Economy, and Why It Matters for Global Capitalism*. Princeton, New Jersey: Princeton University Press, 2009.

John Anthers, *The Fearful Rise of Markets: Global Bubbles, Synchronized Meltdowns, and How to Prevent Them In The Future*. London: FT Press, 2010.

William W. Beach and others, *Obama Tax Hikes: The Economic and Fiscal Effects* (Monograph). Washington, D.C.: Heritage Foundation, 2010.

Ben S. Bernanke and others, *Inflation Targeting: Lessons from the International Experience*. Princeton, New Jersey: Princeton University Press, 1999.

Peter Bernholz, *Monetary Regimes and Inflation: History, Economic and Political Relationships*. Williston, Vermont: Edward Elgar Publishing, 2006.

William Bonner and Addison Wiggin, *Financial Reckoning Day: Surviving the Soft Depression of the 21ˢᵗ Century*. Hoboken, New Jersey: John Wiley & Sons, 2004.

_____, *The New Empire of Debt: The Rise and Fall of an Epic Financial Bubble* (Second Edition). Hoboken, New Jersey: John Wiley & Sons, 2009.

Neal Boortz and John Linder, *The FairTax Book: Saying Goodbye to the Income Tax and the IRS....* New York: Regan Books / HarperCollins, 2005.

Neal Boortz, John Linder and Rob Woodall, *FairTax: The Truth: Answering the Critics*. New York: Harper, 2008.

Jerry Bowyer, *The Free Market Capitalist's Survival Guide: How to Invest and Thrive in an Era of Rampant Socialism*. New York: Broad Side / Harper Collins, 2011.

H.W. Brands, *The Age of Gold: The California Gold Rush and the New American Dream*. New York: Doubleday / Random House, 2002.

Arthur C. Brooks, *The Battle: How the Fight Between Free Enterprise and Big Government Will Shape America's Future*. New York: Basic Books / Perseus, 2010.

_____, *Gross National Happiness: Why Happiness Matters for America – and How We Can Get More of It*. New York: Basic Books, 2008.

James M. Buchanan and Richard E. Wagner, *Democracy in Deficit: The Political Legacy of Lord Keynes*. Indianapolis: Liberty Fund, 1999.

Bruce Caldwell (Editor), *The Collected Works of F.A. Hayek, Volume 2: The Road to Serfdom: Texts and Documents: The Definitive Edition*. Chicago: University of Chicago Press, 2007.

Marc Chandler, *Making Sense of the Dollar: Exposing Dangerous Myths about Trade and Foreign Exchange*. New York: Bloomberg Press, 2009.

Congressional Budget Office, *The Budget and Economic Outlook: Fiscal Years 2011 to 2021*. Washington, D.C.: Congressional Budget Office, January 2011. URL: *http://www.cbo.gov/ftpdocs/120xx/doc12039/01-26_FY2011Outlook.pdf*

Jerome R. Corsi, *America for Sale: Fighting the New World Order, Surviving a Global Depression, and Preserving U.S.A. Sovereignty*. New York: Threshold Editions / Simon & Schuster, 2009.

Clyde Wayne Crews, Jr., *Ten Thousand Commandments: An Annual Snapshot of the Federal Regulatory State*. 2011 Edition. (Monograph). Washington, D.C.: Competitive Enterprise Institute, 2011.

Glyn Davies, *A History of Money: From Ancient Times to the Present Day*. Third Edition. Cardiff: University of Wales Press, 2002.

Glyn Davies and Roy Davies, *A Comparative Chronology of Money: Monetary History from Ancient Times to the Present Day*. (Monograph based on Glyn Davies and Roy Davies, above.) (2006) URL: *http://projects.exeter.ac.uk/RDavies/arian/amser/chrono.html*

Hernando de Soto, *The Mystery of Capital: Why Capitalism Triumphs in the West and Fails Everywhere Else*. New York: Basic Books / Perseus, 2000.

Jared Diamond, *Collapse: How Societies Choose to Fail or Succeed*. New York: Viking Press, 2005.

James A. Dorn (Editor), *Federal Reserve Policy In The Face of Crises* (An entire issue of the Cato Institute's *Cato Journal* with 15 experts writing on this topic.) *Cato Journal*, Volume 27 No. 2 (Spring/Summer 2007).

Peter F. Drucker, *Post-Capitalist Society*. New York: Harper Business, 1993.

Dinesh D'Souza, *The Virtue of Prosperity: Finding Values in an Age of Techno-Affluence*. New York: Free Press / Simon & Schuster, 2000.

Richard Duncan, *The Dollar Crisis: Causes, Consequences, Cures*. Singapore: John Wiley & Sons (Asia), 2003.

Gregg Easterbrook, *The Progress Paradox: How Life Gets Better While People Feel Worse*. New York: Random House, 2003.

Gauti B. Eggertsson, *What Fiscal Policy Is Effective at Zero Interest Rate?* Staff Report No. 402 (Monograph). New York: Federal Reserve Bank of New York, November 2009. URL: *http://www.newyorkfed.org/research/staff_reports/sr402.pdf*

Barry Eichengreen, *Exorbitant Privilege: The Rise and Fall of the Dollar and the Future of the International Monetary System*. Oxford: Oxford University Press, 2011.

_____, *Global Imbalances and the Lessons of Bretton Woods* (Cairoli Lectures). Cambridge, Massachusetts: MIT Press, 2010.

_____, *Globalizing Capital: A History of the International Monetary System* (Second Edition).

_____, *Golden Fetters: The Gold Standard and the Great Depression, 1919-1939* (NBER Series on Long-Term Factors in Economic Development). Oxford: Oxford University Press, 1996.

Barry Eichengreen and Marc Flandreau, *Gold Standard In Theory & History*. London: Routledge, 1997.

Richard A. Epstein, *How Progressives Rewrote the Constitution*. Washington, D.C.: Cato Institute, 2006.

_____, *Takings: Private Property and the Power of Eminent Domain*. Cambridge, Massachusetts: Harvard University Press, 1985.

Niall Ferguson, *The Ascent of Money: A Financial History of the World*. New York: Penguin Press, 2008.

_____, *The Cash Nexus: Money and Power in the Modern World, 1700-2000*. New York: Basic Books, 2002.

_____, *Civilization: The West and the Rest*. New York: Penguin Books, 2011.

_____, *Colossus: The Price of America's Empire*. New York: Penguin Press, 2004.

Peter Ferrara, *America's Ticking Bankruptcy Bomb: How the Looming Debt Crisis Threatens the American Dream – and How We Can Turn the Tide Before It's Too Late*. New York: Broadside Books, 2011.

Ralph T. Foster, *Fiat Paper Money: The History and Evolution of Our Currency.* Second Edition. 2008.

Justin Fox, *The Myth of the Rational Market: A History of Risk, Reward, and Delusion on Wall Street.* New York: Harper Business, 2009.

Kevin D. Freeman, *Economic Warfare: Risks and Responses: Analysis of Twenty-First Century Risks in Light of the Recent Market Collapse* (Monograph). Cross Consulting and Services, 2009. This can be downloaded from the Internet at no cost from *http://av.r.ftdata.co.uk/files/2011/03/49755779-Economic-Warfare-Risks-and-Responses-by-Kevin-D-Freeman.pdf*

or at no cost from *http://www.freemanglobal.com/uploads/Economic_Warfare_Risks_and_Responses.pdf*

George Friedman, *The Next Decade: Where We've Been...And Where We're Going.* New York: Doubleday, 2011.

Milton Friedman, *An Economist's Protest.* Second Edition. Glen Ridge, New Jersey: Thomas Horton and Daughters, 1975. Also published as *There's No Such Thing As A Free Lunch.* La Salle, Illinois: Open Court Publishing, 1975.

_____, *Capitalism & Freedom: A Leading Economist's View of the Proper Role of Competitive Capitalism.* Chicago: University of Chicago Press, 1962.

_____, *Dollars and Deficits: Inflation, Monetary Policy and the Balance of Payments.* Englewood Cliffs, New Jersey: Prentice-Hall, 1968.

_____, *Money Mischief: Episodes in Monetary History.* New York: Harcourt Brace, 1992.

_____, *On Economics: Selected Papers.* Chicago: University of Chicago Press, 2007.

Milton & Rose Friedman, *Free to Choose: A Personal Statement.* New York: Harcourt Brace Jovanovich, 1980.

_____, *Tyranny of the Status Quo.* San Diego, California: Harcourt Brace Jovanovich, 1984.

Milton Friedman & Anna Jacobson Schwartz, *A Monetary History of the United States, 1867-1960.* A Study by the National Bureau of Economic Research, New York. Princeton, New Jersey: Princeton University Press, 1963.

Francis Fukuyama, *The End of History and The Last Man.* New York: Free Press, 1992.

_____, *Trust: The Social Virtues and The Creation of Prosperity.* New York: Free Press, 1996.

James K. Galbraith, *The Predator State: How Conservatives Abandoned the Free Market and Why Liberals Should Too.* New York: Free Press, 2008.

John D. Gartner, *The Hypomanic Edge: The Link Between (A Little) Craziness and (A Lot of) Success in America.* New York: Simon & Schuster, 2005.

Charles Gasparino, *Bought and Paid For: The Unholy Alliance Between Barack Obama and Wall Street.* New York: Sentinel / Penguin, 2010.

Nicole Gelinas, *After the Fall: Saving Capitalism from Wall Street – and Washington.* New York: Encounter Books, 2011.

Pamela Geller and Robert Spencer, *The Post-American Presidency.* New York: Threshold Editions / Simon & Schuster, 2010.

George Gilder, *Wealth and Poverty.* New York: Basic Books, 1981.

Jason Goodwin, *Greenback: The Almighty Dollar and The Invention of America.* New York: John

Macrae / Henry Holt and Company, 2003.

Charles Goyette, *The Dollar Meltdown: Surviving the Impending Currency Crisis with Gold, Oil, and Other Unconventional Investments*. New York: Portfolio / Penguin, 2009.

Alan Greenspan, *The Age of Turbulence: Adventures in a New World*. New York: Penguin Books, 2007.

William Greider, *Secrets of the Temple: How the Federal Reserve Runs the Country*. New York: Simon & Schuster, 1989.

G. Edward Griffin, *The Creature from Jekyll Island: A Second Look at the Federal Reserve*. Third Edition. Westlake Village, California: American Media, 1998.

Alexander Hamilton, James Madison and John Jay, *The Federalist Papers*. New York: Mentor / New American Library, 1961. Pages 280-288. For an online version of James Madison's Federalist Paper No. 44, go to this URL: *http://www.constitution.org/fed/federa44.htm*

Keith Hart, *Money in an Unequal World*. New York: TEXERE, 2001.

Friedrich A. Hayek (Editor), *Capitalism and the Historians*. Chicago: Phoenix Books / University of Chicago Press, 1963.

_____, *Choice in Currency: A Way to Stop Inflation*. London: Institute of Economic Affairs, 1976. This can be downloaded from the Internet at no cost from *http://www.iea.org.uk/sites/default/files/publications/files/upldb ook409.pdf*

_____, *The Counter-Revolution of Science: Studies On The Abuse of Reason*. New York: The Free Press / Macmillan / Crowell-Collier, 1955.

_____, *The Constitution of Liberty*. The Definitive Edition, Edited by Ronald Hamowy. Chicago: University of Chicago Press, 2011.

_____, *Denationalisation of Money: The Argument Refined: An Analysis of the Theory and Practice of Concurrent Currencies*. Third Edition. London: Institute of Economic Affairs, 1990. This can be downloaded from the Internet at no cost from *http://mises.org/books/denationalisation.pdf*

_____, *The Fatal Conceit: The Errors of Socialism*. Chicago: University of Chicago Press, 1991.

_____, *The Road to Serfdom*. Chicago: Phoenix Books / University of Chicago Press, 1944.

Henry Hazlitt, *The Failure of the "New Economics": An Analysis of The Keynesian Fallacies*. New Rochelle, New York: Arlington House, 1959.

_____, *From Bretton Woods to World Inflation: A Study of Causes & Consequences*. Chicago: Regnery Gateway, 1984. This can be downloaded from the Internet at no cost from *http://mises.org/books/brettonwoods.pdf*

W.H. Hutt, *The Keynesian Episode: A Reassessment*. Indianapolis: LibertyPress, 1979.

John Maynard Keynes, *Essays in Persuasion*. New York: W.W. Norton, 1963.

_____, *The General Theory of Employment, Interest, and Money*. New York: Harcourt, Brace & World, 1935.

Arnold Kling, *The Case for Auditing the Fed Is Obvious*. (Monograph / Briefing Paper). Washington, D.C.: Cato Institute, April 27, 2010. URL: *http://www.cato.org/pubs/bp/bp118.pdf*

Gabriel Kolko, *Railroads and Regulation 1877-1916*. New York: W.W. Norton, 1970. Originally published in 1965 by Princeton University Press.

Laurence J. Kotlikoff, *Jimmy Stewart Is Dead: Ending the World's Ongoing Financial Plague with Limited Purpose Banking*. Hoboken, New Jersey: John Wiley & Sons, 2011.

Laurence J. Kotlikoff and Scott Burns, *The Coming Generational Storm: What You Need to Know About America's Economic Future*. Cambridge, Massachusetts: MIT Press, 2005.

Paul Krugman, *The Return of Depression Economics and The Crisis of 2008*. New York: W.W. Norton, 2009.

Joel Kurtzman, *The Death of Money: How the Electronic Economy Has Destabilized the World's Markets and Created Financial Chaos*. New York: Simon & Schuster, 1993.

Arthur B. Laffer, Stephen Moore and Peter J. Tanous, *The End of Prosperity: How Higher Taxes Will Doom the Economy – If We Let It Happen*. New York: Threshold Editions / Simon & Schuster, 2008.

Arthur B. Laffer and Stephen Moore, *Return to Prosperity: How America Can Regain Its Economic Superpower Status*. New York: Threshold Editions / Simon & Schuster, 2010.

John Lanchester, *I.O.U.: Why Everyone Owes Everyone and No One Can Pay*. New York: Simon & Schuster, 2010.

David S. Landes, *The Wealth and Poverty of Nations: Why Some Are So Rich and Some So Poor*. New York: W.W. Norton, 1998.

Louise Levathes, *When China Ruled the Seas: The Treasure Fleet of the Dragon Throne, 1405-1433*. Oxford: Oxford University Press, 1997.

Michael Lewis, *Panic: The Story of Modern Financial Insanity*. New York: W.W. Norton, 2009.

Naphtali Lewis and Meyer Reinhold (Editors), *Roman Civilization: Sourcebook II: The Empire*. New York: Harper Torchbooks, 1966.

Nathan Lewis and Addison Wiggin, *Gold: The Once and Future Money*. Hoboken, New Jersey: John Wiley & Sons, 2007.

Deirdre N. McCloskey, *Bourgeois Dignity: Why Economics Can't Explain the Modern World*. Chicago: University of Chicago Press, 2010.

Bethany McLean and Joe Nocera, *All the Devils Are Here: The Hidden History of the Financial Crisis*. New York: Portfolio/Penguin, 2010.

Karl Marx and Friedrich Engels, *The Communist Manifesto*. London: Penguin Classics, 1985.

John Mauldin and Jonathan Tepper, *Endgame: The End of the Debt Supercycle and How It Changes Everything*. Hoboken, New Jersey: John Wiley & Sons, 2011.

Martin Mayer, *The Fed: The Inside Story of How the World's Most Powerful Financial Institution Drives the Markets*. New York: Free Press, 2001.

Michael Medved, *The 5 Big Lies About American Business: Combating Smears Against the Free-Market Economy*. New York: Crown Forum, 2009.

David I. Meiselman and Arthur B. Laffer (Editors), *The Phenomenon of Worldwide Inflation*. Washington, D.C.: American Enterprise Institute, 1975.

Gavin Menzies, *1421: The Year China Discovered America*. New York: Harper Perennial, 2002.

_____, *1434: The Year a Magnificent Chinese Fleet Sailed to Italy and Ignited the Renaissance*. New York: Harper Perennial, 2009.

Ludwig von Mises, *The Anti-Capitalist Mentality*. Princeton, New Jersey: D. Van Nostrand Company, 1956.

_____, *Human Action: A Treatise on Economics*. Third Revised Edition. Chicago: Contemporary Books, 1966.

_____, *On the Manipulation of Money and Credit*. Dobbs Ferry, New York: Free Market Books, 1978.

_____, *The Theory of Money and Credit*, New Edition. Irvington-on-Hudson, NY: Foundation for Economic Education, 1971.

Stephen Moore, *How Barack Obama Is Bankrupting the U.S. Economy* (Encounter Broadside No. 4). New York: Encounter Books, 2009.

Charles R. Morris, *The Trillion Dollar Meltdown: Easy Money, High Rollers, and the Great Credit Crash*. New York: Public Affairs/Perseus, 2008.

Robert P. Murphy, *The Politically Incorrect Guide to Capitalism*. Washington, D.C.: Regnery, 2007.

Charles Murray, *What It Means to Be a Libertarian: A Personal Interpretation*. New York: Broadway Books, 1997.

Andrew P. Napolitano, *Lies the Government Told You: Myth, Power, and Deception in American History*. Nashville: Thomas Nelson, 2010.

Maxwell Newton, *The Fed: Inside the Federal Reserve, the Secret Power Center that Controls the American Economy*. New York: Times Books, 1983.

Johan Norberg, *Financial Fiasco: How America's Infatuation with Home Ownership and Easy Money Created the Economic Crisis*. Washington, D.C.: Cato Institute, 2009.

Mancur Olson, *The Logic of Collective Action: Public Goods and the Theory of Groups*, Revised Edition. Cambridge, Massachusetts: Harvard University Press, 1971.

_____, *Power and Prosperity: Outgrowing Communist and Capitalist Dictatorships*. New York: Basic Books, 2000.

_____, *The Rise and Decline of Nations: Economic Growth, Stagflation, and Social Rigidities*. New Haven, Connecticut: Yale University Press, 1984.

Ron Paul, *End The Fed*. New York: Grand Central Publishing / Hachette, 2009.

_____, *Liberty Defined: 50 Essential Issues That Affect Our Freedom*. New York: Grand Central Publishing / Hachette, 2011.

_____, *Pillars of Prosperity: Free Markets, Honest Money, Private Property*. Ludwig von Mises Institute, 2008.

_____, *The Revolution: A Manifesto*. New York: Grand Central Publishing / Hachette, 2008.

Ron Paul and Lewis Lehrman, *The Case for Gold: A Minority Report of the U.S. Gold Commission*. Ludwig von Mises Institute, 2007. This can be downloaded from the Internet at no cost from *http://mises.org/books/caseforgold.pdf*

Peter G. Peterson, *Running On Empty: How the Democratic and Republican Parties Are Bankrupting Our Future and What Americans Can Do About It*. New York: Farrar, Straus and Giroux, 2004.

Kevin Phillips, *Bad Money: Reckless Finance, Failed Politics, and the Global Crisis of American Capitalism*. New York: Viking Press, 2008.

_____, *Boiling Point: Democrats, Republicans, and the Decline of Middle-Class Prosperity*. New York: Random House, 1993.

Richard A. Posner, *The Crisis of Capitalist Democracy*. Cambridge, Massachusetts: Harvard University Press, 2010.

_____, *A Failure of Capitalism: The Crisis of '08 and the Descent into Depression*. Cambridge, Massachusetts: Harvard University Press, 2009.

Virginia Postrel, *The Future and Its Enemies: The Growing Conflict Over Creativity, Enterprise, and Progress*. New York: Free Press, 1998.

Raghuram G. Rajan, *Fault Lines: How Hidden Fractures Still Threaten the World Economy*. Princeton, New Jersey: Princeton University Press, 2010.

Joshua Cooper Ramo, *The Age of the Unthinkable: Why the New World Disorder Constantly Surprises Us And What We Can Do About It*. New York: Little Brown / Hachette, 2009.

Ayn Rand, *Capitalism: The Unknown Ideal (With additional articles by Nathaniel Branden, Alan Greenspan, and Robert Hessen)*. New York: Signet / New American Library, 1967.

Carmen M. Reinhart and Kenneth S. Rogoff, *This Time Is Different: Eight Centuries of Financial Folly*. Princeton, New Jersey: Princeton University Press, 2009.

Barry Ritzholtz with Aaron Task, *Bailout Nation: How Greed and Easy Money Corrupted Wall Street and Shook the World Economy*. Hoboken, New Jersey: John Wiley & Sons, 2009.

Wilhelm Röpke, *A Humane Economy: The Social Framework of the Free Market*. Chicago: Henry Regnery Company, 1960. This can be downloaded from the Internet at no cost from *http://mises.org/books/Humane_Economy_Ropke.pdf*

Murray N. Rothbard, *America's Great Depression*. Fifth Edition. Auburn, Alabama: Ludwig von Mises Institute, 2000. This can be downloaded from the Internet at no cost from *http://mises.org/rothbard/agd.pdf*

_____, *The Case Against the Fed*. Second Edition. Auburn, Alabama: Ludwig von Mises Institute, 2007. A version of this book can be downloaded from the Internet at no cost from *http://mises.org/books/Fed.pdf*

_____, *A History of Money and Banking in the United States: The Colonial Era to World War II*. Auburn, Alabama: Ludwig von Mises Institute, 2002. This can be downloaded from the Internet at no cost from *http://mises.org/Books/HistoryofMoney.pdf*

_____, *The Mystery of Banking*. Second Edition. Auburn, Alabama: Ludwig von Mises Institute, 2008. This can be downloaded from the Internet at no cost from *http://mises.org/Books/MysteryofBanking.pdf*

_____, *What Has Government Done to Our Money?* Auburn, Alabama: Ludwig von Mises Institute, 2008. This can be downloaded from the Internet at no cost from *http://mises.org/Books/Whathasgovernmentdone.pdf*

_____, *For a New Liberty: The Libertarian Manifesto* (Revised Edition). New York: Collier Books / Macmillian, 1978.

Michael Rothschild, *Bionomics: The Inevitability of Capitalism*. New York: John Macrae / Henry Holt and Company, 1990.

Nouriel Roubini and Stephen Mihm, *Crisis Economics: A Crash Course in the Future of Finance*. New York: Penguin Books, 2010.

Robert J. Samuelson, *The Good Life and Its Discontents: The American Dream in the Age of Entitlement 1945-1995*. New York: Times Books, 1995.

_____, *The Great Inflation and Its Aftermath: The Transformation of America's Economy, Politics and Society*. New York: Random House, 2008.

Peter D. Schiff and Andrew J. Schiff, *How an Economy Grows and Why It Crashes*. Hoboken, New Jersey: John Wiley & Sons, 2010.

Robert L. Schuettinger and Eamonn F. Butler, *Forty Centuries of Wage and Price Controls: How NOT to Fight Inflation*. Washington, D.C.: Heritage Foundation, 1979. This can be downloaded from the Internet at no cost from *http://mises.org/books/fortycenturies.pdf*

Barry Schwartz, *The Paradox of Choice: Why More Is Less*. New York: Ecco / Harper Collins, 2004.

George Selgin and others, *Has the Fed Been a Failure?* Revised Edition. (Monograph). Washington, D.C.: Cato Institute, 2010.

Hans F. Sennholz, "Inflation Is Theft," *LewRockwell.com*, June 24, 2005. URL:*http://www. lewrockwell.com/orig6/sennholz6.html*

Hans F. Sennholz (Editor), *Inflation Is Theft*. Irvington-on-Hudson, New York: Foundation for Economic Education, 1994. A copy of this book may be downloaded at no cost from FEE's website at *http://fee.org/wp-content/ uploads/2009/11/InflationisTheft.pdf*

Amity Shlaes, *The Forgotten Man: A New History of the Great Depression*. New York: Harper Collins, 2007.

_____, *The Greedy Hand: How Taxes Drive Americans Crazy And What to Do About It*. New York: Random House, 1999.

Julian L. Simon, *The Ultimate Resource*. Princeton, New Jersey: Princeton University Press, 1981.

Mark Skousen, *Economics of a Pure Gold Standard*. Seattle: CreateSpace, 2010.

_____, *The Making of Modern Economics: The Lives and Ideas of the Great Thinkers*. Second Edition. Armonk, New York: M.E. Sharpe, 2009.

Craig R. Smith, *Rediscovering Gold in the 21ˢᵗ Century*. Sixth Edition. Phoenix: Idea Factory Press, 2007.

_____, *The Uses of Inflation: Monetary Policy and Governance in the 21ˢᵗ Century* (Monograph). Phoenix: Swiss America Trading Company, 2011.

Craig R. Smith and Lowell Ponte, *Crashing the Dollar: How to Survive a Global Currency Collapse*. Phoenix: Idea Factory Press, 2010.

Guy Sorman, *Economics Does Not Lie: A Defense of the Free Market in a Time of Crisis*. New York: Encounter Books, 2009.

George Soros, *The Age of Fallibility: Consequences of the War on Terror*. New York: Public Affairs, 2007.

_____, *The Bubble of American Supremacy: The Cost's of Bush's War in Iraq*. London: Weidenfeld & Nicolson, 2004.

_____, *George Soros on Globalization*. New York: Public Affairs, 2005.

_____, *The New Paradigm for Financial Markets: The Credit Crisis of 2008 and What It Means*. New York: Public Affairs, 2008.

_____, *Open Society: Reforming Global Capitalism*. New York: Public Affairs, 2000.

_____, *The Soros Lectures at the Central European University*. New York: Public Affairs, 2010.

Thomas Sowell, *Basic Economics: A Common Sense Guide to the Economy*. Third Edition. New York: Basic Books / Perseus, 2007.

_____, *Dismantling America*. New York: Basic Books, 2010.

_____, *Economic Facts and Fallacies*. Second Edition. New York: Basic Books, 2011.

_____, *The Housing Boom and Bust*. Revised Edition. New York: Basic Books, 2010.

_____, *On Classical Economics*. New Haven, Connecticut: Yale University Press, 2007.

Mark Steyn, *America Alone: The End of the World As We Know It*. Washington, D.C.: Regnery, 2008. *[Full Disclosure: Steyn quotes Lowell Ponte in this book.]*

Joseph E. Stiglitz, *Freefall: America, Free Markets, and the Sinking of the World Economy*. New York: W.W. Norton, 2010.

_____, *Globalization and Its Discontents*. New York: W.W. Norton, 2002.

Nassim Nicholas Taleb, *The Black Swan: The Impact of the Highly Improbable*. Second Edition. New York: Random House, 2010.

Peter J. Tanous and Jeff Cox, *Debt, Deficits and the Demise of the American Economy*. Hoboken, New Jersey: John Wiley & Sons, 2011.

Johan Van Overtveldt, *Bernanke's Test: Ben Bernanke, Alan Greenspan and the Drama of the Central Banker*. Chicago: B2 Books/Agate Publishing, 2009.

Damon Vickers, *The Day After the Dollar Crashes: A Survival Guide for the Rise of the New World Order*. Hoboken, New Jersey: John Wiley & Sons, 2011.

William Voegeli, *Never Enough: America's Limitless Welfare State*. New York: Encounter Books, 2010.

M.W. Walbert, *The Coming Battle: A Complete History of the National Banking Money Power in the United States*. Chicago: W.B. Conkey Company, 1899. Reprinted by Walter Publishing & Research, Merlin, Oregon, 1997.

David M. Walker, *Comeback America: Turning the Country Around and Restoring Fiscal Responsibility*. New York: Random House, 2009.

Jude Wanniski, *The Way the World Works*. New York: Touchstone / Simon & Schuster, 1978.

Jack Weatherford, *The History of Money: From Sandstone to Cyberspace*. New York: Crown Publishers, 1997.

Carolyn Webber and Aaron Wildavsky, *A History of Taxation and Expenditure in the Western World*. New York: Simon & Schuster, 1986.

Janine R. Wedel, *Shadow Elite: How the World's New Power Brokers Undermine Democracy, Government and the Free Market*. New York: Basic Books / Perseus, 2009.

Eric J. Weiner, *The Shadow Market: How a Group of Wealthy Nations and Powerful Investors Secretly Dominate the World*. New York: Scribner, 2010.

R. Christopher Whalen, *Inflated: How Money and Debt Built the American Dream*. Hoboken, New Jersey: John Wiley & Sons, 2010.

Lawrence H. White, *Is The Gold Standard Still the Gold Standard among Monetary Systems?* (Monograph). Washington, D.C.: Cato Institute, February 8, 2008. URL: *http://www.cato.org/pubs/bp/bp100.pdf*

Peter C. Whybrow, *American Mania: When More Is Not Enough*. New York: W.W. Norton, 2005.

Addison Wiggin and William Bonner, *Financial Reckoning Day Fallout: Surviving Today's Global Depression*. Hoboken, New Jersey: John Wiley & Sons, 2009.

Addison Wiggin and Kate Incontrera, *I.O.U.S.A.: One Nation. Under Stress. In Debt.* Hoboken, New Jersey: John Wiley & Sons, 2008.

Aaron Wildavsky, *How to Limit Government Spending...*, Berkeley, California: University of California Press, 1980.

Jonathan Williams (Editor), *Money: A History.* New York: St. Martin's Press, 1997.

Thomas E. Woods, Jr., *Meltdown: A Free-Market Look at Why the Stock Market Collapsed, the Economy Tanked, and Government Bailouts Will Make Things Worse.* Washington, D.C.: Regnery Publishing, 2009.

_____, *Nullification: How to Resist Federal Tyranny in the 21st Century.* Washington, D.C.: Regnery Publishing, 2010.

_____, *Rollback: Repealing Big Government Before the Coming Fiscal Collapse.* Washington, D.C.: Regnery Publishing, 2011.

Thomas E. Woods, Jr., and Kevin R.C. Gutzman, *Who Killed the Constitution?: The Federal Government vs. American Liberty From WWI to Barack Obama.* New York: Three Rivers Press, 2009.

Bob Woodward, *Maestro: Greenspan's Fed and the American Boom.* New York: Simon & Schuster, 2000.

Fareed Zakaria, *The Future of Freedom: Illiberal Democracy at Home and Abroad.* New York: W.W. Norton, 2003.

_____, *The Post-American World.* New York: W.W. Norton, 2009.

Jason Zweig, *Your Money & Your Brain: How the New Science of Neuroeconomics Can Help Make You Rich.* New York: Simon & Schuster, 2007.